BASTARD
BEHIND
THE LINES

The extraordinary story of
Jock McLaren's escape from Sandakan
and his guerrilla war against the Japanese

BASTARD
BEHIND
THE LINES

TOM GILLING

ALLEN&UNWIN
SYDNEY•MELBOURNE•AUCKLAND•LONDON

Allen & Unwin
83 Alexander Street
Crows Nest NSW 2065
Australia
Phone: (61 2) 8425 0100
Email: info@allenandunwin.com
Web: www.allenandunwin.com

A catalogue record for this book is available from the National Library of Australia

ISBN 978 1 76087 587 9

Map by Mapgraphics
Set in 11.5 pt/17 pt Minion by Midland Typesetters, Australia
Printed and bound in Australia by Griffin Press, part of Ovato

10 9 8 7 6 5 4 3 2 1

The paper in this book is FSC® certified. FSC® promotes environmentally responsible, socially beneficial and economically viable management of the world's forests.

For Mum and Dad

CONTENTS

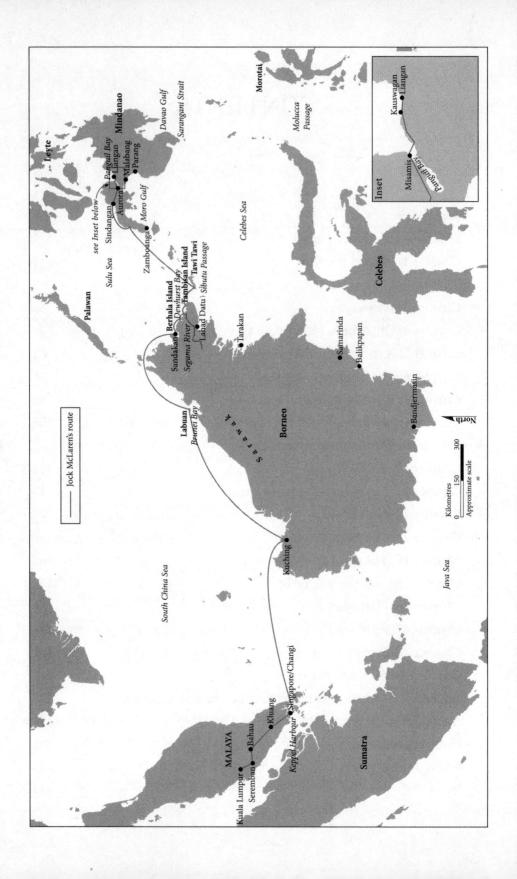

Prologue

CLOAK-AND-DAGGER MAN

––►•◄––

The story of QX21058 Captain R.K. McLaren, MC and Bar, is one of the most astonishing of the war. The only full-length account of McLaren's exploits is Hal Richardson's *One-Man War: The Jock McLaren Story*, written more than half a century ago and based on material supplied by McLaren. It is important to note that Richardson's version does not always align with the various official histories, or with military records, or with other eyewitness accounts. None of these different versions, however, diminishes McLaren's extraordinary courage and inspiring leadership, for which he was widely admired and officially decorated.

One-Man War was presented to the public as a book about Jock McLaren, researched and written by Hal Richardson. According to the cover blurb, the 'amazing' story of McLaren's exploits in Malaya, Borneo and the Philippines 'might have been lost in official files—and even there it was not complete—had not Hal Richardson . . . gone to New Guinea to hear it from the only man who could tell it in full'. In his preface Richardson writes that the book was 'based solely on Jock McLaren's notes and recollections'. The truth, however, is more complex.

'Ybsul', a pseudonymous columnist in the *Bulletin* magazine who knew McLaren well enough to have 'shared a Brisbane hotel-room with Jock for a few months just after the Jap war', revealed that in January 1948 McLaren was 'casting about for a writer' to help with his memoirs.

Letters deposited in the State Library of New South Wales confirm that soon after leaving the army, Jock McLaren began writing a book about his wartime adventures. A handwritten aerogram by McLaren refers repeatedly to 'my MS'. McLaren therefore was not just the source for *One-Man War* but also its original author. But how reliable are his recollections?

Richardson begins with a dramatic account of McLaren's escape from Singapore's Changi prisoner-of-war camp with 'two younger companions, freckle-faced Ginger Burnett and a small dark man named Wilkie, both Queenslanders'. He states that the escape took place 'on the night of the 19th February 1942, the Friday after Singapore fell'. But McLaren, in an intelligence report dated 30 September 1943, puts the date of the escape three weeks later; he also claims that four men escaped, not three. McLaren's report states that on the night of 10 March, 'four personnel including myself escaped, crossed the Straits of Johore, and proceeded Northwards'. The fourth absconder is identified as Private K.P. Kelly of Gordonvale, Queensland. His full name was Kenneth Patrick Kelly and, like McLaren, he was a member of the 2/10th Ordnance Workshop. Private Kelly survived the war and returned to Australia (his name is included in a list of returned POWs published by the *Central Queensland Herald* in September 1945), but his name does not appear anywhere in the pages of *One-Man War*.

Richardson informs us in his preface that McLaren 'read the MS of this book before he was killed'. So either McLaren forgot about Private Kelly, which seems unlikely, or else he agreed to Richardson leaving Kelly out of the story. Either way, the omission of Kelly alerts us to the risks of placing our trust in the 'authorised' version of McLaren's life.

Like any biographer, Hal Richardson brought something of his own life experience, beliefs and prejudices to his book. A professional journalist before joining the Second Australian Imperial Force in May 1940, Richardson was sent to Singapore with the 8th Division and spent four years as a POW at Palembang in Sumatra. Richardson was as marked by his experience of Japanese brutality as McLaren was by his. Asked for his opinion of the war crimes trials conducted by the Allies, Richardson told the *Sun* newspaper that convicted Japanese war criminals 'deserve everything they get, but I don't particularly want to hang them myself. I don't even want to watch it being done . . . but I'm glad they're getting it in the neck, just the same.'

After completing his first draft, Richardson posted the manuscript to Jock McLaren in New Guinea, advising him that if he felt 'unduly misrepresented' he was free to 'make any alterations'. McLaren's only reservation was that the book made him 'appear . . . a hero'. He asked Richardson to 'point out that the fighting and privations were shared by guerrilla fighters, Australians and others, much braver than himself'. Whether he believed that statement or not, Richardson did as he was asked.

One-Man War: The Jock McLaren Story was eventually published by Angus & Robertson in 1957, with a foreword by Australia's wartime head of military intelligence, Brigadier John Rogers. In 1958 a paperback edition was published in London by Panther Books. (The same year *Escape from Hell*, by another Australian soldier, Walter Wallace, was also published in London. The two men fought together in the Philippines, but Wallace's book scarcely mentions McLaren.)

Richardson argued successfully for *One-Man War* to include the citations for McLaren's two Military Crosses, noting that these, together with Rogers' foreword, would give the book 'the full mark of authenticity'.

Some reviewers remained sceptical. '[*One-Man War*] so teems with adventure and excitement,' the *Bulletin* commented, 'with one daring exploit after another, that, obviously authentic though it all is, you have to remember that the fighting Scotch are a race apart to believe it.' A posthumous article in the *Pacific Islands Monthly*, some of whose readers would have known Jock McLaren personally, refers to his 'apparently impossible' escape from imprisonment and the 'fabulous one-man war' that followed.

Despite the question marks over its credibility, Richardson's book is still listed as a primary source for McLaren's entry in the authoritative *Australian Dictionary of Biography*.

According to Richardson, McLaren was 'a fighter first and last' who had 'served with the 51st Highland Battalion in the First World War'. McLaren's obituary in the *Pacific Islands Monthly* also refers to him as a 'World War I veteran'. Captain Ray Steele, who fought side by side with McLaren on the Filipino islands of Tawi Tawi and Mindanao, told broadcasters Tim Bowden and Hank Nelson that McLaren had served in the First World War. But McLaren, born in April 1902, would have been only twelve years old when the war started and sixteen when it ended. During the war the minimum legal age for enlisting in the British army was eighteen, but thousands of under-age soldiers lied about their age, and the army, hungry for manpower, soon learnt to turn a blind eye.

There is no reference to First World War service in McLaren's seven hundred-word entry in the *Australian Dictionary of Biography*, written by Alan Powell, an expert on Australian special operations. Nor is there any mention of it in McLaren's file in the National Archives of Australia. In his signed 'attestation form' for special forces raised for service in Australia or abroad, the answer to question 7 ('Give details of previous military service') is left blank. McLaren's personal data sheet for the Citizen Military Forces mentions his wife and a single dependent child under sixteen, along with his height, weight, chest expansion and dental classification, but when it comes to item 18 ('Previously on Active Service'), there is an 'X' in the box marked 'NO'.

Why would McLaren have told companions, such as Ray Steele, about having served in the First World War while keeping it a secret from the army? The age limit for enlisting in the 2nd AIF in 1939 was thirty-five, although a year later it was raised to forty. McLaren was born in 1902, which put him just inside the limit when he enlisted in 1941. If, however, he had served lawfully in the First World War, this would have made him too old to enlist for the Second World War.

The *Bulletin* columnist 'Ybsul' had no doubt about McLaren's service in the First World War, describing him as having a 'First War bullet-groove along the right cheek-bone'. McLaren, he wrote, had 'gerrymandered his age—on in the first war, and back in the second'.

'Ybsul' went on to say, however, that McLaren had 'tallied up in both schemozzles nine years' active service' (an impossibility, unless McLaren had managed to enlist in the British army at the age of thirteen) and that 'in 1946 he told me he was 49' (in fact McLaren turned forty-four on 27 April 1946).

If Jock McLaren could not be trusted to tell the truth about his age and his First World War service, can we trust him to have told Hal Richardson the truth about his exploits in the Second World War?

Most of McLaren's war was spent out of sight of Australian military authorities, either as an escaped prisoner or as a guerrilla. Between April 1942 and April 1944, his service record lists him as 'missing', then 'reported prisoner of war', and finally 'escaped & on active service—no date given'. Trying to verify the details of McLaren's story from official records is futile, but the soldier who marauds through the pages of *One-Man War* is recognisably the same as the one described in the *Official History of the Operations and Administration of Special Operations—Australia* and in citations for the Military Cross and the US Bronze Star Medal.

If McLaren's memories of combat do not always accord with those of his companions Ray Steele and Rex Blow, theirs do not always accord with each other. Major Tom Harrisson's biographer, Judith Heimann, disputes the accuracy of Blow's recollections, suggesting that information Blow gave to his own biographer about the capture of a Japanese unit on Borneo overemphasised Blow's role and 'nearly eliminates Tom's'. Heimann quotes an entry in Harrisson's diary in which Harrisson notes that by chance he has 'read Rex's bullshit letter on his trip up Trusan after Japs. But he's a nice chap.' It is hard to imagine such anodyne words being used about Jock McLaren.

In his foreword to *One-Man War*, Brigadier Rogers described McLaren as a 'cloak-and-dagger' man. What people knew about him was only what he allowed them to know, and it was not always true. During the three and a half years that followed his escape from Changi, McLaren would cheat death numerous times, alone and in front of witnesses, some of whom would recall events very differently from the way he remembered them.

During their conversations in New Guinea, McLaren told Richardson that he had 'developed a nose for danger, death, treachery and loyalty'—a faculty, Richardson suggests, that 'may account partly for his success in his private war against the Japanese'.

In a letter written shortly before the book was published, McLaren told Richardson, 'Time is running out for me,' By the time those words were printed, McLaren was dead, the victim of a freak accident. Luck, which saved his life so many times during the war, deserted him in the end.

Chapter 1

BEYOND THE WIRE

———◆———

Singapore, Britain's supposedly impregnable fortress in the Far East, was already doomed by the time Private Jock McLaren arrived to defend it. On the evening of 8 February 1942, after advancing 800 kilometres through the Malay Peninsula, the first Japanese divisions crossed the causeway linking Singapore to the mainland. As a member of the 2/10th Ordnance Workshop, McLaren was responsible for supplying, repairing and maintaining artillery equipment, but with Allied resistance collapsing, Australian soldiers assigned to the field workshops were rushed into improvised infantry units. Those who survived the fighting faced the prospect of seeing out the war as prisoners of the Japanese.

A Scot by birth, McLaren had enlisted at the age of thirty-nine in the Citizen Military Forces before transferring to the Second Australian Imperial Force. Captain Ray Steele, who got to know McLaren later in the war, recalled that by the time the two of them met, McLaren was 'already starting to show a few grey hairs. He had a son at Dunkirk. He realised he was probably over the hill as . . . a combat soldier so he joined a non-combatant unit.' Interviewed more than forty years later by documentary-makers Tim Bowden and Hank Nelson, Steele remembered McLaren as 'a leader . . . completely fearless'.

McLaren had no intention of remaining a prisoner. A month after the surrender, McLaren and his mates Ginger Burnett and Edgar Wilkie crawled under the barbed wire surrounding the prison camp at Changi Point. This is where we find him at the start of Hal Richardson's *One-Man War*.

Before the POW camp was sealed off by the Japanese, McLaren had noticed an old sampan—a small, flat-bottomed boat common all over South-East Asia—lying abandoned in the mangroves. With the sentries less than 300 metres away, the fugitives groped for the sampan and dragged it towards the water. In the heavy tropical darkness they hoped to drift unnoticed past the guards, whose banter they could hear in the distance. Their destination was Burma, more than 1400 kilometres to the north.

But the boat timbers were more rotten than McLaren had imagined. The Australians were barely halfway across the strait when a plank broke and the sampan began to sink. Straight ahead lay the island of Palau Ubin, whose quarries had supplied much of the stone used to build the 1000-metre-long causeway between Singapore and the Malay Peninsula. Using shovels they had stolen from the camp as oars, they paddled ashore before pushing the sampan into deeper water and letting it sink.

A series of peaks loomed over the island. McLaren and his companions crept through tall grass to the top of a hill and gazed across at the mainland. Hundreds of lights flickered close to the shoreline. To McLaren, the lights looked like Japanese soldiers with torches scouring the headland for escaped prisoners. As they lay there, the Australians became aware of something else: a smell Richardson describes as a 'strange and clinging stench'.

Behind them, Singapore lay in ruins. Japanese bombs and artillery had reduced parts of the city to rubble. Smoke from burning oil tanks hung over the island. Hospitals overflowed with wounded, and the streets and alleys were strewn with the bodies of dead civilians. British engineers had blown up the causeway in an attempt to block the Japanese advance, but they had botched the job. The gap was barely 20 metres wide, and Japanese soldiers were able to wade across at low tide.

McLaren, Burnett and Wilkie woke at dawn, their legs caked with mud. Daylight revealed that what they had seen the night before was not Japanese soldiers hunting for prisoners but lantern fish-traps set by Malay fishermen. The source of the 'sickening, overpowering odour' was now apparent: lying in the long grass were the putrefying corpses of British and Australian soldiers killed in the first Japanese infantry assaults.

McLaren heard a dog bark, but there was no sign of people. The Australians stayed hidden until dark, then began exploring, hoping to find a sampan or canoe that could carry them across the strait. Eventually they found a dugout canoe, but the sound of Japanese soldiers stalking the mangrove swamp convinced them that it was too dangerous to attempt to paddle to the mainland.

As well as the Japanese soldiers, there were some Chinese civilians on the island. Creeping up to a house on the ridge, McLaren saw a Chinese man in black pyjamas, who ushered him wordlessly inside. Soon afterwards, another Chinese arrived at the house. Younger than the first man, with cropped hair and dressed in a white suit, he spoke some English. There were four hundred Japanese soldiers on the island, he told McLaren. Japanese aircraft flew low over the island, and if the Australians were not careful, they would be spotted. He gave McLaren some fish and rice to share with his companions, who were hiding nearby. The young Chinese promised to come back after dark and take the Australians off the island. There were many Chinese like himself, he said, who were working against the Japanese and would help prisoners to escape. But he warned

McLaren not to trust Malays or Tamils, who he said were sympathetic to the Japanese and were likely to betray any prisoner they found.

The Chinese was as good as his word. That night he paddled the three Australians across the Johore Strait in a sampan, landing them close to a rubber plantation. Before turning back, he gave them fresh supplies of fish, rice and tobacco and repeated his warning against Tamils and Malays, urging them to trust 'only Chinese'.

For a few days they headed north, keeping as close as possible to the main road but hiding in the bush at the first sign of Malays or Japanese soldiers. On the fifth morning a Chinese appeared out of the jungle, startling the Australians as they huddled over a fire. Gesturing to the men to remain silent, he led them to a rubber plantation, where a much older Chinese in a white suit introduced himself in English, promising to take them to meet a group of fighters in the jungle. The 'CP', he said, would look after them, as it was already looking after other escaped soldiers.

More Chinese joined them. 'CP' scouts had been watching the Australians for some time, perhaps ever since they arrived on Johore. According to Hal Richardson, McLaren presumed the old man, who 'looked like a harmless pineapple planter', was referring to a 'Chinese society'. In truth, once he saw the Chinese were ready to share their hot tea and food, he did not care who or what the 'CP' was.

They spent all day and the next night in a rough shelter before following the old man 12 kilometres to a Malay-style timber house. Later, after being given coffee, biscuits and cigarettes, they were taken to a hideout in the jungle. Chinese armed with .303 rifles warned them that Japanese footprints had been spotted nearby and urged them to move deeper into the jungle. Richardson writes that the Australians were 'taken to a jungle camp where they saw about thirty Chinese, all busily cleaning tommy-guns, Vickers machine-guns and British army rifles. Amazingly, standing in a clearing on its own with no indication as to how it had been brought there, [was] a British 25-pounder howitzer.'

McLaren, Burnett and Wilkie were not the only Allied soldiers who had decided to take their chances in the Malayan jungle rather than surrender to the Japanese. During the seven days they spent in the camp, they were joined by other Australians, all brought by Chinese guides. By the time orders came to move, they were part of a large armed party.

Throughout the Malayan campaign the Imperial Japanese Army had committed atrocities wherever it went. The victims were mostly ethnic Chinese. Captain Ray Steele later recorded several civilian massacres in an 'Intelligence report on Malayan prisoners of war' dated 27 September 1943. In January 1942, 'about 250 Chinese were tried and executed in the MERSING, MALAYA area. Their bodies were observed by an AIF working party in July 1942.' In February and March 1942, 'hundreds of Chinese males were tied and executed by MG fire on the beach at Changi'. At Kota Tinggi, Malaya, '300 Chinese coolies were employed by the Japanese on repairing a bridge. They were then lined up and machine-gunned when the work was finished. This happened in Feb 1942 and was observed and reported by Malay Police.'

In her book *And Tomorrow Freedom*, Sheila Ross reports that at Keppel Harbour Japanese troops 'lined up every man, woman and child in the area, mostly Chinese, and gunned them down'. Ross's brother-in-law, Rex Blow, a lieutenant with the 2/10th Field Regiment, was among a group of Australian prisoners of war who saw 'a gory pile of several hundred' Chinese bodies at Keppel Harbour, 'the majority dead, but with many still clawing the air'. Decapitated heads were displayed on the site of the old Singapore General Post Office in Fullerton Square.

Massacres of ethnic Chinese were not simply acts of retaliation against Chinese who had fought with the British; they represented a systematic purge of perceived anti-Japanese elements. Malays and Tamils, long dominated by the more commercially successful Chinese, often proved enthusiastic collaborators. The records of the Singapore garrison commander reveal that on 6 March 1942 alone, 237 ethnic

Chinese Singaporeans were executed as 'spies, weapon holders, defection seekers, communists, holding the Chinese national flag, teachers and holders of the enemy's currencies'.

Many of the victims of Japanese atrocities were women. McLaren recalled seeing flies rising in swarms from what Richardson describes as the 'decomposing bodies of more than a hundred Chinese women and children' beside a road in Johore. The women had been 'chased down the road, ravished, shot and bayoneted. Their children lay sprawled beside them, just as they had been indiscriminately cut down. For miles the wide red road was gruesomely decorated with torn dresses and blouses and with murdered bodies. The Chinese guerrillas marched impassively on, inured to the sight by now.'

At a jungle clearing, the Australians were met by around two hundred Chinese. McLaren noticed a cloth banner that read: 'Welcome, international fighter. Join our anti-Jap League—the Chinese Communist Party.'

There was a parade ground, headquarters, huts and ammunition stores. The Chinese had a good supply of weapons but little knowledge of how to use them; they wanted McLaren to teach them about weapons and tactics. He did what they asked, but as news came through that the Allies had lost Sumatra, then Java and finally Burma, McLaren became restless—'morose and argumentative', in Richardson's words. The Chinese, he reckoned, were more interested in Communist Party ideology than in fighting the Japanese, and in any case he had no desire to spend the rest of the war as a weapons instructor in the Malayan jungle.

The guerrillas' shooting skills improved enough under McLaren's tutelage for them to launch fighting patrols to harass the Japanese. The three Australians joined raiding parties that ventured as far north as Kluang, more than 60 kilometres away, and Kota Tinggi, 30 kilometres to the east. The guerrillas expected reprisals, but the Japanese were wary of being ambushed in the jungle and instead took revenge on the civilian population. The flow of refugees into the jungle camp increased, putting further pressure on supplies. With food running low, raiding all but stopped.

McLaren was still aiming for Burma. He knew that his hosts, if they wished, could pass him up the spider's web of opium trails to Burma and perhaps even China, where he would be able to make contact with Allied forces. But the guerrilla commanders were reluctant to let him go.

Dysentery swept through the camp; the only treatment was opium pills. Beriberi, caused by lack of vitamin B1, left men wasted and barely able to walk. In September 1943, McLaren wrote a detailed intelligence report that Ray Steele carried back to Australia. In the report McLaren wrote that three Australian soldiers were among those who died while in the camp. Finally the Chinese asked McLaren to go for help. McLaren wrote that he stayed at the guerrilla camp for just over a fortnight, from 17 March to 1 April 1942.

Together with two men from the 2/4th Machine Gun Battalion, McLaren, Burnett and Wilkie set off northwards, accompanied by a Chinese guide. After a couple of days the guide left them. McLaren's party decided to keep moving north-west towards Siam, while the machine-gunners headed west to Malacca, hoping to find a boat that would take them to Sumatra. (Captured within hours, the machine-gunners were sentenced to four years' solitary confinement at Singapore's notorious Outram Road Gaol.)

As they headed north, McLaren's plans changed. India now seemed like the most promising destination, but the incessant rain and water-logged ground made it tough going. After finding the railway line that connected Singapore and Kuala Lumpur, they followed the tracks for a while, almost stumbling into a Japanese patrol before retreating into the jungle again. Near Kluang, they made contact with Chinese guerrillas who had been told to look out for them. After two days' rest at a jungle camp, they resumed their trek, keeping to rubber and pineapple planta-tions to avoid enemy patrols on the roads and making use of darkness to elude the guards on the ruined Segamat railway bridge.

Since escaping from Changi, McLaren and his two companions had traversed nearly 160 kilometres of enemy-controlled territory. They had left Johore state and were now in the state of Negri Sembilan. Ahead lay the capital, Kuala Lumpur, and, hundreds of kilometres to the north, the Siamese border.

A few kilometres outside the town of Rompin, McLaren and his companions stopped to rest in a rubber plantation. They were eating breakfast when voices called out to them in Malay, 'Good morning, masters.' Dressed in traditional sarongs, the Malays seemed friendly enough, although McLaren noticed some of the group melt away as the rest stood around talking. Deciding it was time to go, the Australians slipped back into the jungle just as the Malays returned, accompanied by Malay police. The guerrillas had warned them to trust only Chinese, but Malaya was full of Malays; it was not possible to hide from all of them.

The next day, another Malay—a middle-aged man—appeared before them. Promising to help the Australians despite the risk of being killed by the Japanese, the man led them to a jungle clearing. In return for a few Malayan dollars in payment, he agreed to buy food and bring it to them. While the Malay's eagerness to please made him suspicious, McLaren knew they could not risk walking into a town to buy food for themselves.

A few hours later the Malay returned as he had promised, but not alone. Instead of bringing food, he brought with him a handful of Malay policemen armed with rifles and bayonets. McLaren tried to talk the policemen into letting them go, but it was no use: the Japanese were paying twenty-five dollars a head for captured Allied soldiers. Driven by truck to Bahau, not far from Rompin, the Australians were taken to a military prison and hauled before a captain of the Kempei-Tai, the Japanese military police.

Known for its brutal interrogation methods, the Kempei-Tai was given the task of rooting out all resistance to Japanese military rule. Singapore's

Outram Road Gaol, where the two Australian machine-gunners had been sent after being captured, was a Kempei-Tai interrogation centre.

It was clear to McLaren that the Kempei-Tai captain wanted all three of them shot, but the garrison commander would not agree to it. Eventually the captain strode out of the guardhouse in disgust. McLaren could not help noticing the British First World War ribbons on the commander's tunic, which matched those he wore on his own leather belt. It turned out that they had been won not by the commander himself but by his father and that the commander was merely following Japanese tradition by wearing his father's decorations.

Impressed, perhaps, by the sight of the ribbons on McLaren's belt, the commander told the Australians to sit down. He ordered a guard to bring them food. Most of the prison guards were regular soldiers who were recovering from battle wounds. McLaren recalled them giving up their own beds to the prisoners and sleeping on the guardhouse floor. According to Richardson, 'For two days ... the Australians were pretty well treated.'

It 'did not last. Before dawn on the third morning, Jock McLaren was dragged before the commander. Arranged on a table were identity discs and pay books belonging to McLaren, Burnett and Wilkie. The commander demanded to know where they had come from. When McLaren declined to answer, he was struck over the head with a ruler and told he would be shot. It was not an idle threat: prisoners unfortunate enough to be recaptured were often summarily executed. McLaren looked across the table and told the commander that if he wanted to shoot him, he should go ahead and do it.

A curious scene followed in which, Richardson writes, 'The commander stared steadily at him for a minute, then pulled an English Three Castles cigarette from a tin, shoved it into McLaren's mouth, and lit it', remarking: 'You very good soldier ... You escape from Nippon army. More better you become soldier for Nippon and for me.'

After boasting that 'Nippon never prisoner', the commander invited McLaren to explain his own 'teachings' about a soldier's duty. 'To fight as long as we can,' was McLaren's reply. 'If we are taken prisoner, then we must be as big a nuisance as possible, and escape if we can.' In Richardson's account of the meeting, the commander 'nodded his head slowly. "Ah soka," he said. "You very good soldier." '

The frontline soldiers 'treated the prisoners much more kindly than did the occupation guards, who had not actually fought during the war and made up for that deficit by brutality'. In his September 1943 report, McLaren described the treatment at Bahau as 'fairly good' and wrote that 'Food here was good as we got extra food from individual soldiers'. When a truck arrived on 15 April to take the three Australians away, the soldiers 'gave them tobacco and an almost affectionate farewell'. McLaren often told Richardson, 'They were the best Japanese I ever met.'

From Bahau the Australians were taken to the larger town of Seremban, not far from the coast, and imprisoned in the guardhouse at the old AIF headquarters. McLaren's report states that food was 'of bad quality' and that there was '[p]lenty of face slapping'.

For three days the Australians lay around the guardhouse at Seremban. On the fourth day they were thrown in a truck and driven to the town gaol, where they were put in separate cells, each with a cement slab for a bed. For six consecutive mornings they were taken outside and put up against a high stone wall while a sword-wielding Japanese officer ordered a firing squad to take aim. Each time the officer rescinded his own order and the Australians were marched back to their cells. Every day they were given a small bowl of rice and a few sips of stagnant water. It seemed almost a blessing when they were finally taken from their fetid stone cells and delivered by truck to the sprawling Pudu Gaol in the capital, Kuala Lumpur.

Hal Richardson writes that Pudu housed about three hundred and fifty British and Australian prisoners of war—'unshaven, wasted and diseased'—as well as civilian prisoners. In his intelligence report, McLaren mentioned 'over 500' prisoners confined in buildings intended to house seventy during the 'British Regime'. The POWs were kept at first in the women's section of the gaol. The exercise yard, which had been very small to begin with, was soon dug up to provide pit latrines. Before long, practically every square metre of outdoor space had been dug up for latrines. With dysentery rife, the prisoners switched to the bucket system—a 'great improvement', according to McLaren. Treatment by the Japanese prison guards was generally 'fair', although McLaren reported that guards assigned to working parties 'did some beating up on occasions'.

Rations were scarce, and almost every man in the gaol suffered from beriberi or some other vitamin deficiency. Nevertheless, after the solitary confinement of Seremban and the isolation of the guerrilla camps, McLaren was glad to be among soldiers again. Weekly concerts were allowed, and one guard commander even had a piano brought into the gaol, which 'improved the entertainments'.

Later the supply of pork ceased and the prisoners were given beef, until that too 'became unfit for human consumption'. McLaren soon realised that the key to staying alive would be getting himself assigned to the working parties that went into the city to load scrap iron and other materials for the planned Siam–Burma railway. Outside the gaol, prisoners were able to scavenge for extra food, while those too sick to work were unlikely to survive. McLaren gives the names of four Australian soldiers who died at Pudu between January and September 1942; one hundred and one British prisoners died in the same period. Many had been in dire physical condition when they were brought in owing to having 'lived in the jungle for months'.

McLaren, Burnett and Wilkie were well enough to work, but as known escapees they were forbidden to go into the city. Trapped inside the overcrowded and disease-ridden gaol, they knew they would be lucky to survive. As well as beriberi, McLaren began to show signs of pellagra, caused by a lack of vitamin B3. Its classic symptoms are often described as the 'four Ds': diarrhoea, dermatitis, dementia and death. McLaren's condition was steadily worsening when a rumour began to circulate that all inmates were going to be moved. Hardly a day went by without some rumour or other doing the rounds of the prison, but this one turned out to be true. In October 1942, McLaren, Burnett and Wilkie found themselves back in Changi.

Chapter 2

MATA-MATA 142

Despite its notoriety, there were far worse Japanese POW camps than Changi. The camp had a decent hospital, and by mid-1943 many prisoners would have access to electric lighting and running water. Rohan Rivett, an Australian journalist and broadcaster who was captured on Java after escaping from Singapore, remembered the few days he spent at Changi as being 'like a holiday'. The official Australian history of the war describes the camp as having 'a pleasant suburban atmosphere'.

Since the POWs at Changi were nominally under the control of their own officers, there was less contact between guards and prisoners and consequently less opportunity for violence. Albert Thompson, a corporal in the Royal Australian Engineers, wrote in his diary that there was 'no scraping and bowing, no lashing and no interference whatever'.

Outside the camp, the Kempei-Tai was ruthless in its suppression of anti-Japanese activity, and ethnic Chinese were regularly pulled in for interrogation. From its headquarters in the old Art Deco YMCA building, the Kempei-Tai set up an island-wide network of spies and informants. Those accused (sometimes falsely) of subversion or sabotage faced torture and summary execution. Yet despite the dangers, some Chinese communist spies had stayed behind in Singapore to keep communications open to the guerrilla camps in Malaya.

McLaren's first priority was to become healthy again, and he was soon crawling through the wire at night to forage for extra food. Through a Chinese labourer, McLaren was able to make contact with one of the communists—a 'well-to-do citizen', according to Richardson, who would meet him at night outside the wire and give him food.

After nearly being caught by a sentry, the Chinese began sending his daughter instead, hoping that if anything went wrong the Japanese would fall for the story of a romantic tryst. Eager to join the communist guerrillas in the jungle, she tried to persuade McLaren to come with her, but he turned her down. His health was much worse than it had been a year earlier, and McLaren knew all too well the deprivations he would have to endure while living with the communists.

Singapore was now operating as a staging post for the mass transfer of prisoners of war to work in Japanese coal mines or on construction projects such as the Siam–Burma railway. In March 1943, word got around that a working party known as E Force was being organised at Changi and that its destination would be Borneo. This was another rumour of great interest to McLaren. While in Pudu Gaol, he had befriended an English prisoner who had worked for a shipping company on the trade routes around Borneo. The Englishman had told McLaren about a string of tiny islands that extended south-west from Mindanao in the southern Philippines towards British North Borneo (now Sabah). Local traders used small sailing craft to travel between these islands and the north-east coast of North Borneo.

McLaren's first escape had convinced him that reaching India through Malaya, Siam and Burma was impossible. It was not just the distance or the difficulty of obtaining food. Even if he were able to hide from the Japanese, there would be Malays ready to turn him in for the reward money. Escaping by boat to Sumatra, as some Australians and others had attempted to do in the days before Singapore fell, was out of the question now that Java and Sumatra were both under Japanese control. If McLaren was going to make a successful escape, it would have to be from Borneo. He pulled every string he could to make sure his name was on the draft.

On 28 March 1943, E Force, comprising five hundred British and five hundred Australian prisoners of war, sailed out of Singapore's Keppel Harbour on a small tramp steamer, the *de Klerk*, bound for Kuching in Sarawak. It was while waiting at the Singapore waterfront that McLaren met Lieutenant Rex Blow.

When he was interviewed forty years later by Bowden and Nelson, Blow described McLaren as a 'tall gangly Scotsman. He still had quite an accent. He was a tough-looking old bugger but you could see immediately that he was quite a character.'

Blow sat on the end of a box, with as many possessions as he could carry. 'I was trying to make myself as comfortable as I could,' he told Bowden and Nelson. 'We were waiting for the boat and Jock sat at the other end of the box and we started talking.'

That conversation on the Singapore docks would shape the course of the war for both men, but its significance continued long after the fighting was over. From now on there would be another witness to McLaren's adventures, another account of the events McLaren described to Hal Richardson.

Rex Blow was an easy man to talk to. Captain Athol Moffitt described Blow in his diary as a 'tall, good-looking chap with an easy manner and a wicked smile on his face'. But there was steel behind his charm.

It did not take long for McLaren and Blow to discover that each was planning to escape. Blow's co-conspirators were Captain Ray Steele of the 2/15th Field Regiment and Lieutenant Miles Gillon, an officer from the 2/10th Field Regiment. Like Blow, Ray Steele would later record a series of interviews with Bowden and Nelson for their radio documentary about Australian prisoners of war. Steele recalled that he 'very soon found out that Rex Blow and Miles Gillon, who were both in the camp but from a different unit, had the same idea [of escaping]. We started to talk about getting away and very soon it became known amongst the other fellows that there was an escape being planned. They started to call us the Escape Club, or the Dit Club, dit being Morse for E and E being for Escape.'

Blow had been thinking of little else since the surrender. One of his many schemes involved persuading a Chinese driver to smuggle him across the causeway in a vegetable truck, then travelling up the west coast of Malaya and stealing a boat to carry him across the Bay of Bengal to India. Not surprisingly, no amount of money was large enough to persuade a driver to take them across the causeway. Another plan involved sailing a boat directly from Singapore to Ceylon or India. In preparation, Blow and three other men had managed to stockpile tinned food, quinine tablets and assorted weapons and ammunition. The plan was abandoned after an identical attempt by two other prisoners failed. The absconders were caught and handed over to the Japanese; both were shot.

The physical condition of E Force was better than that of its predecessors, C and D Forces, which had been sent to Japan and Thailand respectively. In her book *Sandakan: A Conspiracy of Silence*, Lynette Silver writes that the 'vast majority' of prisoners in E Force came from combat and engineering units and had spent months employed on working parties around Singapore. Strict medical examinations had weeded out the sick. As a result, the men were generally fitter and there were fewer 'old blokes'. (Ironically, one of the 'old blokes' was McLaren himself.)

When war was declared, Rex Blow had been working at the Commonwealth Trading Bank in Brisbane; Hal Richardson suggests that, after looking him over, McLaren had doubts about whether Blow was physically tough enough to attempt an escape.

While it was true that Blow worked behind a desk at the bank, he was a champion swimmer; nearly six feet tall, he had been swimming competitively until shortly before he sailed with the 2nd AIF to Malaya. Blow had first made news as a nine-year-old in the 1927 Grafton public schools' swimming carnival, and throughout his school years the *Grafton Examiner* reported regularly on his feats in the pool. In 1934 the Brisbane *Telegraph* noted that the now Brisbane-based swimmer was 'improving at an amazing rate and seems sure of a brilliant future'. Blow won state swimming titles and there was talk of him competing in the Olympic Games, but after being picked to represent Queensland in the 1939 Australian championships in Melbourne, he made the startling decision to pull out, saying he 'did not feel disposed to make the trip at his own expense'. In September 1939, declaring his 'ardent desire to meet Hitler face to face', Blow enlisted in the 2nd AIF. Seventeen months later, he sailed to Malaya as an artillery officer. In September 1941, *Truth* reported that Blow had 'got himself a charming English bride, as a side activity to war service with the AIF'. How much of his life story Blow told Jock McLaren as they sat on the docks at Singapore is unknown, but if McLaren suspected Blow of being too soft to survive outside the wire, he would soon realise his mistake.

On board the *de Klerk*, the number of would-be escapers was growing. As well as Ray Steele and Miles Gillon, Blow had recruited a young lieutenant, Charlie Wagner, a former Sydney bookmaker who had served in the militia before being posted to Malaya with the AIF in February 1941. As an intelligence sergeant, Wagner played a crucial role in the ambush of a large Japanese force during the fighting in Malaya, penetrating enemy lines to gather accurate information about Japanese positions. Later he returned to the area to help bring out survivors. For his 'coolness, courage and devotion to duty', Wagner had been awarded the Distinguished Conduct Medal. Five days before the Allied surrender, he was commissioned lieutenant. Not only was Charlie Wagner an exceptionally brave soldier but also he spoke fluent Malay—an invaluable asset for any prisoner contemplating escape.

As the *de Klerk* steamed slowly towards Borneo, the group acquired one more member, Sapper Jim Kennedy, a colleague of McLaren from the 2/10th Ordnance Workshop. McLaren had tried to persuade Kennedy to join his escape from Changi more than a year earlier, but on that occasion Kennedy had turned him down. This time he was eager to go.

Lynette Silver writes that while on board the *de Klerk*, Captain Steele spoke to the senior Australian officer, Major John Fairley, about seizing the ship and sailing it to Australia. Charlie Wagner was all for it, but Fairley was unconvinced, saying he doubted the ship had enough fuel to make the trip. While expressing 'grave reservations' about the viability of such a plan, he put it to the senior British officer on E Force, Lieutenant Colonel Whimster, who 'turned on his heel and went below, eliminating the possibility of any further discussion'.

The voyage from Singapore to Sarawak took only a few days. After disembarking at Kuching, the five hundred Australians were marched several kilometres to an aerodrome where British civilians from Sarawak, Brunei and North Borneo had been interned with some Dutch civilians and another three hundred Australian soldiers from Singapore. Among the latter was an officer from McLaren's old unit, the 2/10th Ordnance Workshop, who had been transferred six months earlier from the POW camp at Sandakan in what was then British North Borneo. Hal Richardson reports the officer gripping McLaren's hands as he listened 'gravely' to McLaren's escape plans. "'Look here, Jock, you made it once, and you can make it again, and this time you'll get away with it. Now here, take this and don't argue." He pressed twenty-eight dollars into McLaren's fist. "You'll make it, all right, and I've got just the chappie to help you. Come along with me.'"

The 'chappie' was one of the civilian internees, the British governor of North Borneo, Robert Smith. Hearing that McLaren was planning to escape, Smith urged him to seek help from a former member of the North Borneo Armed Constabulary, Mata-mata (police agent) 142. Together with many other members of the colonial constabulary, Mata-mata 142 had been kept on by the Japanese. They wore wide cotton armbands inked with their identification number. According to Smith, Mata-mata 142 was pretending to work for the Japanese but in reality was working against them.

As well as memorising the policeman's number, McLaren assiduously gathered snippets of information—on tides and currents, the loyalties of the local population, and edible plants—that could be useful to him in his escape attempt.

Meanwhile, McLaren and Lieutenant Blow were put to work, along with the other Australian prisoners, unloading cement from a cargo ship, the *Taka Maru*, that had been chosen to transport the Australians 800 nautical miles around the coast to Sandakan.

On 14 April, the prisoners, still caked in cement dust, were loaded into the holds, one of which had headspace of only 1.2 metres. According to Richardson, there was 'one boiler on deck to cook for the five hundred men. Five rude latrines decorated the stern. As the men marched aboard in the afternoon sun, the rain came pelting down . . . and the wet cement stiffened into thin plaster-like casts that took the hair from the prisoners' bodies when they tried later to peel it off.' Lynette Silver notes that prisoners were rarely allowed to visit the latrines and that when they were, 'the contents of the tins leaked onto the troops below decks'.

For three days the *Taka Maru* steamed north-east along the coast of Sarawak, stopping at the island of Labuan (where the prisoners were allowed to wash in the ocean) before rounding the tip of North Borneo into the Sulu Sea. Fairley and his second-in-command, Major Carter, had been detained in Kuching, and Captain Rod Richardson was now the Australians' commanding officer. Steele again suggested hijacking the ship, but the idea was quickly rejected. According to Sheila Ross, 'none of them were sailors, none knew the area and they felt that too many of their fellow POWs would be against them anyway'.

In his book *Death on the Hellships*, Gregory Michno recounts a conversation between Captain Steele and Captain Richardson: '"Let's take the ship over!" said Steele. "There are only 20 guards—we can handle them and we'll head for the Celebes!" Richardson refused to agree. "It's my job to get these men home," he said.'

McLaren seems not to have mentioned either hijacking proposal to Hal Richardson, perhaps because he did not know about them. Although he would finish the war as a captain, in early 1943 Jock McLaren was still a private soldier. Officers and men were kept separated on the ship, and it would have been difficult for McLaren and Blow to communicate during the voyage.

On 21 April 1943, the *Taka Maru* finally dropped anchor at Berhala Island, a rugged and picturesque strip of land lying at the entrance to Sandakan Bay. The island was roughly a kilometre wide and 4-kilometres long. In his interview with Bowden and Nelson, Ray Steele described the island as 'lush' and recalled that 'you could hear birds'. At its northern tip, a horseshoe bay fringed with coconut palms was walled by sheer sandstone cliffs. Steele remembered being told that the Australians would not be on the island for long and that the Japanese were building more huts in the main camp at Sandakan. The beauty of the scenery seduced some prisoners into thinking they might even enjoy their time on Berhala Island.

The Pacific war had caught the British inhabitants of Sandakan unprepared. A tiny volunteer force protected a white population (often described as 'European', although it included Australians) of only around a hundred. Their response to the Japanese attack on Pearl Harbor had been to round up Japanese nationals at Sandakan and intern them in the old quarantine station on Berhala Island, where they would be kept until a camp could be built to house them on the mainland. After the Japanese took over, 'European' civilians replaced Japanese civilians as internees on

Berhala Island, although some essential personnel, such as the Australian Dr Jim Taylor, were kept under 'house arrest' and allowed to carry on their occupations. The Japanese took an inventory of the hospital's stores of drugs, but Taylor was given permission to dispense and sell drugs to the locals. According to evidence given by Lieutenant Rod Wells to the War Crimes Board of Inquiry, 'by paying in his own money and faking entries in the drug stores book, [Taylor] was able to obtain small supplies for the use of the POW camp'.

In the words of the 1946 report, 'Awards to helpers British North Borneo', written by Major Harry Jackson, 'The diet which was supplied to the Internees by the Japanese was a poor one and assistance from Sandakan town to those on Berhala Island began almost immediately. The "key" personnel through local native assistants were able to smuggle food, money and comforts into the camp.'

In January 1943 the civilian internees were taken off Berhala Island and transferred to Kuching in Sarawak, leaving the quarantine station empty to receive the Australian prisoners from the *Taka Maru*.

As the POWs were herded off the ship, word came back that the Japanese were searching all prisoners. McLaren hung back: as well as a miniature map of South-East Asia in his pocket, he had a revolver and twenty rounds of ammunition sewn into the collar of his gas cape. He was banking on the guards becoming bored and careless by the time they reached him.

It was not only McLaren whose palms were sweating. Rex Blow had managed to hold on to his escape kit: quinine tablets, bits and pieces of a wireless set, a .38 revolver with 45 rounds of ammunition, all secreted among his personal belongings. While on board the *de Klerk*, Blow had hidden the revolver by tying it to a piece of string and hanging it down one of the ship's wind vents.

The Australians were taken by barge across the bay to Berhala Island and lined up along the beach. Fortunately the sand was soft and, with

Gillon keeping watch, Blow was able to bury most of his gear before the guards reached him. There was not much he could do about the radio condenser, which was too big to bury, so he held out his pack, with the condenser hidden under the flap, and hoped.

From the deck, McLaren could see the Japanese guards poking and prodding each prisoner in search of contraband. Once ashore, he made straight for the oldest guard he could see. After throwing his cape on the ground, he waited for the guard to inspect his pack. On discovering a pencil in McLaren's pack, the Japanese looked pleased with himself. McLaren asked half-heartedly for the pencil back before reaching down and grabbing his cape off the sand. Holding it by the collar, he gave it a brisk shake before the guard waved him on. McLaren relaxed. Compared with others they had experienced, this search had been unusually thorough, although the Japanese had been mainly looking for writing materials. Preoccupied with pencils and paper, the guards failed to prevent Australian officers (who were entitled to more baggage than other ranks) from smuggling in the components of a complete wireless set.

The wooden buildings of the quarantine station were surrounded by double wire fences a couple of metres apart. The land behind the camp was well covered with vegetation and climbed to a densely forested mountain ridge. McLaren and Kennedy liked the look of it. The Australians were told they would be cutting timber for the main camp at Sandakan, just across the water. Before they could begin this task, they had to get the quarantine station camp in order. Food, as usual, was the number one priority, and McLaren and Kennedy made sure they were on the first working party to go searching for timber to build a wooden fish trap.

From up on the ridge, they could see the whole of Berhala Island. One thing immediately caught McLaren's eye: a cluster of buildings further along the coast, beyond the quarantine station. The Australians did not know it yet, but those buildings housed the island's leper colony. On the beach, unguarded, was a dugout canoe—a canoe, McLaren told Kennedy, that could carry them to freedom. All they would need was a pair of wooden paddles. As soon as they found suitable pieces of wood, they began whittling them into paddles with pocket knives.

The next day the Japanese camp commandant, Captain Susumi Hoshijima, delivered his customary welcoming speech, a variation on the speech he had given to B Force nine months earlier: 'You have been brought here to Sandakan to have the honour to build for the Imperial Japanese Forces an [aero]drome, you will work, you will build this [aero] drome if it takes three years. I tell you, I have power of life and death over you, and you will build this aerodrome if you stay here until your bones . . . rot under the tropical sun.' According to Private Nelson Short, one of only six Australians to survive the Sandakan death marches, Hoshijima told the Australians, 'If any of you escape, I will pick out three or four and shoot them. The war will last 100 years.'

The speech, according to Hal Richardson, was translated by 'a wizened Japanese interpreter named Yamamoto, who had been a jockey in civilian life and had ridden in Australia'. Lynette Silver calls the interpreter Ozawa and describes him as a 'Formosan civilian', although she agrees that he was small. There is no evidence that Ozawa had been a jockey, let alone ridden in Australia, but Canberra author Anthony Hill, in a 2011 speech to the families of Sandakan POWs, asserted that the diminutive interpreter was 'nick-named "Jimmy Pike" after the jockey'.

Richardson writes that at the end of the war both the commandant and his interpreter 'hang[ed] themselves with their mosquito nets after surrendering to the allies'. This is not true. The Sandakan commandant, Captain Hoshijima, was found guilty of war crimes and executed. What happened to Ozawa the interpreter is harder to say. The National Archives file of Warrant Officer William Sticpewich, another of the six death march survivors, includes some 'notes on the interrogation of Takakawa [i.e. Captain Takakuwa, who took over as commandant from Hoshijima in May 1945]'. Under the heading 'Trek to RANAU', Sticpewich asks:

'Who ordered the killing of OSAWA the interpreter. (American subject) over 15 years residence in USA. Was it for the reason you suspected him of being pro allied.'

Whatever the eventual fate of Hoshijima's interpreter, it was still three years away. During those three years, Ozawa would continue to play a significant role in events at Sandakan. McLaren, meanwhile, listened to the commandant's 'welcome' speech for clues to his own fate. Among Hoshijima's melodramatic threats and scoldings, the commandant revealed a vital piece of information: their stay on Berhala Island was only going to be temporary; before long the Australians would be transferred to the mainland to work on the aerodrome.

Hoshijima warned the prisoners against trying to escape. If his men did not recapture them, he said, they would die in the jungle. In both cases there would be reprisals against those left behind. The Australians had heard it all before. 'We all had our ideas about what it was best to do,' Blow told Bowden and Nelson. 'I don't think any of us wanted to be stupid. We realised that if you made a mistake and were caught, you weren't going to get a second chance. We sat around discussing it for hours on end.'

Between the POW camp and the shoreline was a small guardhouse shared by the Japanese guards and former constables of the North Borneo Armed Constabulary, still wearing their colonial uniforms. McLaren saw a 'well-built man, aged about twenty-nine' watching the prisoners as he patrolled the perimeter. He noticed that the man wore the number 142 on his armband. This was the person Governor Smith had told him to look out for.

The number 142 belonged to Corporal Koram, a Murut tribesman from the deep interior of Borneo. While masquerading as a trustworthy servant of the Japanese, Koram had continued to help civilians interned on Berhala Island. Six months earlier he had been disciplined by the Japanese for carrying messages between Berhala and Eight Mile Camp on the mainland, where POWs from B Force had already been put to work building the new aerodrome. Despite the reprimand, he was now acting as a guard for the newly arrived Australian POWs in E Force. (According to Silver, after being arrested twice and gaoled for a fortnight, Koram had been warned that next time he would be shot—a threat that persuaded him to 'curtail' his activities for a while.) Realising that his role as a guard would make it easier for him to come and go, Koram had even agreed to spy on the prisoners for his supposed new masters.

Waiting for Koram to come near him alone, McLaren whispered Governor Smith's name. Koram murmured back, 'Tonight'. Returning a few hours later, Koram drew McLaren a rough map in the sand, indicating the Filipino island of Tawi Tawi, around 120 nautical miles east of Sandakan, where he said guerrillas were fighting the Japanese. Koram was in contact with the guerrillas through a Chinese-Filipino trader, Wong Mu Sing, who had traded in sandalwood in Borneo before the war. Mu Sing was now an anti-Japanese agent whose fleet of *kompit* (ocean-going sailing craft) and power boats visited Sandakan every ten days or so with trading goods and a lot more besides. The guerrillas on Tawi Tawi, Koram told McLaren, were able to communicate with Australia by wireless. If McLaren wanted to escape, that should be his destination.

By now Blow, who spoke some Malay, had struck up his own friend-ship with Koram. Like McLaren, Blow had been quick to volunteer for wood-collecting outside the camp. With Koram acting as guard, the two found plenty of opportunities to talk. It was through his conversations with Koram that Blow heard about the guerrillas fighting on Tawi Tawi. The wood-hunting expeditions were useful in other ways, too, enabling Blow, as he later recalled, to do 'a pretty good reconnaissance of the island'. Koram promised to help Blow and his companions to escape, but only when he judged that the time was right.

Before Koram had the chance to act on his promise, an extraordinary thing happened. The 'fearless, compact Constabulary NCO' was fishing from his *prahu* (a traditional Malay sailing boat) when a US submarine surfaced alongside him. Greeting him from the conning tower was Corporal Alberto Quadra, who had been fighting with US soldiers operating as guerrillas on the Philippines. Thanks to Mu Sing, the guerrillas knew about the Australian prisoners on Sandakan. Quadra handed Koram a letter and asked him to deliver it, according to Major Jackson's report, to 'any white man he saw'. He also told Koram that if anyone wanted to escape, 'this was their chance'. If they were interested in joining the guerrillas, Mu Sing could arrange for them to be picked up by a US submarine and taken to Tawi Tawi.

In Jackson's words, it was a 'good thing that Koram was the one to have the experience and not a pro Jap native'.

Koram took the letter to Dr Jim Taylor, the district surgeon and principal medical officer of the North Borneo Trading Company. Born in Yass, New South Wales, Taylor worked at Sandakan hospital and was the central figure in the civilian underground, an organisation that until now had been mostly occupied with smuggling food and medicines to internees and prisoners. Taylor, in turn, asked Koram to deliver a letter to Captain Lionel Matthews, who had arrived the previous year with B Force and was now intelligence officer for the Australian prisoners at Eight Mile Camp. The doctor was also aware of Blow's escape plans. He asked Koram to pass on Quadra's message to the officers in Blow's escape group.

Awarded the Military Cross for bravery during the Malayan campaign, Captain Matthews had cunning to match his courage. A few months earlier, camp doctors had become worried about the number of men losing their sight as a result of vitamin A deficiency. In the absence of cod-liver oil and yellow vegetables, palm oil offered a way to improve vitamin A levels. When the Japanese gave permission for a working party to collect nuts from palm oil trees, Matthews nominated himself and three signallers to join the group. With no guards supervising the nut collectors, Matthews used the opportunity to set up a jungle 'postbox' in a large tree not far from the police station.

The tree became a meeting place for Captain Matthews and members of the civilian underground. It was through these meetings that Matthews learnt that some of the Chinese community were in touch with Filipino guerrillas on Tawi Tawi and other islands. Matthews also used his jungle postbox to make contact with Dr Taylor and with Governor Smith, who at that time was still interned on Berhala Island. With Taylor's help, Matthews had set up a system for smuggling life-saving drugs—including vitamin B to treat beriberi—into Eight Mile Camp.

Through Koram, Steele was able to get a message to Captain Matthews telling him about his plans to escape with Blow, Gillon and Wagner. There was no question of Matthews joining the escape, but Steele asked him for any help he could provide. While Matthews was not in a position to offer much, others were.

Chapter 3

WALLACE

⟫━⟪

Corporal Koram and Dr Taylor were not the only civilians risking their necks to help the Australian POWs at Sandakan. Two employees at the hospital, Peter Raymond Lai and Richard Low, were helping Taylor smuggle drugs to sick prisoners at Eight Mile Camp. According to Lieutenant Wells's evidence to the War Crimes Board of Inquiry, between September 1942 and July 1943, Dr Taylor sent 'almost weekly' supplies of medicines and equipment, including Atebrin, quinine, ether, sterilised bandages, iodine and other disinfectants, surgical instruments as well as extra food for the sick, and 'intelligence information regarding troop movements and other items of military interest'.

As well as medical supplies, Taylor sent chemicals needed to operate a secret wireless set that had been built by a handful of prisoners under Captain Matthews' direction at Eight Mile Camp. When not in use, the wireless was wrapped in a groundsheet and hidden at the bottom of a disused latrine. After building a receiver, the Australians built a transmitter. Both devices worked, although the transmitter was hidden after being successfully tested and was never used.

The receiver would be an invaluable—but highly dangerous—source of news on the progress of the war. Jackson writes that 'although Capt. Matthews was careful in the disposition of the news, many of his brother officers and PW [prisoner-of-war] helpers were not so discreet. In fact, as time went on many of them became extremely careless and it was only luck that prevented the Japanese from discovering the secret in the early days of the receiving set.'

As the demands of civilian internees and POWs grew, Taylor had been forced to expand his group of civilian helpers. Ernesto Lagan, a detective in the Japanese-controlled police, became an important figure, along with three brothers from a local Eurasian family, Alex, Paddy and Johnny Funk. The Funks lived less than 2 kilometres from the Eight Mile POW camp. Twenty-five-year-old Alex used to visit the camp and was befriended by Captain Matthews. In her affidavit to the War Crimes Board of Inquiry, Helen Funk described how her son Alex brought Matthews 'medical supplies, food and radio spare parts, a pistol and some ammunition'. Matthews also 'gave Alex some photo negatives of pictures of the camp and Alex had them developed for him. Messages and these photographs were taken by Alex and sent by native boats to some Americans hiding at Subu Island in the Philippines.' According to Helen, this went on 'for nearly a year'.

Ernesto Lagan was instrumental in fundraising for the internees and POWs, with the money going to pay for food, medicines and other necessities. 'Even the lowliest of coolies often contributed a few cents to Lagan and his assistants,' Major Jackson wrote in his report. Lieutenant Wells, in his evidence to the board of inquiry, recalled that Mrs M.Y. Cohen, a 'wealthy jewess' who owned a department store in the town of Sandakan, contributed a considerable sum to a secret fund organised by Dr Taylor to 'provide assistance for special POW cases such as escapees'. Taylor's secret fund, Wells told the board, would be 'of great assistance in the ultimate escape of Capt. Steele and his party'.

As well as smuggling contraband to the prisoners, civilians were acting as go-betweens and messengers between Berhala Island and Eight Mile Camp, with coded messages often passing through many hands before being delivered or left for collection at the jungle postbox. The main courier was Mohammed Salleh, who before the war had been watchman for the quarantine station and neighbouring leper colony. Duped by Salleh into believing that he was anti-British, the Japanese had kept him on. From his hut at the end of the jetty, Salleh kept watch on Japanese movements while passing on intelligence and contraband to the Australians.

In an attempt to mitigate the increasingly unhygienic conditions of the Berhala Island camp, the Japanese guards regularly took the prisoners to bathe in the sea. During these bathing excursions, they warned Salleh not to speak to the Australians, who they said were 'very bad men'. Salleh played along so convincingly that, in the words of the Jackson report, 'the Japs formed the opinion that . . . any propaganda on their part . . . to embitter him as an Asiatic against the white man, as far as they were concerned, met with the maximum of success. Little did they realise the cunning that existed within the skull of the diminutive Salleh.'

The Australian prisoners at Berhala Island often asked Salleh to sell their belongings for them and use the proceeds to buy food and medicines. In his report Jackson writes:

Although Salleh was a poor man he said that there was no need for that and refused to accept their belongings. He used to visit Dr Taylor daily for the purpose of bringing medicine back to the island. He used to return to Berhala at about 1400 hrs daily and always brought something back with him for the PW which he gave to them after telling them that they were to divide it amongst themselves.

By now Corporal Koram had arranged for the Filipino trader Mu Sing to pick up the officers' group and take them by boat to Tawi Tawi. In preparation for the escape, Koram made regular trips to the mainland, returning with dried fish and prawns, noodles and rice, which the prisoners stockpiled along with medicines and other equipment. But when the escape plan was put to the commanding officer of Eight Mile Camp, Major Fleming, he rejected it, insisting that all prisoners remain at Sandakan.

Blow had already passed up one opportunity to escape. When the Japanese invaded Singapore, he could have left by boat rather than be taken prisoner but, according to Sheila Ross, Blow's colonel had 'begged' him to stay with his men, and he had done so. Now, however, 'they were no longer a unit and they all felt it was a case of every man for himself'. Blow was not going to throw away the opportunity to escape from Sandakan. The same went for Steele, Gillon and Wagner. As for McLaren, his mind had been made up long ago. He did not need anyone's consent, and he was not asking for it. Nor was he relying on catching a ride—with Mu Sing or an American submarine captain or anyone else. McLaren had been betrayed once already, in Malaya, by a stranger he had trusted to help him escape but who had handed him over to the Japanese instead. He was not going to make the same mistake again.

McLaren's preference was to find (or steal) a boat and paddle to Tawi Tawi, but he knew that he and Kennedy would not be able to paddle to Tawi Tawi by themselves: the distance was too great, and they would not have the stamina. They would need a third man to share the load. The person McLaren chose was Sergeant Rex Butler, a former buffalo shooter who, according to Hal Richardson, could 'shoot a buffalo's eye out at fifty yards'. (An intelligence report by Steele, Wallace and Kennedy dated 20 March 1944 describes Butler as an 'exceptional rifle shot—known to have scored four hits on planes'.)

On the question of timing, however, McLaren was willing to compromise. He understood that if his party and Blow's were to make separate breaks, the first to go would trigger a reaction by the Japanese that would make it impossible for the second to get away. Told by Blow that the officers were not quite ready to go, McLaren apparently replied, 'OK. We'll hold our horses for a while.'

What McLaren did not know when he agreed to put his plans on hold was that his group and Blow's were not the only ones plotting an escape.

Artillery Sergeant Walter Wallace was an ingenious scrounger. While imprisoned at Eight Mile Camp, he had made himself useful to Captain Matthews by acquiring parts needed to build the secret wireless. Wallace's plan to escape dated back almost to his arrival at Sandakan. Nothing could sway him from his mission, not even the recapture of five Australians from the 2/29th Battalion who had escaped from Sandakan in July 1942. All five were in a pitiful state from beriberi, malaria and other skin diseases. After a spell in the Sandakan gaol, the men were taken to Kuching, where they were held for three months inside wire mesh cages. Put on trial for attempted escape, they were eventually sentenced to between six months' and six years' imprisonment. One of the men, Corporal Fairey, died at Changi Gaol in June 1944.

Four more would-be Australian escapers were recaptured having barely made it beyond the perimeter of the Sandakan aerodrome. They were part of a group of six that had escaped around the same time as Fairey's party. The remaining two were caught about 80 kilometres along the coast from Sandakan. All six were tried at Kuching and sentenced to four years at Singapore's Outram Road Gaol. Three would not survive their captivity.

In light of the savage beatings the men received when they were recaptured, senior officers at Sandakan counselled extreme caution to any prisoner contemplating escape, but Sergeant Wallace was undeterred.

Wallace had confided in the trader Mu Sing that he was determined to escape. He had also spoken to another member of the underground, nineteen-year-old Chin Piang Syn, whom the Australians nicknamed 'Sini'.

Sini worked as a clerk in the Japanese store at the aerodrome. His youth and small size made him seem more innocent than he was. The Japanese let him wander freely between Eight Mile Camp and Sandakan, unaware that he was acting as a courier for the prisoners. His apparent impunity meant he was entrusted by the underground not just with the usual money and cigarettes but also with maps and letters. After dropping them in the jungle postbox, Sini would leave a sign at the aerodrome to alert the Australians that a delivery awaited collection. According to Lynette Silver, Sini brushed off warnings about the dangers of his actions, telling Captain Ken Mosher, 'I know what will happen if the Japanese catch me, but I must do my duty. I am British and I am also a Boy Scout.'

Convinced that his best chance of escape was by sea, Wallace had been eager to make his break as soon as possible, but Sini held him back, insisting (according to Jackson) that he first travel to Tawi Tawi himself to see if what they had heard about the Filipino guerrillas was true. Wallace doubted that Sini was capable of undertaking such a journey, but Sini told him he would accompany Mu Sing on his next trip back to Sitangki (a small island off Tawi Tawi) and see the situation for himself. Although sceptical, Wallace gave him two letters for the guerrillas to pass on to the Allied authorities—a reckless act that would later earn him a severe reprimand from Major Fleming.

On 15 March 1943—more than a month before McLaren, Blow and the rest of E Force landed at Berhala Island—Sini set out in a small boat with Mu Sing and his wife, Halima. From Sandakan to Sitangki was a hazardous trip for such a vessel. The sea around North Borneo was infested with pirates, mostly Moro tribesmen from the Philippines. A party of pirates stopped Mu Sing's boat and robbed the three of everything except their clothes. They failed, however, to find Wallace's letters, which Sini had hidden in his shoes.

According to Jackson, the party reached Sitangki on 21 March. Sini and Mu Sing were picked up by the Japanese the day after they landed and asked why they had come. They told their interrogators that they had been robbed by pirates and had put in at Sitangki for protection, promising to leave as soon as they were released. The Japanese believed their story and let them go, but before leaving, Sini made sure Wallace's letter found its way to the guerrillas for delivery to the Allies.

Back in Sandakan, Wallace did not believe that Sini had actually been to Sitangki, but it made no difference to his plans. He was determined to break out: it was just a question of when. On 30 April, nine days after the arrival of E Force on Berhala Island, Wallace made his move. In Major Jackson's disapproving words, 'Unfortunately Sjt Wallace was impatient to escape and he did not take [Sini's] advice to wait until he gave the word.' Sini was said to have been 'amazed' when he heard the news, while Mu Sing and Ernesto Lagan recommended an immediate search.

Wallace had taken with him two signallers, twenty-one-year-old Howard Harvey and thirty-two-year-old Theodore MacKay. They crawled under the wire at around 9.30 p.m., planning to head roughly south to the coastal town of Lahad Datu, where they hoped to find a boat to take them to Tawi Tawi. Wallace was carrying a pistol and home-made dagger as well as two hundred dollars in cash, maps, a compass and food. They would have to cover around 170 kilometres, crossing rivers and swamps and a jungle-covered mountain range to reach Lahad Datu. If the trek proved to be too difficult, Wallace planned to double back and make contact with the underground in the hope of obtaining a boat.

Even with maps and a compass, the three men found the going too hard. After days of wading through swamps and beating their way through jungle, they discovered they had travelled a mere 11 kilometres from Eight Mile Camp. Wallace switched course, leading the party north-east in the direction of the aerodrome, but Harvey and MacKay were exhausted. With their rations gone, the two signallers decided to float downstream on logs, leaving Wallace to continue alone on foot. After several more days, he too gave up and plunged into the river, drifting with the current before running aground on the bank just a kilometre or two from the aerodrome. There was no sign of Harvey or MacKay, but a cigarette packet lying in the mud told Wallace that Japanese soldiers patrolled the riverbanks.

Around 8 p.m. on 11 May, Heng Joo Ming's de facto wife, Siti, heard a voice calling from outside the house. Joo Ming, a geologist before the war, had a job supervising local labourers at the aerodrome. He was also a central figure in the Sandakan underground. As well as providing rations for Wallace's escape, Joo Ming had been the source of many of the radio parts that found their way into the secret wireless at Eight Mile Camp. If Wallace could trust anyone, it was Joo Ming. After hearing the noise, Siti went outside and found Wallace standing there naked but for a pair of swimming trunks. Ushering him into the house, she told Joo Ming that 'Wally Wallace' had arrived.

Wallace and Joo Ming spent most of the night discussing what to do next. Before dawn, Wallace was taken to a shelter built by Corporal Koram and two other policemen in the jungle. Here Wallace would be safe from the Japanese search parties combing the area. With Siti bringing him food, Wallace spent his days in the jungle shelter, visiting Joo Ming's house only at night.

It was not until a week later that Joo Ming told Sini what had happened. The immediate reaction from the underground was to insist on getting Wallace away to Tawi Tawi as soon as possible. The dangers of being at large were brought home when Joo Ming returned one afternoon from the aerodrome with the grim news that Wallace's fellow escapees, Harvey and MacKay, were dead. After drifting downstream, the two men had come ashore a few kilometres from Eight Mile Camp, only to be spotted by a group of Malays. Two pretended to help, saying they would find the Australians a boat, while the rest stayed. When the two Malays returned, they brought with them two truckloads of Japanese soldiers. Armed with nothing but stones, Harvey and MacKay tried to fight them off, but they were quickly subdued and tied up. Ray Steele recalled being told that the two men had been beheaded. According to Japanese testimony cited by Lynette Silver, they were driven to a secluded spot where Harvey was shot to death, while MacKay was shot and then bludgeoned to death with rifle butts.

Jackson gives a different account, writing that the two signallers were seen near a kampong, or native village, and were 'betrayed by natives to the Japanese who ordered a search party from Mile 8 to . . . apprehend the escapees . . . Lt Moritake and Sjt Shoji together with some Formosan guards in two motor trucks were soon in the area, Harvey and Mackay were shot dead by a Japanese named Nagura as they were about to load a native boat . . . Wallace seemed to have vanished into thin air.'

The two bodies were dumped at the edge of the aerodrome. The shooting had been heard by prisoners working at the aerodrome, but it was only when Private Frank Martin was sent to identify the bodies that the Australians and Heng Joo Ming were able to confirm their fate.

Major Fleming, then the senior officer at Eight Mile Camp, gave yet another account of their deaths in his handwritten affidavit to the War Crimes Board of Inquiry. Fleming recalled being 'ordered to the airport to identify bodies of two Australian soldiers who had been shot while attempting to escape. I identified HARVEY and McKENZIE [after going absent without leave under his real name, MacKay had re-enlisted under the name McKenzie] who were lying in rough coffins. I was not allowed to touch anything. The men were covered by blankets and these were lifted so that I could only see the faces and chests of the deceased. As far as I could see there were no signs of violence beyond bullet wounds.'

Fleming asked the Japanese how his men had died and was told that they had been spotted in a Malay village 'collecting coconuts'. After being called on to stop, Harvey and MacKay 'ran and were shot'. When Fleming asked what had happened to Wallace, the Japanese replied that he was lying 'badly wounded' in Sandakan hospital.

Desperate, but not wounded, Wallace was now pleading with Captain Matthews to be allowed back into Eight Mile Camp, but Matthews refused. Strict head counts by the Japanese meant it was impossible for a missing man to reappear suddenly.

According to Hal Richardson, Koram approached McLaren and said, 'Something will have to be done about that third Australian outside Sandakan who is being taken care of by the Chinese. They might turn him over to the Japs.'

'Bring him across,' McLaren is said to have replied, although it is unlikely that the decision was his to make.

At any rate, the onus was now on Dr Taylor, who was keeping Wallace supplied with food, to arrange for his removal from Sandakan. An attempt was made to get him off the mainland to rendezvous with a boat that could take him to Tawi Tawi, but after the rendezvous craft failed to appear, Wallace had to return to his lair in the jungle. A few days before the end of May, Joo Ming's father-in-law and another fisherman rowed Wallace out to sea, hoping to transfer him to a boat manned by Mu Sing, Corporal Koram and another policeman, but again the rendezvous did not happen and Wallace had to go back. The decision was now made to move him to Berhala Island, where Koram and Salleh could keep him hidden until parties led by McLaren and Blow were ready to make their escapes. A few days later Joo Ming rowed him across the harbour and delivered him into Koram's care. All Wallace could do now was wait.

Wallace was not a popular man. Years later Blow remembered him as a 'difficult bloke'. Ray Steele said:

We had no alternative but to take him with us because if he'd been left there he would have died or been discovered. There was no point in taking him into the camp because he wasn't on the rolls. He was a fellow that had had a fairly mixed life . . . he was a prison warder, and you know what Australians think about policemen and prison warders . . . He was a big man . . . a bit of a bully . . . He liked to make idiots of the troops when he was training them.

In spite of all this, 'he was an Australian, he was a volunteer soldier, he was with us, and he needed help'. For as long as Wallace was hiding on Berhala Island, Blow and Charlie Wagner continued to slip under the wire to bring him food.

From time to time McLaren saw Burnett, one of his two partners on the ill-fated escape from Changi, and encouraged him to join the group. But Burnett had lost his appetite for escape. In the account McLaren gave to Richardson, Burnett said, 'The war will be over soon, so why throw your life away? I'm too young to die in the jungle. You'll never get away with it.'

It was a mistake, and Ginger Burnett would pay for it with his life. The third member of the Changi escape party, Edgar Wilkie, would survive the horrors of being a prisoner in South-East Asia only to be worked to death in a labour camp in Japan. Only Jock McLaren would ever see Australia again.

With Wallace still in hiding, word reached the men of E Force that the move to Sandakan was scheduled for 1 June 1943. The seven who had made up their minds to escape—Captain Steele; Lieutenants Blow, Gillon and Wagner; Sapper Kennedy, Driver Butler and Private McLaren— understood that once they were on the mainland, the odds against escaping would be much higher. Their best and perhaps their only chance of success was to escape while they were still on Berhala Island.

According to Steele, McLaren's group was preparing to go early. Steele recalled the news throwing Blow's group into a panic. 'We had to find them and say, "For God's sake don't go. We've got a party too. Can we all go together?"'

McLaren agreed to wait. In the event, the transfer to Sandakan was delayed by four days. News went around the camp that the move would definitely take place on the morning of 5 June. That meant the escape had to happen on the night of the 4 June.

It was clear that Wallace would have to go with them. Eight, however, was too many to fit in one boat. Nor was there enough food for eight men. The group had managed to stash enough food for seven men for ten days. Now they needed more food and at least one more boat.

Chapter 4

OH, AMERICANO, AMERICANO!

———⟶•⟵———

The new plan was for the four officers to hide out with Wallace at Koram's jungle shelter and wait for the *kompit* that would carry them to Tawi Tawi, while the other three—McLaren, Kennedy and Butler—paddled away in a canoe to be picked up by a native boat and transferred to a US submarine. Koram and Salleh had already 'borrowed' a large boat belonging to the leper colony, which they had dismantled and hidden in the jungle. According to Major Jackson, this was a 'ruse' to convince the Japanese that the whole party had departed by sea, although the officers would still be hiding on the island. Little did the lepers know that in addition to the hidden boat they would also be supplying the canoes.

According to Ray Steele, after the evening meal the gates to the camp were left open and prisoners were 'encouraged' to use the latrines. At that time it was still light. Once the gates were shut, no prisoner was allowed out of the camp for any reason.

Since arriving on Berhala Island, McLaren and Jim Kennedy had given themselves the job of collecting kindling to light the cooking fires. The camp guards had grown used to seeing them walk out of the camp gates carrying a wooden box on shafts. Richardson describes McLaren and Butler bowing 'awkwardly' to a Japanese guard as they carry the box of firewood, supported on two home-made wooden oars, out of the camp. Suddenly they hear a 'fierce cry' from the guard. Richardson asks, 'Had other Japanese found the clothing and supplies hidden in the undergrowth beyond the camp?' The two Australians fear the worst, but fortunately the cry turns out to be nothing more sinister than a shouted salute from the sentry to his NCO. The third member of McLaren's party, Sapper Kennedy, follows a few minutes later, and the three meet at the latrines, dropping through the holes on to the beach below before digging up their hidden supplies and heading for the high ground behind the bay.

Sheila Ross's account in *And Tomorrow Freedom* is even more suspenseful than Richardson's. It starts on the night before the escape, with the officers smuggling supplies and equipment outside the wire to be picked up when they leave. Aware that guards regularly patrolled the camp perimeter, Blow had arranged for Koram to create a distraction by talking to them. Blow and his companions 'lay flat just inside the wire, all the gear beside them, till the guard and Koram passed, then began to move . . . no sooner had they done so than a glinting bayonet confronted them.' Ross speculates that the guard on patrol duty 'knew of Koram's friendliness towards the POWs and did not entirely trust him' and, after completing his patrol, had suddenly backtracked on the inside of the wire, leaving Koram 'powerless' to warn his friends.

The quick-thinking intelligence officer, Charlie Wagner, 'stuck his fingers down his throat and began vomiting violently':

Owing to the cracked corn they were being fed, stomach pains and vomiting were not uncommon and not long before, Charlie had been genuinely ill. He clutched himself, staggering towards the guard, narrowly missing being run through by his bayonet, demanding that he be taken to hospital and making such a show that while the man's attention was diverted, Rex and Miles were able to bolt under the wire, dragging the supplies with them . . . the Japanese were terrified of any kind of disease and Charlie had played on this.

Charlie Wagner's performance earned him a brief hospitalisation while buying time for his companions to crawl back under the wire. McLaren and Kennedy then smuggled out the remaining supplies in their 'firewood' box.

On the night of the escape, they were again forced to improvise. According to Ross, the ship that had been due to transport the prisoners from Berhala Island to the mainland tied up at the jetty on the afternoon of 4 June. The seven absconders had planned to drop through the latrines into the mangrove swamp below, then scuttle quickly along the beach until they reached cover. But with the beach now in full view of Japanese guards posted on the ship and on the jetty, they had to loiter until dusk 'in the muck and mangrove' before making their move. The 'stench and slime were revolting', but they barely noticed them until later, when they cleaned themselves up.

In Lynette Silver's version, the escape from Berhala went off without a hitch. The seven Australians 'had no trouble leaving the compound . . . just as the main gate was due to be closed for the night, the group made its way to the camp latrines, built native-style out over the sea. It was a simple matter to drop through the seat and on to the tidal flats below. A quick dash across the mangroves to the jungle and they were free.'

Jackson merely records that 'at 2000 on the night of 4 June the four officers and the three other ranks escaped from the Berhala compound'.

Although it was not yet dark, and the camp guards were no more than 50 metres away, the men got away unnoticed. According to Ray Steele, the other prisoners at the latrines knew there was an escape in progress and 'gathered round in groups so we couldn't be seen shooting through the holes'.

The seven gathered at the place where Wallace was hiding, around half a kilometre from the camp. After that, they split up. McLaren, Butler and Kennedy were going to steal a canoe from the leper colony and head for Tawi Tawi, leaving the rest to follow in a few days' time. But none of the three was a strong swimmer. Blow and Wagner were excellent swimmers, so it fell to them to steal the canoe.

As a result of their careful reconnaissance of the island, Blow and Wagner knew exactly where the lepers moored their canoes, several hundred metres offshore. The pair swam out, clambered aboard and started to pull in the anchors. In his interview with Bowden and Nelson, Blow described the anchor as 'three lumps of metal joined together with a bit of wire'. Pulling it up made 'a hell of a clang'. The noise 'woke the lepers up. They came down and asked what we were doing. We told them we were going fishing. We realised it would take them some time to go and get the Japs from the camp.'

Sheila Ross writes that the lepers were 'understandably ... not convinced' by the fishing story. They pursued Blow and Wagner along the beach as they towed the canoes towards McLaren and his mates, who were 'holding another group of irate lepers at bay with their paddles'.

Richardson supplies some dialogue: 'No, no, masters ... Do not take our boat. We have to catch the fish to eat. We shall die. No, masters ...' But the Australians had come too far to stop now. 'Blow and Wagner climbed cautiously in after the others, as the lepers hobbled after them, alternately threatening and pleading,' Richardson writes. 'McLaren and Butler, seating themselves side by side, dug their crude paddles into the water and paddled furiously.'

After rounding the point of the bay, Blow and Wagner dropped over the side and sank their canoe in the deep water before swimming for shore. According to Ross, they hoped that by the time they got back to the beach 'the lepers would have given up the chase and gone back to bed'. If so, they were mistaken. 'The lepers were certainly not in bed. The instant they reached the shore Rex and Charlie heard the sound of shouting. And the voices were Japanese. There was no going back along the beach. Diving back into the sea they swam as rapidly as they could away from the shouting, back round the cliffs.'

From the point where they came ashore, the only way back to the place where they were to meet Steele, Gillon and Wallace was straight up Berhala's towering pink cliffs—a climb of about 160 metres, in the dark. Somehow they made it up the cliffface, only to collapse exhausted at the top. They did not rendezvous with their three comrades until the next morning. 'The others were a bit worried about us,' Blow recalled, 'but we had to shake off the lepers first.'

According to Lynette Silver, it was not until morning that the Japanese found out about the escape. Instead of carrying out a normal headcount, the camp guards had ordered the prisoners to number off. In an attempt to bamboozle them, the Australians called out their numbers at random, rather than in numerical order, but before long the guards cottoned on to the fact that they were seven men short and sent search parties to scour the island.

Jackson's report credits the lepers with ensuring the success of the 'ruse'.

To clinch the ruse the lepers had been persuaded to approach the Japanese . . . and tell them that they had seen seven white men raising the sail and departing . . . The lepers played their part well and gave a graphic description of the wretched Orang Puteh (white men) hauling up a sail on their boat and heading out to sea in a Northerly direction. The Japanese immediately ordered a fast motor launch to make the necessary search.

Hal Richardson, Sheila Ross and Lynette Silver all contradict Jackson's version, suggesting that the lepers were too angry about the theft of their boats to do any favours for the men who had stolen them.

Jackson, in preparing his 1946 report, had the unique advantage over the three published authors of being able to interview a wide range of eyewitnesses to the events he was describing while their memories were still fresh. But at least some of the witnesses had something to gain from speaking to Jackson: a minute paper for the Department of the Army records that Jackson paid out 292 pounds, two shillings and sixpence to 'Natives for services rendered to Australian Ps.W'.

As well as identifying individuals who had helped Australian prisoners, Jackson's report gave a precise account of the events that led to the two Sandakan death marches. By the time Jackson arrived, the Japanese had been defeated and Britain was back in control of its colonies, including Malaya. Whether or not the lepers on Berhala Island were actively seeking a share of the Australian rewards, it seems highly unlikely that they would have told a serving Australian officer about having informed the Japanese that Australian prisoners were attempting to escape. Not only would this have ruled them out of any share of the reward money but it could also have exposed them to some form of reprisal. A more plausible explanation is that in recounting the story of the stolen boats, they subtly recast their unheroic role in order to convince Jackson that it was all a 'ruse' to deceive the Japanese.

Silver, who lists Richardson's book in her bibliography but not Ross's, rejects Jackson's 'ruse' and concludes instead that while the 'irate lepers' told the Japanese about the prisoners having made off with their canoes, the Japanese 'did not suspect that four of the absconders, as well as Wallace, were still on the island'. (In their interviews with Bowden and Nelson, Blow and Steele both said the opposite, insisting the Japanese knew that at least some of the fugitives had not left the island.)

In any case, it was not only the Allies who offered rewards. The Japanese commandant, Captain Hoshijima, visited the watchman, Mohammed Salleh, on the morning the breakout was discovered. Hoshijima knew from reports that the guards had been cultivating Salleh, and he had come to the conclusion, as Jackson put it, that 'the Imperial Japanese Army had a true friend in Salleh'. He offered Salleh a thousand dollars for any information that led to the capture of the missing Australians. As Jackson notes in his report, to a poor man like Salleh, a thousand dollars was 'a sum of fabulous proportions'. Salleh went to great lengths to say how much it would mean to him to receive such a huge sum, telling Hoshijima how much he hated the 'white man' and promising to turn the fugitives over to the Japanese even if there was no reward. Hoshijima went away convinced of Salleh's loyalty. Japanese search parties continued to press him for news of the prisoners, visiting Salleh three times a day and each time being told, 'I am sorry that I have not seen the white men. I wish I could, I would love to have the reward.'

What the Japanese did not know was that while they were pestering the watchman for information, he was helping Koram feed the prisoners. According to Jackson, when Salleh visited the mainland, he and Koram used to go together to Dr Taylor's house to pick up food. Koram showed Salleh the spot where the officers were hiding, and every day Salleh 'put the food in five different places, at the same time signifying his presence by mewing like a cat'.

Although she does not mention Salleh's mewing, Lynette Silver retells the story of Salleh's dissembling to the Japanese soldiers virtually as Jackson told it, quoting the watchman's 'I am sorry' act word for word from Jackson's 1946 report. By then Salleh had more than proved his loyalty to the Allies. The watchman was among those arrested and tortured by the Kempei-Tai in the orgy of retribution that followed the escapes from Berhala Island. He was eventually sentenced to twelve years in prison.

As McLaren, Butler and Kennedy paddled away from Berhala Island, Wallace and the officers hunkered down to wait for the boat that Koram had promised would take them to Tawi Tawi. Mu Sing had boats in port waiting for Koram to give the word, but on realising that seven prisoners had escaped, the Japanese ordered all private vessels out of Sandakan harbour.

As well as landing dog teams on Berhala Island to search for the absconders, the Japanese circled the island with launches to prevent them from getting away by boat. According to Ray Steele, a boat was supposed to come for them on the first night, but it did not arrive. Each night the Australians went down to the shore, but each night they were disappointed.

In his interview with Bowden and Nelson, Blow recalled Japanese planes 'flying over all the time' searching for the Australians' hideout. Koram had promised to come back on the fifth day with food, but there was no sign of him. Blow was worried that Koram had been picked up by the Japanese.

McLaren's party had problems of its own. The men had no sails or long oars, and propelling a dugout canoe with crude home-made paddles was back-breaking work. As Hal Richardson depicts the scene, '[E]ndless trudging with the rough paddles across the water dulled the thoughts of the three men, who were so immersed in the slogging toil, that if one of the historic galleons that sailed these waters hundreds of years before had hove to beside them, they would barely have noticed.'

Japanese spotter planes made it too dangerous to venture out in daylight, so after paddling all night they would pull into a bay and stay hidden until dark. At Dewhurst Bay the Australians 'scaled coconut-trees and pulled out the soft cabbage-like foliage—known as "millionaire's fruit salad"—and ate it with raw fish', Richardson writes. 'Sway-backed, long-snouted wild pigs came grunting round their hiding-place, and McLaren tried out his revolver, but if he hit them they went plunging speedily back into bamboo and the trailing rattan palms. They tried to catch the small jungle crabs that scuttled noisily across the leaf carpets on the banks of the shallow, quick-flowing stream, until a plane roared over, and it was their turn to scuttle for cover.'

Near the mouth of what McLaren believed to be the Segama River, they encountered some native men in an outrigger canoe. A similar encounter with locals had led to McLaren's recapture in Malaya and, more recently, had cost Howard Harvey and Theodore MacKay their lives at Sandakan. McLaren had every right to be wary, but rather than avoid the local men, he and his companions went out to meet them. According to the account McLaren gave Richardson, when he told the men his name they 'shouted with glee', recognising it as the name of a 'good man' who worked for the Borneo Timber Company. 'My cousin,' McLaren told them, drawing on a 'vague memory' of a relative who lived in the area before the war. This fortuitous meeting resulted in a hearty meal of 'fish and native sweet potatoes' followed by a relaxing day watching orang-utans.

From the Segama River they headed to Tambisan Island, where they spent several days resting before trying to cross the treacherous Sibutu Passage, a 30-kilometre-wide channel separating Borneo from the islands of the Sulu Archipelago, one of which was Tawi Tawi.

According to Richardson, their first attempt to cross the passage failed when heavy seas threatened to overwhelm the canoe, forcing them to turn back to Borneo. On the night of 12 June they tried again, and when morning came they caught their first sight of what they hoped was Tawi Tawi but was actually the neighbouring island of Sanga Sanga. They landed there before realising their mistake and moving on. That afternoon, as they beached their canoe on Tawi Tawi, a native boy paddled towards them on an outrigger, prompting an encounter reminiscent of McLaren's meeting a few days earlier with the group of locals at the mouth of the Segama River.

McLaren was again greeted like a liberator. The young native boy 'came thrusting through the sea, waist-deep ... Salt water, or tears, streamed down his brown face, and he kissed each of the three haggard white men, crying out "Oh, Americano, Americano!"'

Assured that there were no Japanese on the island, McLaren and his companions followed the boy further around the coast until they ran into a 'junk like a craft out of a fairy tale'. The boat was laden with fruit— mounds of pineapples and bananas—which the Filipino sailors started hurling, not in anger but in celebration. 'The three Australians sat silent and bewildered,' Richardson writes, 'while cries of welcome rang out across the narrow channel; then a shower of fruit poured down on them, bouncing off the side and cascading over their heads and shoulders, filling the boat until it began to tilt under the load.'

What happened to the *prahu* that was supposed to meet the three Australians and deliver them to a rendezvous with a US submarine? According to Major Jackson's report, the plan had been for the party of three 'other ranks' to be picked up and taken to Kuala Kinabatangan, around 60 kilometres along the coast, where Koram would 'supervise their embarkation on an American submarine'. Jackson reports that the meeting with the *prahu* happened as planned 'at around 9 p.m.' on the night of the escape and that it reached Tanjong Aru at 10 p.m. and Kuala Kinabatangan at 3 a.m. While he does not confirm the rendezvous with the submarine, he states that 'Kennedy, Butler and McLaren reached Tawi Tawi on 14 June'.

Lynette Silver writes that the *prahu* arrived well before the agreed time of 3 a.m. but 'the submarine was unable to surface because a Japanese motor torpedo boat was in the area. As dawn was only three hours away, the escape party had no alternative but to try and make it to Tawi Tawi. The following night, when the submarine was able to surface, Koram delivered a letter to the commander, along with the message that the escapees had gone on alone.'

None of this corresponds with the account that McLaren gave to Hal Richardson, or with the story Blow told to Bowden and Nelson. Richardson does not mention the men transferring from the dugout canoe to a *prahu* or any subsequent rendezvous with a US submarine. Blow told Bowden and Nelson that McLaren and his companions paddled their canoe by night along the Borneo coast while taking cover during daylight in the dense coastal mangrove swamps. At some point they took their chances on the stretch of open sea between the coast of Borneo and Tawi Tawi. The one fact that all four accounts agree on is that on either 13 or 14 June 1943, McLaren, Butler and Kennedy landed safely on Tawi Tawi.

Suspecting them of being German spies, the Filipino guerrillas contacted Australian authorities by radio and reported the arrival of three men claiming to have escaped from a Japanese POW camp at Sandakan. A message came back asking, according to Hal Richardson, for their 'full names and army numbers, where they had lived in Australia, and who had lived in the houses next door and opposite to their own'. The wireless cross-examination went on for several nights until Australian military intelligence was satisfied that the escapees were who they said they were.

With their credentials confirmed, McLaren and his companions initially had 'nothing to do on Tawi Tawi . . . but relax, their only serious worry being the fate of the other escape party, of whom nothing had been heard'.

The reason for this was that the four officers and Wallace were still holed up on Berhala Island. The hiding place Koram had prepared for them was not as safe as it appeared. According to Sheila Ross, Blow was horrified to discover that the lepers were cultivating a vegetable garden just below their shelter, cutting the trees back ever further until the Australians had to cross a clearing to reach the nearest stream—a trip they dared risk only in the early evening, after the lepers had gone home. Worse, the lepers brought a dog with them to work every morning. The fugitives 'could hear the animal prowling around, could see him through the foliage, head down, tail wagging, following their scent, to stop a little short of their funk hold and . . . bark and bark'. It was only a matter of time, they were sure, before one of the lepers came to investigate.

Ten days passed before Koram was able to visit them. By then, their rations were almost gone. Koram told Blow that the Japanese knew they were still on the island. However, they believed the Australians were better armed than they actually were (their only firearm was Blow's .38 revolver). Koram warned them that the Japanese had issued the lepers with binoculars and that soldiers were searching the island with tracker dogs. He suspected, however, that the Japanese were scared of being ambushed and would prefer to let the fugitives starve to death. 'The Japs were scared stiff of the jungle,' Steele told Bowden and Nelson. 'By then the combat troops had moved on. The new guards were base wallahs, unfit for combat duty. They didn't like jungles so they didn't go too far into it, dogs or no dogs.'

At Koram's suggestion, the five moved back to the hideout previously occupied by Wallace, in an area the Japanese had already searched. Throughout this time, they made no attempt to contact the prisoners in the Sandakan camp.

'It was a difficult three weeks because it wasn't such a big island and therefore we couldn't sing out, and we couldn't light a fire for obvious reasons,' Ray Steele recalled. 'We had to talk in a whisper for practically all the time.'

An elaborate plan was devised to get the officers and Wallace off the island. It began with a visit by the Filipino soldier Alberto Quadra to his brother Bernard on Sandakan, supposedly on a 'trading mission'. It was Alberto who had startled Koram some weeks earlier by emerging from the conning tower of a US submarine that surfaced next to his fishing boat. As Jackson noted, the Japanese at Sandakan were 'naturally suspicious' of visitors from the Philippines, but anti-Japanese agents in the customs office persuaded them that Quadra was harmless. The truth, however, was that he had come to Sandakan in response to Mu Sing's request for help in getting the Australian escapees away from Berhala Island. Ernesto Lagan, the police detective, had been busy collecting funds from underground supporters to give to the Australians, and by 24 June nearly everything was in place for the escape. The Japanese had wound back their search for the five men and were no longer patrolling the sea around Berhala Island. 'We knew the launches had stopped,' Steele told Bowden and Nelson. 'Every other night we could hear them going round and round and round.'

Mu Sing, Koram, Moo Jing and other senior figures in the underground decided that the escape should happen two nights later, on 26 June. Before leaving, Blow gave Koram his watch—the only item of value he had—as a token of gratitude for the extraordinary personal risks the Murut tribesman had taken to help the Australians.

'We had arranged a meeting point near a few coconut trees,' Blow recalled. 'It was easy to distinguish even at night. We had to go there at dusk and smoke these dreadful cigars that Koram had brought us and wave them in a circle every minute or so. By midnight we were sick of these cigars. Then we saw a boat gliding in. By morning we were well along the coast . . . we pulled into a beach and hid among the mangroves.'

The 8-metre-long *kompit* was more seaworthy than McLaren's dugout canoe, but it was also more conspicuous. Once adrift in the Sibutu Passage, the sailing boat would be easily visible to Japanese ships en route to North Borneo. Although the Australians did not question the loyalty of Alberto Quadra, they were less certain about his Moro crewmen. Blow had a compass but the Moro pilot was navigating by the stars. When a whole night passed without their position changing, the prisoners immediately suspected a double-cross.

Sheila Ross suggests the *kompit* was actually heading back towards Borneo and that Blow forced the Moro pilot to turn the boat around by putting a gun to his head. Perhaps that is what he told her, but the story he told Bowden and Nelson in 1983 was slightly different. In his tape-recorded interview, he said that it was a cloudy night and that the pilot, while attempting to steer by the stars, had inadvertently sailed 'in a bit of a circle'. He could not remember putting a gun to the pilot's head. In any case, Quadra's Moro crew soon had a chance to demonstrate their loyalty.

On the second day out from Berhala Island, Quadra spotted smoke on the horizon. A Japanese warship was steaming towards them. Quadra ordered the Australians to lie down flat under a false floor while the crew hurriedly covered them with bags of rice. As Quadra kept up a running commentary on the warship's approach, Blow pleaded with the crew to 'give [the Japanese] a wave, smile, laugh—do anything!' Quadra had lowered the sail and put up an atap roof to give the impression that the crew was merely out fishing. If they were going to be sold out by the Moros, this was the moment. With the Australians immobilised under heavy bags of rice, they would have been helpless to prevent the Moros from shouting out a warning to the Japanese. But as the warship came alongside, the Moros played along, smiling and waving to the Japanese sailors, while the five Australians struggled to breathe under the cargo of rice. The Japanese officer, watching through binoculars, was deceived. Without bothering to come down, he waved the *kompit* on its way.

It took four days for Blow's party to reach Tawi Tawi (McLaren's group had taken ten). A small native boat took them ashore. When they finally landed, hordes of Filipinos came down to welcome them. It appeared to be common knowledge on Tawi Tawi that Quadra had gone to Sandakan to fetch them. According to Sheila Ross, a 'guard of honour of fierce-miened Moros carrying spears, *bolos*, *kerises*, home-made shotguns and rifles, sprang to attention at the command from a sergeant and saluted after a fashion'.

McLaren recalled rushing down to the shore to greet the officers as they arrived. He told Richardson he had recognised Blow from a distance by his 'fair hair'. Blow was convinced that McLaren's party had 'given us up. They thought we'd been caught.' To celebrate the Australians' reunion, their Filipino hosts laid on a feast and plied them with bamboo tubes filled with fiery coconut wine called *tuba*.

The guerrilla chief on Tawi Tawi was Lieutenant Colonel Suarez. Richardson describes him as a 'swarthy middle-aged man, whose partly Spanish ancestry showed in his features and bearing'; Sheila Ross portrays him as 'very tall, dark, half-Spanish and possibly half-Moro'. After interviewing the Australians, Colonel Suarez officially inducted them into the 125th Infantry Regiment of the US Forces in the Philippines, otherwise known as the Filipino guerrilla army. According to the March 1944 intelligence report by Steele, Wallace and Kennedy, the eight AIF men were invited by Suarez to 'undertake training of 125 Inf Regt pending further advice from HQ SWPA [South West Pacific Area]'. At the same time, 'particulars' of the eight Australians were sent by courier to guerrilla headquarters on Mindanao.

Several of the Australians had been looking forward to returning home, but the guerrilla leadership on neighbouring Mindanao would be in no hurry to make this happen. For the time being, McLaren and his companions were more valuable to the Allied war effort where they were.

Chapter 5

A SORRY COLLECTION OF MEN

⸺⸻⸺

It was more than two and a half years since the Imperial Japanese Army had invaded the Philippines. The US commander, General Douglas MacArthur, had initially intended to defend the whole of Luzon, the country's largest and most prosperous island and home of its capital, Manila. However, the success of Japanese landings on the west and east coasts of Luzon, and the consequent risk of being caught in a huge pincer movement, forced MacArthur to revert to War Plan Orange (WPO), the retreat to Bataan. Conceived long before the war, WPO had been endlessly pored over by American officers-to-be at West Point, as well as by visiting Japanese exchange students. MacArthur had opposed it since the mid-1930s. The plan proposed a series of delaying actions in central Luzon to hold up the enemy advance while the bulk of US and Filipino forces were with-drawn to the Bataan Peninsula, west of Manila, where they would dig in until relieved by the US Navy. The attack on Pearl Harbor on 8 December

1941 put paid to this fanciful scheme, and from early January 1942 the US and Filipino troops found themselves trapped in desperate rearguard actions on Corregidor Island and the Bataan Peninsula. They were still holding on in both places when President Roosevelt ordered MacArthur to evacuate to Australia, where he was made supreme commander of the South West Pacific Area, in charge of all Allied naval, land and air forces.

Inadequately supplied, and with their numbers depleted by disease and malnutrition, the troops defending Bataan were doomed. The Japanese commander, Lieutenant General Masaharu Homma, halted his attack during February and March to refit and reinforce his army. When the attack resumed, the Americans were rapidly overwhelmed. Bataan fell on 9 April 1942.

Homma had expected a total capitulation and was furious when the US surrender on Bataan was not extended to American soldiers throughout the Philippines. On 6 May, after a savage two-day assault, the Japanese captured Corregidor Island.

When MacArthur's successor, Lieutenant General Wainwright, requested terms for the surrender of his troops on Corregidor, the Japanese refused to accept the surrender unless it included all US forces in the Philippines. Torn between surrendering and disobeying an order, most of Wainwright's commanders reluctantly complied, but some resolved to fight on as guerrillas. Among them was Wendell Fertig, a Colorado-born mining engineer living in Manila when he was called to active duty with the US Army in June 1941. Fertig had been sent to Mindanao in late April 1942 to help with the destruction of highways and bridges. Defying General Wainwright's order to surrender, Fertig set about uniting the disparate guerrilla groups on Mindanao under his command.

In the beginning the guerrilla forces suffered from a shortage of arms and equipment. From March 1943, US submarines began delivering weapons and other supplies from Australia, but it took time for Fertig to transform his guerrillas into an effective military force. Until then, their chief value lay in intelligence rather than combat, especially the observation of Japanese ship movements through a network of coast-watch stations.

The small band of guerrillas on Tawi Tawi led by Colonel Suarez was enthusiastic but lacked basic military skills. Wallace, McLaren, Butler and Kennedy were given jobs as instructors, teaching the guerrillas the basics of infantry work, rifle work and signalling. In order for them to 'command respect and discipline', Suarez promoted all four to be senior to the Filipino NCOs whom they were instructing. Captain Steele became Suarez's second in command, Wagner was given responsibility for intelligence, while Blow and Gillon were made field commanders.

Wallace remained a divisive figure. In his tape-recorded interview, Steele said that Wallace 'never saw an angry man or fired an angry shot for the whole of the war'. Although he was valuable as an instructor, 'when it came to anything fair dinkum, Wallace was never there. On the two or three occasions when the Japs did land on Tawi Tawi, Wallace . . . took off up to the hills with his troops . . . with the excuse [of having] to save the signals equipment.'

While Blow and Steele were often scathing about Wallace, Colonel Suarez had a high opinion of him. When recommending Wallace for promotion in July 1943, Suarez wrote: 'Our troops are greatly indebted to this man for the excellent instruction he had given wherein he spends practically 24 hours a day, to improve the men . . . I consider Sgt Major Wallace the best instructor we have.' In his 'report on activities' dated 15 October 1943, even Steele had to concede that Wallace 'spent much of his own time in instruction and was highly respected for his military knowledge in all subjects'.

Jock McLaren, now with the rank of acting sergeant, was soon herding his fighters up and down the emergency trails to familiarise them with escape routes that would be needed in the event of large-scale Japanese landings.

After two American guerrillas arrived from Mindanao with a powerful wireless, the Australians helped build an observation post on top of Thumb Hill, a promontory that afforded a perfect view of Japanese ships moving between the islands. Largely thanks to Wallace, the guerrillas became expert in both Morse and semaphore signalling. Intelligence about ship sightings was conveyed by flag signals to the wireless operators further down the hill, who dispatched it to guerrilla headquarters. From there it was sent to the Americans, who could pass the information to MacArthur's headquarters in Australia or direct to submarines patrolling the sea lanes.

Far out to sea, McLaren often saw Japanese ships slide beneath the waves after being struck by torpedoes. Sooner or later, he knew, the Japanese would wake up to the presence of guerrilla spotters. After that, it would not take long for them to identify Thumb Hill as the likely observation post. Then the Australians, with a few dozen rifles and a couple of thousand rounds of ammunition, would be in trouble. Food was plentiful enough where they were, but there was not enough to sustain them for long if they had to retreat and hide out in the interior.

The first Japanese to come ashore turned out not to be soldiers but sailors who had survived the overnight sinking of a large merchant ship. 'They were a sorry collection of men, burnt by explosion and sun, rowing thankfully into Batu Batu [the capital], expecting the tender commiseration and attention of a Japanese occupying force,' Richardson writes. 'Instead, they found Batu Batu in the hands of their enemies. They climbed sheepishly out of the lifeboats and huddled together, leaving their dead behind, rolling in the red-tinged water that swilled in the boats.'

Blow, in his interview with Bowden and Nelson, recalled the survivors landing on a nearby island after drifting for fifteen days without food or water. After some of the islanders came across to Tawi Tawi and told the Australians that there were 'lots of Japanese' on their island, Blow went over to pick them up. He said they 'didn't have much fight in them'.

Blow had the bedraggled crewmen loaded on to a couple of *kompit* and took them back to Tawi Tawi for questioning.

Walter Wallace refers to the incident in his book, *Escape from Hell*, but writes only that the Japanese sailors were 'herded into a large bamboo stockade'. It is hard to believe that Wallace would have been unaware of what happened next.

As Sheila Ross puts it,

Now came the problem: what to do with them? They certainly couldn't let them go free to spread the word that they were there, training the guerrillas. There were no such things as POW camps on Tawi Tawi and, despite the impression given by the initial welcome feasts [for the Australians], food was far from plentiful on the island; certainly there was none to spare for unwanted Japanese. They knew exactly what their fate would be were they to be handed over to the locals, too many of whom had suffered at their hands. Even the now hardened Australians were too squeamish for that.

In his book *Fighting Monsters*, Richard Braithwaite, whose father was one of the few to escape from Sandakan, notes that Japanese captured by Allied soldiers were routinely executed. Senior commanders did not always discourage this. In 1943, General Sir Thomas Blamey, the Australian commander of Allied land forces in the Pacific under General Douglas MacArthur, told the *New York Times*, 'Fighting Japs is not like fighting normal human beings. The Jap is a little barbarian . . . We are not dealing with humans as we know them. We are dealing with something primitive. Our troops have the right idea of the Japs. They regard them as vermin.'

Dr Mark Johnston, author of a symposium paper on wartime Australian attitudes towards the Japanese, notes that 'the killing of unarmed, sleeping, sick or wounded Japanese was common. Although official pressure was put on troops to take prisoners, the Australian front-line soldiers—like their American counterparts—had little desire to do so.' He goes on:

At the jungle training school at Canungra, recruits were told that the Japanese was 'a cunning little rat', who was 'full of little ruses and tricks'. Australians were unwilling to take Japanese prisoners largely because of distrust born of bad experiences, with Japanese offering surrender and then acting as human bombs by detonating concealed explosive. The thousands of Australian soldiers who passed through Canungra were advised to shoot any Japanese surrendering with their hands closed. Frank Rolleston recalls that an apparently defenceless Japanese carrying a white cloth at Milne Bay was shot down on the grounds that 'we were not prepared to take the slightest risk with an enemy that had proved to be the limit in deception and treachery'. The fact that Australian wounded, and the stretcher bearers who carried them, could expect no immunity from enemy fire was a major source of criticism, as was Japanese bombing of medical facilities. Thus a medical officer wrote about a tent 'ward' attacked by enemy aircraft in Papua: 'When the smoke cleared the twelve [patients] were still in the tents, but each one was dead—killed by the deliberate sub-human fury of Tojo's men.'

In his interview with Bowden and Nelson, Ray Steele made it clear that the Japanese treatment of Allied POWs was in their minds as they considered what to do with the captured sailors. In addition, Blow and McLaren had both witnessed Japanese atrocities against civilians in Singapore and Malaya.

In Richardson's account, it was McLaren who took the decisions, despite the fact that two officers, Lieutenant Wagner and Captain Steele, were present at the interrogation. McLaren 'ordered the survivors to line up, and questioned them through a Moor [Moro?] woman who had once been married to a Japanese. He asked them about their ship and destination. Charlie Wagner stood beside him, listening to the replies, occasionally throwing in a question.' All the prisoners answered 'readily' except for one man, whom McLaren remembered seeing in a Japanese army tunic 'with the badge of a two-star private' when he landed, but who was now 'coatless and dressed like the others'.

'Get your tunic,' said McLaren abruptly. The Japanese looked at him with his mouth twisted down in contempt, strolled arrogantly away, and returned wearing his tunic.

'What's happened to your two stars?' asked McLaren with a thin smile.

In Japanese the soldier denied he had any rank and then as he watched McLaren's smile and Wagner's serene face, burst into tears.

'You cut off my head,' he said.

'You bastard!' said McLaren. 'You can speak English.'

McLaren and Wagner quickly agreed that they had 'no ammunition to waste' on shooting the prisoners and not enough food to keep them alive.

'It's all very well saying you should liberate prisoners if you can't feed them,' said McLaren, 'but what's to stop them killing you, once they're loose in the jungle? And if they catch you, will they liberate you?' He smiled mirthlessly, remembering the swollen bodies of women and children scattered along the road to Kulai, and the screaming of the tortured in Pudu Jail. 'I've seen too much of their little ways.'

The Japanese were 'liberated' with the sword.

Captain Steele told Bowden and Nelson that the crewmen were 'quite an embarrassment to us'. Although initially reluctant to describe what had happened to the captured sailors, Steele was eventually persuaded to speak by Bowden and Nelson, who assured him that enough time had passed for the story to be told (or rather retold, since Hal Richardson's version was published in 1957).

According to Steele, the Australians were well aware of how the Geneva Convention required prisoners of war to be treated, and of how the Japanese had disregarded the convention in their own treatment of prisoners. He told Bowden and Nelson that this knowledge 'eased their conscience a bit'. The Australians 'got what information we could' out of the sailors, 'which was nothing, and then . . . we had a great old argument as to what we were going to do with them'. As the senior Australian officer, Steele decided that 'if anyone was going to stick their neck out it was up to me'. He recalled that with the help of some Filipino guerrillas, the Australians put the Japanese sailors in boats and took them out to sea. Most were killed with *parang*, or Malay machetes. As Steele put it in his interview, 'We pushed them overboard and then cleaved their skulls in. Anyone who looked like he wasn't dead or was going to get in again, I shot him. We disposed of the bodies and that was all we could do.'

Rex Blow gave a different account of the incident to his sister-in-law, Sheila Ross. In her book she writes that the guerrillas 'loaded as many of the [Japanese] as they could into boats, took them out to sea and after hitting them on the back of the head threw them overboard'.

The rest were beheaded, which was undoubtedly a cleaner and quicker job. There was one Filipino who was a wizard at wielding a *bolo*—the heavy Moro knife—and there were few of them who had any qualms about executing an enemy. And who could blame them? The Japanese were blindfolded and stood at the edge of an uncovered manhole over a sewage pit; the head came off with one stroke, clean as a whistle every time. Body and head were united in the sewage and the lid replaced. None of the Australians liked the thought of cold-blooded execution, but, as they were to say many years later, what else could they have done?

Under questioning from Bowden and Nelson, Blow was a good deal more circumspect. 'They sort of died for one reason or another' was all he would say about the fate of the Japanese crewmen.

The unedited tape-recordings of interviews with Blow, Steele and many other former prisoners of the Japanese are held by the Australian War Memorial. Hank Nelson used these interviews to write a book he called *Prisoners of War*. The book includes Steele's frank account of the killings but omits Blow's evasive answer.

Richard Braithwaite comments in his book that Steele, a friend of his father, was a 'good man' who 'found himself committing a war crime in a totally pre-meditated way'. He goes on:

War, particularly guerrilla warfare, puts good people in that sort of situation. I find it most admirable that Ray had the moral courage to talk about it explicitly. I find the half-joking sort of way Rex Blow, an outstandingly brave soldier, talked about the same incident, less attractive. Hank Nelson was worried about including the piece in the radio documentary but Ray was happy, even though theoretically he could be prosecuted for war crimes.

Chapter 6

THE SANDAKAN INCIDENT

Back on Berhala Island, members of the Sandakan underground waited anxiously for news of the latest escape. Eventually, in early July, a man arrived in Sandakan from Tawi Tawi and told Mu Sing that all the Australians had made it safely to the Philippines. He delivered a letter from the escapees and another from one of the guerrillas. Mu Sing gave both letters to Koram, who showed them to Dr Taylor and Captain Matthews.

Relieved to know that all eight had reached Tawi Tawi, the pair could now start planning the next breakout. Sapper Ted Keating had been plotting his escape for some time and had done a deal with Charlie Wagner for the pair of them to escape together, along with three of Keating's mates. At the last minute, however, Wagner had changed his mind and gone with Blow instead, leaving Keating and his friends fuming. As long as the fate of Blow's party remained unknown, Keating had been willing to put off his own escape. Now he decided he had waited long enough.

There were other groups besides Keating's eager to try their luck. Sergeant Adair Macalister Blain was the federal Member of Parliament for the Division of Northern Territory. Together with Staff Sergeant James and Driver Scott, Blain had been asking Taylor for help to escape but, like Keating, he had been told to wait. Now both groups were ready to go. Mu Sing and others in the underground were making plans for the escapes while at the same time organising something much more dangerous: an armed uprising. This would be timed to coincide with a breakout by Australian POWs assisted by Corporal Koram and other members of the former North Borneo Armed Constabulary.

According to Lieutenant Wells' detailed evidence to the War Crimes Board of Inquiry, the Filipino guerrillas had responded to Matthews' request for arms with 'two machine guns, about twenty-seven rifles and about two thousand five hundred rounds of ammunition to be used in conjunction with the police arms in the event of any Allied move in the vicinity of Sandakan'.

The Sandakan uprising was, in turn, to be part of a larger revolt that would include insurrections in Jesselton, 300 kilometres away on the island's north-west coast, and in the south.

The underground had stockpiled guns and ammunition smuggled into Sandakan by the Filipino guerrillas, who would also join in the revolt. According to the Jackson report, the plans were 'very much in the early stages' and few prisoners even knew about them, although caches of rifles and machine guns had been hidden in 'strategic spots' close to Eight Mile Camp.

Before either the escapes or the uprising could take place, disaster struck.

Heng Joo Ming, who had hidden Wallace after his escape from Eight Mile Camp, was making money on the side by selling rice he had brought over from the islands. After an argument with his business partner, the two fell out, and the partner and an accomplice tried to blackmail Joo Ming

over his involvement with the underground. When Joo Ming refused to
pay up, the disgruntled blackmailers decided to tell a man called Jack
(or Jackie) Lo everything they knew.

According to Jackson, Jack Lo 'had the appearance of a bad type of
Chinese and his looks did not belie him':

[H]e was an untrustworthy and villainous man and was employed
by the Japanese as a spy. He was always anxious to serve his Japanese
masters. His hatred of the [prisoners of war] and anybody who had
dealings with them was well known. There were many among the local
population who were anxious to keep in with Lo, in him they saw their
chance of popularity with the Japanese. Jack Lo also had many who
were willing to come to him with information.

Joo Ming's falling out with his partner was to have calamitous results,
not just for him but for the whole of the Sandakan underground.

On 17 July 1943, Joo Ming was arrested and taken to the Sandakan
headquarters of the Kempei-Tai, where he was interrogated and tortured.
As Jackson writes:

[After] bashing [him] and throwing him around the room Ju-Jitsu-
style they spreadeagled him on the ground. A cloth was placed over
his face and one of the Japs continued to pour water into his mouth
until he was virtually waterlogged, then another Japanese jumped
from a chair on to his distended stomach, and so the 'water torture'
made its debut to Sandakan. Joo Ming's father-in-law, Jakariah, was
also brought in and subjected to torture. The Japanese soon began to
hear some names.

Among the names they heard were those of Mu Sing, Dr Taylor, Captain
Matthews, Paddy Funk, the police detective Ernesto Lagan—and Koram.

Sini, the young Chinese who had scoffed at danger by telling Captain Ken Mosher 'I am British and I am also a Boy Scout', was picked up by the Kempei-Tai in the early hours of 18 June. Sini had acted as a messenger for the underground as well as playing a key role in Wallace's escape. There was much he would have been able to tell the Japanese. For four days he was hurled around the walls and tortured without mercy by 'ju-jitsu experts working in relays', but he revealed nothing. Thrown into a room with Mu Sing, Captain Matthews and Dr Taylor, he was finally persuaded by the others to save himself by putting the blame on them. As Jackson put it, 'They wanted someone to remain alive and eventually tell the story.'

At 7 a.m. the next day, the Japanese took Ernesto Lagan to the Sandakan Civil Hospital and ordered him to arrest Dr Taylor and another doctor. After initially refusing, Lagan was forced to obey. Then he too was arrested. All three were taken to Kempei-Tai headquarters. Dr Taylor was savagely tortured but, according to Jackson, 'refused to divulge anything or admit anything. The Japanese practice of slashing a wooden sandal, previously rubbed in wet sand, across the face soon had Dr Taylor's face looking like a piece of raw meat. A middle-aged man of small stature, it seems impossible that Dr Taylor was able to survive the terrific floggings that were meted out to him.'

In his book *Fighting Monsters*, Braithwaite suggests that the doctor 'did not receive the harsh torture the others did', speculating that he might have been 'treated more leniently in deference to his greater age [forty-four to forty-nine years during the war]'. This is contradicted by Lieutenant Wells, who was imprisoned with Taylor at Sandakan and later at Kuching while both were awaiting trial. According to Wells' affidavit to the board of inquiry, Dr Taylor received 'the worst flogging of any prisoner, the scars of which were still evident at Kuching'.

There was no mercy for Ernesto Lagan, who suffered appalling violence. Before long the Japanese had extracted 'a considerable amount of information from him, also a signed statement implicating many'.

But the Kempei-Tai was still not satisfied. After delivering Lagan's 'bloodstained clothes' to his wife, they bullied and threatened her for information about her husband's activities. In particular, they wanted to know if he ever stayed out all night. Mrs Lagan had already burnt his diary and continued to deny any knowledge of his activities while the Japanese ransacked the house for incriminating evidence. When they could not get anything out of her, they started on her children, promising her nine-year-old son 'chocolates and presents if he told them something about his father's habits'. But Mrs Lagan had already warned her children not to fall for the Japanese 'ruses of kindness', and the boy held his tongue. A Japanese guard was left at the house for fifteen days, but Mrs Lagan maintained her silence.

When she was finally allowed to visit her husband in gaol, he was in a bad way—'very thin and pale and . . . devoid of any strength', in Jackson's words. Dismissing the cuts and bruises all over his body as the result of a 'fall', Lagan asked his wife to sell his clothes and use the money to buy food for his fellow prisoners. 'The only brightness which comes out of the darkness that was the PW story in North Borneo, is the loyalty, devotion and sacrifice of the majority of the inhabitants of that country,' Jackson commented in his report.

Koram was tortured, too (Jackson says that he suffered a 'severe form' of the water torture), but he told the Kempei-Tai nothing, although Lagan had implicated him in helping the eight Australians escape. Astonishingly, Koram succeeded in escaping himself, by climbing out of the lavatory window during a break in his interrogation. (As a result of Koram's escape, the prisoners were no longer allowed to go to the lavatory after dark but, as Lieutenant Weynton put it, 'had to urinate through the open window of the room in which we were locked up'.)

Like the Australian officers on Berhala Island, Koram did not draw attention to himself by fleeing but instead went to ground. Lieutenant Wells told the inquiry that Japanese patrols 'made long treks into the jungle looking for Cpl Koram, whose arrest would have seriously complicated the case'. For about a week Koram hid so close to his captors that, according to Lynette Silver, he was able to survive on food 'stolen from the Kempei-Tai's own larder'.

When the searches tailed off, Koram moved to a hideout close to the Sandakan reservoir, living on rations supplied by two of his police colleagues while he recovered from being tortured. Before leaving Sandakan he set light to a Japanese fuel store. His destination was Kota Belud on the north-west coast of Borneo, about 70 kilometres from Jesselton. En route he brazenly called in at a Japanese outpost on the Labuk River where he explained that he was conducting a census of the local population. He was sent on his way with cigarettes, food and three native helpers to carry his gear. Having given the Japanese a false destination far to the south, he continued on his way to Kota Belud. According to Jackson's report, Koram then travelled to Keningau, about 170 kilometres south, and on to his father's home in Pensiangan, close to the border of Sarawak.

About nine months after his escape, Koram returned to Keningau and 'virtually surrendered himself to the Japanese', who sent him back to Jesselton. There he was locked up for eleven days before being taken to Kuching. 'Whilst he was here,' Major Jackson writes, 'he told the Japanese that he had assisted some Australian PW to escape, he said that some of these PW were returning to Borneo and he wanted to help the Japanese as he now realised how wrong he was in trying to plot against his Japanese masters.' As the watchman Salleh had demonstrated, the Japanese were highly receptive to such talk and convinced themselves, in Jackson's words, that Koram was a man who 'could be of value to the Emperor's cause'. In this they were much deluded.

At Sandakan, meanwhile, more members of the civilian underground had been rounded up. Paddy Funk was arrested at the point of a bayonet and taken to Kempei-Tai headquarters, where he was beaten and tortured.

When he lost consciousness during a bout of water torture, the Japanese brought him round by injecting him with a stimulant, then started again.

Paddy's brother Alex, who had been under pressure from the Japanese to spy for them, told his mother he planned to hide out in the jungle, but he was picked up by the Kempei-Tai before he could make his escape. According to Helen Funk, Alex was 'beaten for four days and nights' before being brought home. She 'saw his face badly swollen, a part of his ear was missing and his clothing was bloody'. Helen had been hiding letters and photographs belonging to Captain Matthews but wisely burnt them after Alex's arrest. The Kempei-Tai did not leave Alex alone for long. After forcing him to reveal where he had hidden a rifle and some ammunition, they took him away and gave him the water torture. Helen Funk would never see her son Alex again.

On 20 July, Alberto Quadra's brother Bernard was arrested. Two days later the Japanese, having forced Joo Ming under torture to admit to supplying Wallace with wireless parts, raided Eight Mile Camp. The next day it was the turn of the loyal watchman Mohammed Salleh to be arrested.

Captain Matthews was working in the vegetable garden when the Japanese came looking for the wireless. Having been named by both Ernesto Lagan and Joo Ming Heng, Matthews was certain to be arrested.

The search was a catastrophe for the Australians, although the searchers missed Matthews' pistol and five rounds of ammunition, which another officer had managed to hide at the bottom of a cupboard. But other incriminating items were found. They included a set of news summaries compiled by Lieutenant Wells, the officer in charge of the radio.

Listening in the dark, and taking down notes on paper that had survived the Japanese purge of writing materials, Wells put together regular bulletins that were then rewritten and delivered to the senior Australian officer, Major Fleming, for censoring. Summaries, written in a rudimentary code, were sent each week by courier to Dr Taylor. Although warned of the risks, Wells did not bother to hide these summaries before sending them, believing they were safe enough kept in his socks. It would not take long for the Kempei-Tai to decipher the contents and guess the source of the information.

A second, more thorough search followed forty-eight hours later. Neither the wireless receiver, still hidden at the bottom of the disused latrine, nor the transmitter was discovered, but the Japanese found a number of documents, including maps belonging to Captain Matthews and a notebook. There were three maps: one of the town; another of the area around Eight Mile Camp with information about military installations and troop strength; and the last marking the homes of Japanese civilians. Together, they pointed to plans for some kind of insurrection.

When the POW working parties returned to the camp, they were met by the commandant, Captain Hoshijima. Interviewed by Tim Bowden and Hank Nelson, Wells recalled Hoshijima standing on the back of a vehicle: 'I thought he was about to address everybody. He just called out those two words I'll never forget, "Lieutenant Wells".' According to Jackson, Hoshijima told Wells, 'You are a very stupid boy for writing those things in your diary.' He then 'smacked Wells heavily around the face and head ... twisted a handkerchief that Wells had around his neck and besides nearly choking him he continued to give him a severe beating. He asked Wells where the radio set was but Wells denied that there was one.'

Lieutenant Wells kept up his denials, leading Hoshijima on a fruitless search around the camp before deciding that giving up the transmitter might enable him to save the receiver. He gambled on the Japanese not realising that the valves they had found belonged to a transmitter, not a receiver. Hoshijima called a parade at which, Wells told Bowden and Nelson, he 'took me to the top of the platform where the *tenkos* [roll calls] were held. He asked the whole camp to look at me, and said they would not see me again. And that was the last time I saw my lovely friends who went on the Ranau death march.'

As punishment for the 'radio plot', several officers and men were thrown in the 'cage'—described by Jackson as standing on 'stilts about two feet off the ground . . . it measured approximately 6' × 5' × 4' [and] was constructed of wood with wooden bars and had barely enough head room for a sitting man.' Although the rest were released after a few days, Lieutenant Gordon Weynton was twice sent to the cage and in both cases was left there for two weeks.

At Kempei-Tai headquarters, the POWs and the civilian members of the underground were held in a large room, forced to sit upright and cross-legged from 7.30 in the morning until 9.30 at night. As Wells recalled:

> It was a horrifying place because you could hear the groans and the cries from people being interrogated. Every morning the Kempei-Tai would have their meeting for the day, and always there was a quietness. Then all the chairs were pulled back. You'd know the meeting was over, and you'd think, 'Who's for it now?' You'd hear the clumping down the stairs and in would come in one of the Kempei-Tai. He would just signal with a gesture and you knew that you were in the box that day . . . And this went on for months, from July to November.

One of the Chinese, Wong Yun Siew, known as 'Pop', had been accused by the Kempei-Tai of having obtained valves for the camp wireless. Pop Wong denied it, and continued to deny it even after another inmate confessed to giving the valves to him. The Japanese did not believe Pop Wong, and for nearly a week he was tortured with everything the Kempei-Tai had: the water torture, the log torture, being slapped with the wet sandy slipper, cut with a sword scabbard and threatened with decapitation. By the end of it, Lynette Silver writes, the chief Kempei-Tai torturer, Sergeant Major Ehara, nicknamed 'the Bulldog', 'could only believe that Pop Wong was insane'.

Pop knew that the Japanese treated the mentally-afflicted well ...
When Ehara beat him he laughed, when given food he threw it away,
when ordered to sit at attention he threw himself down the stairs with
a wild-eyed look, or he sang. He even drank his own urine—not to
add to the impression he was mad, but because he had heard that
ingesting it would help heal internal injuries. The Japanese, quite
convinced that he had gone ... mad, stopped the interrogations
and confined him to Sandakan's Buli Sim Sim Mental Asylum.

... At the end of three months, having convinced everyone,
including the other inmates, that he was an 'orang gila', a madman,
he was fined and released. Once outside, he continued his charade by
taking off his trousers, urinating and then walking the length of the
main street with his trousers in his hands, laughing and shouting ... It
was all too much for the Japanese. They returned his fine and told him
to go away and buy some medicine ... Once out of sight, Pop slipped
quietly away and hid at a plantation near the 15-mile peg until the
Japanese had forgotten all about him.

Jackson comments drily in his report that 'Pop Wong's acting probably
saved him a lot of misery and pain'.

His accomplices did not escape so easily. '[T]he list of people arrested
grew as more Asiatics and Australian PW were gathered in by the
sadistic Nipponese,' Jackson writes. Captain Matthews had no doubt
about what was in store for him. After another of the Funk brothers,
Johnny, was arrested in September, Matthews tapped out a message for
him in Morse code: 'If anything happens to me, Johnny, and if you ever
happen to meet my wife, or any Australians, tell then that I have died
for my country.'

From the information they extracted from civilians, the Kempei-Tai
realised there must be another wireless hidden in the camp. As well as
wanting to discover the second wireless, they were determined to find

out everything they could about the planned rebellion. Convinced that Captain Matthews was the ringleader, they demanded to know whether his superior, Major Fleming, was also involved.

Lieutenant Wells, the wireless genius, was dragged in for further interrogation. Kept in solitary confinement for three weeks, on starvation rations, Wells would not admit anything. In mid-August Ehara took over his interrogation. One day Ehara asked Wells whether he was hungry. When Wells said he was, Ehara and his henchmen forced him to consume 'three or four cupfuls' of uncooked rice. Then they pushed a garden hose down his throat and filled his stomach with water. 'About three or four hours later the pain became excruciating as the rice swelled within the stomach.' Part of Wells's intestine came out of his body, but Wells 'managed to push it back by hand'. Then the interrogation continued.

> On another occasion the interviewer produced a small piece of wood like a meat skewer, pushed that into my left ear, and tapped it in with a small hammer. I think I fainted some time after it went through the drum. I remember the last excruciating sort of pain, and I must have gone out for some time because I was revived with a bucket of water . . . the ear was very painful; it bled for a couple of days, with no medical attention. But fortunately for me it didn't become infected. Eventually it healed, but of course I couldn't hear with it, and I have never been able to hear since.

When Wells still refused to confess or to name other Australians involved in the insurrection, he was handcuffed and hung by the wrists from a rafter above his head so that his knees nearly touched the floor. A rafter was then placed across his ankles. While one of the Kempei-Tai flogged him, another jumped on the rafter, rocking it like a see-saw. The effect of this torture, Wells told the board of inquiry,

[was] to stretch your arms or legs and almost break the ankle bones, by making you kneel with the fore part of your foot on the ground, with the rafter across the ankles on each edge. It pulled all the flesh away from the ankle. They apparently thought this amusing and persistently asked me to admit that Major Fleming ... had organised with the help of Capt Matthews and myself a revolt, and the names of persons in the camp possessing firearms or otherwise assisting.

When Wells refused to break, the Japanese turned their attention to Lieutenant Weynton. In his evidence to the War Crimes Board of Inquiry, Weynton described what he called the 'rather unpleasant affair' of his torture.

They took me on to the verandah and tied me to the end of an upright. I was tied facing the wall with my hands above my head. I was kneeling and the guards placed a bit of 4 inches by 2 inches planking about 10 feet long across the back of my legs. A member of the Kempei-Tai stood on each side and see-sawed. Another chap hit me on the back of the head with a riding whip trying to get information. I passed out. The next thing I knew a bucket of water splashed over me and they were kicking me in the ribs to make me get up.

Like Wells, Weynton tried to trick the Japanese into believing that what they had found was the receiver rather than the transmitter. By now, however, the Kempei-Tai had extracted confessions from some of the Chinese who had brought wireless parts into the camp. This information convinced them that the Australians were hiding a second receiver. They burnt Weynton with lighted cigarettes in an effort to force a confession out of him. He told the board of inquiry:

All the time that this had been going on there was a Kempei-Tai sitting down taking it all down in Japanese. The interpreter was a chap named Osawa [i.e. Ozawa, who had translated Hoshijima's welcoming speech]. They compiled a dossier about 1½ inches thick on me . . . All told I was interrogated for about six weeks, not every day but on and off. Interrogations would start about 9 o'clock and they would knock off for lunch, then might go on until 3 o'clock the following morning.

Throughout the time they were in the hands of the Kempei-Tai—seven months, in Lieutenant Weynton's case—the prisoners were forced to sit all day to attention, legs crossed and arms folded across their chest. For five minutes each morning and afternoon they were allowed a break for 'physical culture'. Anyone caught leaning back or not sitting to attention would be taken out of the cell and bashed.

Although forbidden to talk, the Australians managed to communicate by tapping out Morse messages on their thighs or their chest. By this means they were able to 'compare notes' on what they had told their interrogators so that each would know what it was possible to say without incriminating themselves or others. Wells recalled that one sentry, noticing the Australians tapping away, indicated to the relieving guard that Captain Matthews 'had gone a little crazy and might turn dangerous'.

By the middle of September, the Japanese decided they knew enough. Fifty-two civilians and twenty prisoners of war were taken by ship to Kuching to stand trial for crimes that ranged from insurrection and helping prisoners to escape to supplying birthday cakes and trafficking in poultry. Five judges were sent out from Singapore to preside over the trials, but before the first trial could begin the Japanese had to deal with something far more dangerous than the imagined insurrection at Sandakan.

On 9 October 1943, a force of around a hundred Chinese guerrillas attacked administration buildings, police stations and Japanese army facilities in the coastal town of Jesselton (now Kota Kinabalu), wiping out the fifty-strong Japanese garrison. At the same time around two hundred native fighters from the offshore islands landed and burnt the warehouses. The leader of the guerrillas, Albert Qwok, had travelled to the Philippines more than once to make contact with Colonel Suarez, but had not been able to persuade the Filipino guerrillas to send him the weapons he needed.

Jock McLaren recalled Qwok (he misremembered the name as Qwong) visiting Tawi Tawi and offering money to the guerrillas to cross the straits and join the uprising. According to Richardson, the guerrillas believed the rebels did not have a chance: although they might have been able to take Jesselton and hold it briefly, the Japanese were certain to send reinforcements to recapture the town.

'Good God!' McLaren is said to have exclaimed when he heard Qwok's proposal. 'This man's mad. I thought I was mad but . . .'

Having failed to obtain arms or support from the guerrillas on Tawi Tawi, Qwok's rebels had to fight the Japanese with *parang* and spears.

The initial battle for the town was over in a few hours. As well as killing the Japanese garrison, the rebels set fire to the main jetty. According to Lynette Silver, the man responsible for torching the jetty was none other than Corporal Koram. Qwok's rebel force, comprising local Chinese, Malays, Eurasians and Indians, had the run of Jesselton and its surroundings for a day before withdrawing.

Five days after the uprising, the Japanese hit back, sending troops to retake the town and bombing nearby villages. Fighting continued for another two months, but in the absence of arms and reinforcements for Qwok's rebels, there was only one possible outcome.

In his book *Rising Sun over Borneo*, Keat Gin Ooi writes that companies of soldiers from Kuching, together with the Kempei-Tai and native police, descended on Jesselton and its surroundings to hunt down the renegades and their supporters. 'Native inhabitants of islands such as Suluk, Udar,

Dinawan, Mantanani and Mengalum . . . [who] were known to number among the rebels and sympathizers, suffered island-wide extermination. Altogether an estimated 4000 people died in the reprisals.'

By mid-December it was all over for Qwok and his fighters. Cornered in a valley, Qwok surrendered to Japanese troops on 19 December in order to save the valley's inhabitants. According to Ooi, a consignment of weapons 'booked and paid for' arrived just ten days later from the Philippines.

Handed over to the Kempei-Tai, Qwok endured every kind of torture but refused to implicate anyone, stoically insisting that he alone was responsible for the uprising. On 24 January 1944, Qwok and his four top lieutenants were beheaded at Petegas; the remaining guerrillas were machine-gunned to death. Ooi writes that of 131 rebels sent to prison at Labuan, only seven were still alive at the end of the war. More were tortured and beaten to death at Batu Tiga gaol.

As Ooi notes, conquering Jesselton for a day had come at a high price. '[Qwok] and his comrades paid . . . with their lives as well as the lives of their supporters and many other lives as entire *kampung* [villages] along the west coast were exterminated.'

While the Japanese were rounding up those behind the Jesselton uprising, the Kempei-Tai were busy fine-tuning the evidence against those involved in what they were calling the 'Sandakan Incident'.

For nearly two months the accused had been held at Kuching Gaol, a place 'infested with lice and bugs'. In the last week of December, they were taken in parties from the gaol to Kempei-Tai headquarters in a convent opposite the Kuching radio station. Questioned on minute points of evidence, they discovered that the case against them was even stronger than they had imagined, thanks to distortions introduced by the translator, Ozawa. Weynton told the board of inquiry that Ozawa 'had deliberately misinterpreted statements made by me to the Kempei-Tai officer, the object apparently being to make the position seem worse than it really was'.

Weynton was furious to be informed by the Japanese that he had incriminated Major Fleming, his then commanding officer at Sandakan. 'At no time had I mentioned Fleming's name to Osawa,' Weynton wrote in a sworn affidavit, 'but he appeared to believe in his own mind that Fleming had something to do with it, and attempted to distort the evidence to that effect ... I do not think that any notice was taken of the denials I made.'

The Kempei-Tai also questioned Weynton closely on the broadcasts he had listened to on the camp radio, especially those describing Japanese losses in the Battle of the Bismarck Sea. 'They ... questioned me closely on the station that I had listened to, and they seemed rather surprised that I had not listened to or taken any notice of Tokio [sic] broadcasts but preferred the BBC broadcasts.'

During the trial, Captain Matthews and his fellow prisoners were crowded into 'fowl pens', forced, as usual, to sit cross-legged from early morning until late at night. Among the group was Mrs Cohen, who had given so generously to Dr Taylor's 'secret fund' to aid escaping prisoners. According to Lieutenant Wells, she was 'subject to the same rules and regulations as the male prisoners, being on one occasion beaten by a guard for failing to sit to attention'.

The accused were tried in batches before a panel of judges, but were allowed no defence counsel. The trials generally lasted around an hour, and both the verdicts and the sentences were decided in advance. One of the Australians, Sapper Ted Keating, did not survive long enough to see his own trial. It was Keating who had planned to escape with Charlie Wagner before Wagner changed his mind and went with Blow. Already suffering from a hideous tropical ulcer, he had gone down with dysentery on the ship to Kuching. Keating's condition had steadily deteriorated, and he died on 11 February 1944 before he could face court for passing letters and conspiring to escape.

Weynton was never formally told of the charge against him, although he assumed it was 'in connection with the radio'. Marched into the courtroom with four others, he immediately asked for a defence counsel, but the judge laughed at him and refused. After the prosecutor demanded a sentence of eight years, the court retired for ten minutes to consider its verdict. Weynton was found guilty and sentenced to ten years' penal servitude. The whole trial—for Weynton and his four companions—took just forty minutes.

Captain Matthews and Lieutenant Wells were tried on 29 February. They knew that they were on trial for their lives, although they had not been told the wording of the charges, which related to rebellion, espionage and other offences. Alongside them were three non-commissioned officers, Sergeant Alfred Stevens and Corporals McMillan and Roffey, all charged with violating POW regulations. Silver reports that all five were recorded by the court as pleading guilty but adds that this was later denied by Wells. In any case, all five were found guilty. No appeals were allowed.

The faked evidence against Matthews was damning. According to Wells, Ozawa had not confined himself to translating the record of interrogations conducted by the Kempei-Tai but carried out some questioning of his own. To begin with, Ozawa asked Matthews for the name of the commanding officer of the Australian POWs at the time they arrived in Sandakan and for the names of his senior officers. Matthews was willing to answer both questions because he knew the Japanese already possessed nominal rolls of the battalions. When Ozawa then asked him to write down the command structure of the Australian force, Matthews replied that the Japanese already had this information, but Ozawa insisted that he had to provide it himself. Matthews did as he was told. When they arrived in Kuching, Matthews was shown a statement allegedly made by him, saying: 'The following was my organisation of the camp in accordance with the plan to riot against the Japanese.' At his trial Matthews denied having made this confession, but the accusation was never withdrawn. Wells believed that 'it was on this information that Matthews was eventually executed'.

The next day the principal members of the Sandakan underground were brought before the judges. After a two-hour trial, two members of the North Borneo Constabulary, Sergeant-Major Yusup and Sergeant-Major Yangsalang, were each gaoled for fifteen years; Mohammed Salleh, the watchman, was given twelve years; Sini eight; Paddy Funk six; and his brother Johnny four. The remaining defendants, including Ernesto Lagan, Heng Joo Ming, Wong Mu Sing and the third Funk brother, Alex, were remanded until the following day.

On 2 March, Matthews, Wells and the three NCOs stood in court to hear their sentences. Matthews and Wells expected to be beheaded. Weynton told the board of inquiry that while they were all in the cell awaiting sentencing, 'we were given demonstrations a number of times how to lop people's heads off. They were quite convinced we were all to go and we were too.'

Wells, in particular, was astonished to hear his sentence: twelve years' solitary confinement with hard labour. His survival was the result of an extraordinary bureaucratic bungle. Regulations required Japanese army headquarters at Kuching to obtain permission for the executions from the Southern Army command in Saigon. A signal was sent seeking permission to execute two European officers and eight 'native' civilians, but the reply that came back from Saigon authorised the execution of only one European: as Matthews was the senior officer, the court decided that he should be the one to die. According to Lynette Silver, 'Saigon had sanctioned the executions as requested, but the Japanese cypher clerk in Borneo had typed 1 in place of 2. Wells owed his life to a typographical error.'

Weynton was sentenced to ten years. He and Wells spent the rest of the war in Singapore's Outram Road Gaol. Dr Taylor was a fellow inmate.

Jackson records that as Matthews passed the cages, 'the gallant Captain Matthews signified to his fellow prisoners that he was to be executed. He calmly divided his food and possessions with his fellow prisoners before being taken out for execution.'

Eight members of the Sandakan underground were executed alongside Captain Matthews, among them Ernesto Lagan, Joo Ming, Mu Sing and Alex Funk.

Jackson writes that 'Capt. Matthews retained his valiant bearing to the end. He faced the firing squad unflinchingly without an eye bandage, side by side with the eight loyal Asiatics, on 2 March 1944. He was buried in a grave by himself but the other eight were buried in a common grave.' Matthews was posthumously awarded the George Cross to go with the Military Cross and bar that he had already won for his courage in the Malaya campaign and later in the battle for Singapore.

The families of the civilians executed or imprisoned for their roles in the 'Sandakan Incident' continued to be persecuted. In the words of the Jackson report, they were 'left without means of support and many of their homes were destroyed or ransacked after their arrest'. In two cases young wives were forced to work as Japanese 'comfort women' to avoid starvation. Children died of malnutrition and parents 'died of worry'.

When the Japanese searched the home of Koram's colleague Sergeant Yusup, they discovered pencil drawings of Captain Matthews, Winston Churchill and the King and Queen. They beat Yusup's wife until she choked up blood. According to Jackson, she went back to her kampong in 1944 'still suffering from the effects of the treatment she had received at the hands of the Kempei-Tai. She was unable to get any medicine and subsequently died before the release of her husband from prison.'

Alex Funk's widow was not told until October 1945 that her husband had been executed in March 1944. Detective Ernesto Lagan's

British, Indian, Australian and Malayan forces were forced to retreat as Japanese troops, many on bicycles, swept down the Malay Peninsula. (State Library of Victoria)

Above: Australians from the 8th Division fought a desperate withdrawal after two Indian brigades were nearly wiped out at the Battle of Slim River. (State Library of Victoria) *Right:* Japanese troops in tankettes advancing on Singapore. Private Jock McLaren disembarked with his unit, the 2/10th Ordnance Workshop, two weeks before the first Japanese divisions crossed the causeway into Singapore. (State Library of Victoria)

Buildings in Singapore destroyed by Japanese bombing. The city was already in ruins when General Wavell issued his command that 'There must be no question or surrender'. (State Library of Victoria)

A rubber factory in Singapore incinerated by British troops ahead of the Japanese invasion. Jock McLaren was among the Australians ordered to surrender when Singapore fell on 15 February 1942. (State Library of Victoria)

Left: A sketch of Changi Gaol by cartoonist and prisoner of war Ronald Searle. McLaren and two (or perhaps three) fellow Queenslanders escaped from Changi in 1942 and were recaptured weeks later in Malaya. (State Library of Victoria) *Right:* Letters from Australian POWs acknowledging the help of local people while they were captives of the Japanese at Sandakan. Rex Blow and his companions, who hid on Berhala Island for weeks before escaping to the Philippines, all signed the typed letter. (State Library of Victoria)

A street scene in Sandakan, c. 1925. Civilians living in Sandakan risked their lives to smuggle food, medicine and radio parts into the nearby POW camp. Towards the end of the war the town was completely destroyed by Allied bombing. (State Library of South Australia)

American soldiers approaching the beachhead at Leyte. Australian aircraft, warships and landing craft played significant roles in the Leyte landing. (State Library of Victoria)

The liberation of the Filipino island of Mindanao by American troops. The site chosen for US landings on the west coast of Mindanao was changed after McLaren and Blow convinced General Eichelberger that guerrillas already owned the area.

(State Library of Victoria)

General Blamey and General MacArthur. The pair had a sometimes fractious relationship. Blamey spoke to McLaren and Blow about the possibility of rescuing Australian POWs at Sandakan, but the idea was vetoed, probably by MacArthur. (State Library of Victoria)

Australian and Royal Netherlands Indies soldiers on the beachhead at Tarakan. Left out of MacArthur's reconquest of the Philippines, Australian troops played a central role in the invasion of Tarakan. (State Library of Victoria)

Australian troops check a line of amphibious ducks used for the invasion of North Borneo. McLaren and Blow both led intelligence operations with Z Special Unit ahead of Allied landings. (State Library of Victoria)

Australian artillerymen in alligators making for the beach during the landing at Balikpapan, on the east coast of Borneo. McLaren conducted a one-man surveillance operation before the invasion, paddling in by canoe to examine the enemy's shore defences. (State Library of Victoria)

From 1944 RAAF Beaufighter squadrons island-hopped across the Pacific in support of US landings. Here Australian airmen chat to a local fisherman on Sanga Sanga, where Jock McLaren landed in June 1943 after escaping by canoe from Berhala Island. (State Library of Victoria)

With its long range and endurance, the Catalina flying boat performed many roles for the RAAF. McLaren flew over Balikpapan in an RAAF Catalina to search for a suitable drop zone for the Platypus VI team.
(State Library of Victoria)

Private Reg Sparks of Melbourne, who spent three and a half years in a Japanese prisoner-of-war camp in Singapore, taking a sword from a Japanese non-commissioned officer at the end of the war. (State Library of Victoria)

Captain Jock McLaren (centre) on Berhala Island with an Australian inspection party in October 1945. A local Chinese has just pointed out a Japanese dummy anti-aircraft gun. (AWM 121752)

Major Rex Blow (second from left) at Malabang airfield in 1945 with US guerrilla commander Colonel Wendell Fertig (far right) and another US guerrilla leader, Colonel Charles Hedges (second from right). (AWM 072919)

Surrender of the Japanese aboard USS *Missouri* on 2 September 1945.
General Blamey signs on behalf of Australia while General MacArthur,
Supreme Commander South West Pacific, looks on. (State Library of Victoria)

The trial of a Japanese prisoner in a tent on Morotai. Between 1945
and 1951, Australia conducted three hundred war crimes trials in eight
locations in the Asia-Pacific. Captain Hoshijima, the commandant at
Sandakan, was convicted of murder and hanged. (State Library of Victoria)

26-year-old widow suffered a nervous breakdown and was still in 'poor health', depending on charity, when Jackson visited Sandakan in 1946, while the wife of another policeman, Inspector Guriaman, 'died of a broken heart a week after his arrest'.

Chapter 7

PERMISSION TO PROCEED

———➤●◄———

While the Japanese laid waste to the organisation that had enabled their escape, the eight Australians on Tawi Tawi bided their time. Their motive for escaping from Sandakan had been to get home, but for now they were content to make themselves useful training Colonel Suarez's guerrillas. Their headquarters—a native hut with an atap roof, open windows and doors and a few chairs scattered around—became known as Anzac House.

A detailed chronological record compiled by Steele, Wallace and Kennedy as part of their March 1944 intelligence report shows that their responsibilities went well beyond training. The entry for 1 August 1943 shows how a reconnaissance mission to a nearby island led to a successful attack on a Japanese submarine chaser.

1 Aug 43—Capts HAMNER and STEELE and A/WO.II WALLACE visited BONGAO to complete reconnaissance of 1050 ft hill for

coast-watcher station. At 1500 hrs Japanese armoured sub-chaser carrying depth charge racks, 4 in[ch] naval gun, machine guns and searchlight docked at BONGAO. About 30 Japanese aboard (60–70 ft long). Word sent to BATO BATO by native courier. Lieut WAGNER, A/Sgts KENNEDY and McLAREN and three Filipino [fighters] with Browning Automatic Rifle and four rifles left BATO BATO at 1900 hrs.

It was dark when the three Australians reached Bongao, which had once hosted a US naval base. (Wallace did not take part in the action, commenting in his book that he and two companions were 'very sorry' to have 'lost the chance of joining in the fun'.) They made straight for the harbour and found the submarine chaser taking on supplies. All night they lay low, making certain of the number of Japanese on board. Japanese footwear was highly distinctive, and Hal Richardson includes an evocative detail about the 'slithering sound of Japanese rubber shoes on the steel deck'. Before dawn the guerrillas took up positions in the ruins of an old Spanish fort with a commanding position over the narrow entrance to the harbour.

The crew paraded before starting the engines. McLaren estimated there were thirty-five Japanese, but the guerrillas had surprise on their side. As the submarine chaser passed below their position, McLaren and his companions started firing. As Richardson writes,

[Their opening burst] shattered the morning calm and three men toppled on the bridge. Kennedy raked the wheel-house with an automatic rifle. Glass shattered, wood splintered, and Japanese ran in panic across the deck. For a minute there was pandemonium, then black smoke poured from the stack as the ship veered back onto a course for the open sea ... Their work done, the Australians climbed into their outrigger and sailed back to Batu Batu.

The chronological record, presumably based on Kennedy's eye-witness testimony of the encounter, confirms that the submarine chaser was 50 yards away when the Australians opened fire at just after 6.30 a.m. It reports: 'Eight Japs seen to fall, including Captain and other officers on the bridge. Upper works, wheelhouse and bridge badly smashed.'

While the attack on the submarine chaser burnished the Australians' fighting credentials, it provoked reprisals from the Japanese that went on for several days. Less than an hour after the attack, a Japanese dive bomber dropped six bombs on the guerrilla barracks at Batu Batu and machine-gunned the town. Four Filipino guerrillas were killed. At 4 p.m. a much larger Japanese ship anchored a kilometre offshore at Batu Batu. Expecting an enemy landing, the guerrillas manned defences and evacu-ated the town, but no troops appeared. Later a party led by Rex Blow took pot shots at two Japanese boats creeping up the Malum River.

Twice the next day Japanese dive-bombers dropped bombs on Batu Batu and Thumb Hill and machine-gunned the town, this time causing no damage or casualties. A Japanese gunboat lobbed shells harmlessly on the waterfront before moving off. The same day fifty Japanese soldiers 'landed and burned and machine-gunned' on the tiny island of Manuk Mangkaw, just south of Tawi Tawi.

To prepare for a possible assault by Japanese troops, the guerrillas had practised drills in which they dispersed and hid in the bushes while a decision was made about whether or not to engage the enemy. In his conversation with Bowden and Nelson, Blow recalled one or two troop transports arriving at Tawi Tawi with a force of around five hundred soldiers. He said that at the sight of the Japanese 'most of our soldiers disappeared ... we decided there wasn't much percentage for us to face 500 well-armed Japs, so we watched them go by. They looted and burned everything they could lay their hands on and then left.'

Although Japanese troops rarely set foot on Tawi Tawi, pro-Japanese Moros were a constant menace. The Muslim Moros were a famously belligerent people, having resisted Spanish, American and now Filipino rule. Some joined the guerrillas, but pro-Japanese Moros in the north of the island harassed Suarez's force and terrorised locals who supported them.

With Blow in command, a small party of guerrillas set off to attack the hostile Moros, who were camped near an old Spanish fort in the Dungun River region, around 30 kilometres from Batu Batu. The guerrilla group included McLaren, Miles Gillon and Rex Butler (but not Wallace, who, in his own words, 'reluctantly . . . had to remain behind and await results'). Passing through cultivated land, they planned to circle behind the Moros, but the Moros were nowhere to be seen. Blow, convinced that 'cunning' and 'treachery' were the Moros' defining characteristics, believed they would skulk away and avoid a fight. McLaren was not so sure.

According to Sheila Ross, the party spent more than an hour plodding through the mangroves, knee-deep in mud, before Blow decided to give up and return to the clearing.

> But they had underestimated the cunning of the Moros . . . The patrol never reached the clearing. [The Moros' leader] Datu Mohamed and 50 of his men were waiting in ambush on the outskirts. The first burst of fire sent Miles Gillon sprawling into the earth, wounded in an arm and both legs . . . a moment later Rex Butler was hit in the shoulder, the bullet passing down his body and out through his back.

A medical certificate of death signed by Blow records that the bullet 'entered his right shoulder and from his position . . . would have passed through his heart. He died almost immediately.'

Blow told Bowden and Nelson, 'We attacked them from the rear. We hadn't realised . . . how wily the Moros were, and of course they let us through . . . but we couldn't find any of them. It wasn't till we started back that they got between us and where we were going. They ambushed us . . .

Butler was killed and Miles Gillon was hit.' According to both Richardson and Sheila Ross, Rex Butler's last words were: 'They've got me.'

During the battle one Filipino guerrilla dashed out to join the Moros; Richardson writes that McLaren 'shot him dead as he ran'. (The intelligence report by Steele, Wallace and Kennedy notes that the deserter was 'found to be related to [the] Moro leader'.) One of the remaining Filipinos crawled out to retrieve Butler's automatic rifle while the Moros kept up a 'continuous barrage of blood-curdling yells and taunts'.

The Moros were confident, Richardson writes, 'because their leader was in possession of a valuable *anting-anting*—a magic charm which he believed protected him from bullets'.

> There were *anting-antings* for protection against aircraft, kris, or any other danger. This particular one was guaranteed protection against bullets. So the *datu* [chieftain] came out of the cover scornfully, his gun raised to remove Blow's fair head from his broad shoulders with a blast. Blow's tommy-gun raked him across his body, the bullets sending him spinning back into the bushes.
>
> The magic of the *anting-anting* gone, the Moros withdrew in panic up the hill.

To Blow, the Moros' retreat—when the guerrillas were running short of ammunition—'just didn't make sense'. McLaren had a better understanding than his superior of the peculiar mix of courage, pragmatism, clan allegiance and superstition that informed the Moros' actions. To him, their panicked flight after the death of their leader made perfect sense.

McLaren and Blow did what they could for the wounded Gillon, tearing up their shirts to make bandages before setting off on the arduous journey—'through miles of mangrove, over high country, through the cold of the hills, and the mosquito swarms of the coast'—back to Batu

Batu. McLaren was no doctor, but the skills he had learnt as a vet kept Gillon alive. Using a sliver of sharpened bamboo and the needle he always carried with him, McLaren cleaned the rusty iron and buckshot out of Gillon's wounds. Reluctantly they left Rex Butler's body behind.

Having driven off the Australians, the Moros returned to the scene and decapitated Butler. The Japanese gave them a reward of 2000 pesos and impaled the Australian's head on a spike on the garrison island of Jolo.

Rex Butler had been extremely popular with his guerrilla colleagues, respected for what Steele called his 'quiet efficiency and knowledge of bush-craft' as well as for his extraordinary marksmanship. In his intelligence report Steele states that Butler was 'held in such esteem by all ranks' that Colonel Suarez had 'applied to HQ 10th MD for the name of BATO BATO to be changed to CAMP BUTLER'.

Driver Butler was not the only guerrilla casualty that day. The intelligence report notes that the body of the Filipino deserter was found after the battle 'minus arms'. Although Richardson does not mention this discovery, he goes on to describe a skirmish with Japanese troops, after which the body of a dead guerrilla was found with 'both his flanks cleanly cut off, as though to provide steaks from the thin dusty rump'. Were they different accounts of the same incident? McLaren claimed to have witnessed cannibalism, and confessed that he might even have taken part in it. He told Richardson of having seen 'Filipino fighters' (Richardson does not identify them as Moros) take the heart out of dead enemy soldiers, 'drink the blood and eat the liver and even, on occasions, put a freshly severed Japanese head into a pot of coffee and boil it. There were to be times when, though he did not know for certain and felt it would not be polite to ask, he thought the flesh he was eating as a guest of a native guerrilla might not be from an animal.'

If Blow ever witnessed something similar, he kept the knowledge to himself. Throughout his life, however, he spoke freely about his distrust of the Moros, even those fighting on his side. 'In a set piece,' he told

Bowden and Nelson, 'they'd always sneak around the back and kill either you or the Japs. The Moros were never good to train.' While there was no way of compelling the Moros' loyalty, Blow said that it was possible to 'make somebody disappear'. The threat of reprisals, however, meant they had to be 'careful' because, as Blow put it, 'if you knock one Moro off, his whole clan would want to take revenge'.

Suarez's fear that pro-Japanese Moros might attack Batu Batu was one reason why he had turned down Albert Qwok's plea for support in the Jesselton uprising, but there were others. So far the Japanese had shown little interest in destroying the guerrillas on Tawi Tawi, but that attitude could change. With food and medicines running low, and many fighters sick with malaria, the guerrillas were barely capable of defending their own camp, let alone mounting a suicidal raid on the Japanese in Jesselton.

The Australians continued to man the observation post on Thumb Hill and join occasional sorties against the Moros in the north, but they were all becoming impatient to leave. In the end, Ray Steele told Bowden and Nelson, they 'got fed up with Tawi Tawi. Nothing much was going on ... Every now and again the Japs would send a few planes over or a few hundred men to scour the island, but there was nothing very big and we didn't seem to be achieving much.' In late August 1943, Steele wrote to Colonel Fertig on Mindanao, asking him to contact AIF headquarters for instructions. It would be almost November before they were given permission to leave.

The Japanese had now woken up to the strategic value of the island. For a while the Australian observers on Thumb Hill had been reporting to headquarters about naval movements around Tawi Tawi. They suspected that the Japanese were planning to build a naval base, possibly to establish a secure withdrawal route in the event of the tide turning against them in New Guinea and other islands further south.

Hal Richardson suggests that these reports of naval activity were not taken seriously, either by guerrilla headquarters in the Philippines or by Allied High Command. According to Richardson, High Command believed that the Japanese had far too strong a grip on the islands to Australia's north for their commanders to think of pulling back. If they had been considering a withdrawal, the argument went, the Japanese would not have allowed any guerrilla forces to remain behind their lines but would have destroyed them as they rolled south.

For more than a week Japanese aircraft raided the island, bombing Batu Batu to ruins and machine-gunning anything that moved. Ships and launches regularly attacked coastal villages, driving the civilian population to seek safety inland.

The guerrillas' intelligence officer, Charlie Wagner, ordered the arrest of a Filipino officer suspected of supplying the Japanese with information. Sheila Ross writes that the traitor was found with a copy of a map that could only have come from the Japanese headquarters on Jolo. 'His trial was brief and summary execution followed.' The following month, according to Steele's report, a 'civilian pro-Jap' was found guilty by the Staff Judge Advocate and 'executed by order of CO'.

Tawi Tawi was not the only island attacked by Japanese planes. Siasi was bombed and shelled for eight days ahead of a landing by fifty pro-Japanese Moros led by Datu Idris (or Idiris). Three weeks later, according to Steele's report, the *datu*'s force had grown to five hundred, 'looting, burning, raping, holding women to ransom and sending livestock to Jap garrison at JOLO'.

Idris claimed to have an agreement with 'my superiors, the Japanese' that all those resisting the Japanese 'will be killed and those who surrendered even [if] he is an officer should not be killed'. In a propaganda letter translated into English and included in Steele's intelligence report, the *datu* advised 'my brethren Christians, Chinese mestizos and Moros' that 'although you have attempted to attack and kill me, if you surrender to the Japanese, I swear that I keep no bad feeling toward you and I forgive you all'. A postscript contained information the Moro chieftain claimed to have obtained 'secretly' about the progress of the war: the

Americans were 'hard up and suffering' because the English had 'no more strength'. Asia belonged almost entirely to the Japanese, who had already landed in Australia, while Russia was now 'almost taken by the Japanese and Germans'. (According to Steele, Japanese propaganda was 'weak and boastful' and most civilians considered it 'laughable'.)

In October, a Chinese junk carrying a cargo of sugar appeared off Tawi Tawi. When the guerrillas went out to investigate, they found the boat was sailing under Japanese orders. After forcing the boat into Batu Batu, they plundered its valuable cargo. McLaren and Blow both recalled sacks of sugar being piled on the jetty before being stockpiled around the devastated town.

The guerrillas had scarcely finished unloading the junk when a lookout raised the alarm. In the darkness Japanese ships were sliding towards the harbour. As they had rehearsed, Suarez's men gathered up their food and weapons and headed into the hills behind Batu Batu. Gunboats raked the barbed-wire entanglements on the shoreline while naval ships further off lobbed shells into the town.

As dawn approached, barges crammed with infantry moved in. As Richardson describes it, the Japanese soldiers, '[h]elmeted, heavily armed with bayonets fixed', plunged into the shallow water 'hunched up as though expecting some returning fire, stumbling at the double through the mangroves' before dividing up, with half heading into the town while the rest followed their native guides into the jungle.

Their objective was the radio hut used by the guerrillas to transmit information sent down from the observation post on Thumb Hill, but the Japanese arrived too late. The radio operators had dismantled their equipment as soon as the shelling started, hiding or burying the components in the jungle and leaving behind 'only a useless collection of old radio telephone equipment'.

Richardson writes that an old Moro cook, 'a half-blind, grey-haired, loyal old guerrilla fighter, carrying a useless radio battery, came jogging along the road into the very face of the approaching Japanese force. He could see them only as a blur. He never knew what hit him. It seemed as though two thousand machine-guns had opened up to send him rolling, jerking in the spurting dust . . . they shouted frenziedly as they cut down the blind, tired old man, then stormed up and crowded around his body.'

According to Sheila Ross, Blow was dismayed by the way the Filipino guerrillas fled into the jungle rather than take on the enemy, finding the performance—after all their training—'desperately disappointing'. But Suarez's men were following their well-established drill of dropping back into the hills in order to assess the enemy's strength. The number of Japanese troops who came ashore that night was estimated by McLaren at 'about two thousand'. Richardson writes that 'as soon as the conquering party embarked and sailed away, the guerrillas came down from the hills'.

But the Japanese navy had not finished with Tawi Tawi. Richardson reports a fleet of camouflaged Japanese minesweepers 'meticulously sweeping the bay' on the morning after the attack. Whether Allied High Command wanted to believe it or not, the Japanese were evidently making preparations to use the area as a naval base.

According to Steele's intelligence report, the seven AIF men were 'relieved from duty' with Colonel Suarez's 125th Infantry Regiment on 15 October 1943, with permission to proceed to Wendell Fertig's head-quarters on Mindanao 'if they so desired'.

Steele recalled later that Suarez 'wasn't very happy at all and did all he could to persuade us to stop there'. For the Australians, however, leaving Tawi Tawi was the first step in the long journey back to Australia. Steele reminded Suarez that they had escaped from Sandakan with the intention of going home and that it was their duty to get word back to Australia about the fate of the 'poor devils' in Borneo and Singapore. 'Once he could see we were adamant,' Steele told Bowden and Nelson, 'he co-operated.'

On 28 October 1943, Colonel Suarez issued 'Special Order No. 73' transferring the AIF party from Tawi Tawi to the Tenth Military District on Mindanao.

The Australians organised a *kompit* to take them up through the islands lying to the north-east between Tawi Tawi and Mindanao. The first boat 'leaked like a sieve' and almost disintegrated within a day of their setting out, forcing them to go back for another. It was a perilous trip, since some of the islands either housed Japanese military bases or were regularly visited by Japanese patrols. Blow and McLaren survived several close encounters with Japanese naval ships before reaching Mindanao. Landing on the tip of the Zamboanga Peninsula, in the far west of Mindanao, they were met by a party of Fertig's guerrillas. According to Richardson, Japanese soldiers had just withdrawn after pillaging the town, but that did not stop the locals from serving up a welcoming feast even more extravagant than the one that had greeted them on Tawi Tawi—'a feast', as Sheila Ross puts it, 'to put all previous feasts to shame'.

But the conditions on Mindanao were not like those on Tawi Tawi. Ray Steele could feel the tension in the air. He and his companions had arrived in a war zone.

Chapter 8

MINDANAO

Let down by the American surrender, many Filipinos on Mindanao and other islands initially collaborated with the Japanese. In his book *US Army Special Operations in World War II*, David Hogan writes that one US Navy lieutenant 'pessimistically estimated that in the spring of 1942 only about 20 per cent of the Filipinos supported the Allied cause'.

Colonel Fertig's biographer, John Keats, suggests that the level of collaboration with the Japanese was much lower. 'Some raced to embrace the Japanese,' he writes. 'Their number was small, and almost exclusively restricted to those of wealth who sought to save what they could for themselves by taking office in the Japanese-created civil government—an instrument which did not govern, but confiscated. Others accepted rank in the puppet Bureau of Constabulary—a police militia—and others engaged in business with the Japanese.'

But the legacy of America's brief colonial rule in the Philippines was nothing like that of the Dutch in the Netherlands East Indies, where three centuries of colonial exploitation had left the native population deeply embittered towards its former rulers. Many Filipinos continued to feel a sense of loyalty towards the United States. Hogan suggests that these people felt a 'familial, almost mystic sense of obligation to America' and that this attraction 'found expression in the idolization of MacArthur, whose dramatic flair, embodied in his promise to return, captured the Filipino imagination'.

The Japanese occupation of the Philippines began with a concerted attempt to break this 'mystic' bond between the Filipinos and their former colonists. The Japanese-installed puppet government quickly declared its independence, and Filipinos were lectured about the great economic benefits to be gained from belonging to the Japanese-led Greater East Asia Co-Prosperity Sphere. But the pretence of brotherhood and the illusion of shared prosperity quickly broke down under the reality of an increasingly oppressive occupation.

In his monograph 'The American influence on the Mindanao resistance during the Second World War', Michael Balis writes that the Japanese assigned just 10,000 occupation troops to rule more than a million Mindanaoans. These were not the combat veterans who had conquered the island. By July 1942, the frontline soldiers had been withdrawn from Mindanao to fight and die elsewhere. The garrison troops who replaced them consisted largely of Koreans and Formosans who had been conditioned by the brutal treatment they received at the hands of their Japanese superiors.

These troops treated Filipino civilians harshly, extorting food and resources to support Japan's war effort and failing to discriminate between pro-Japanese Filipinos and those loyal to US rule. The historian Stephen N. Sams has shown how the Japanese 'demanded total obedience from the populace, slapping and beheading Filipinos who failed to bow or salute Japanese officers quickly enough'.

The occupation force was not strong enough to stop bandit violence, and in some provinces law and order collapsed. The '108th Division Unit History', dated 9 June 1944, states that Japanese troops 'were not interested in keeping law and order and could not have done so had they so desired as their influence extended only within the towns which they garrisoned. Crimes of all kinds were common under their very noses.' In Lanao Province, 'Japanese Commanders simply laughed when told of stories of brutality, murder and looting. They made no effort whatsoever to enforce any form of law and order.'

As early as June 1942, Christians living in the interior had been forced to move to the coast for protection, while Moros living in the interior were unable to go near the coast. In Kauswagan, Christians were driven out, and only Moro merchants and traders remained. Lawlessness by Moro brigands became so widespread that, in the words of a contemporaneous report, the 'History of the Mindanao Guerrillas', compiled by the Tenth Military District Headquarters, 'no Christian was safe in localities in or adjacent to Lanao. Slave traffic was carried on in undiminished scale and the Moros were bent ... [on squaring] accounts mostly imagined with the Christians living in the province.'

According to the unit history, the Japanese 'paid little attention' to the depredations of Moro bandits in the southern part of Lanao Province, where 'outlaw elements ... took advantage of conditions to establish slave markets ... Raiders from the interior carried on a thriving slave business between the Zamboanga coast ... and Lanao. Evidence is available on two parties that returned to Lanao with between ninety and one hundred Christian and Sulano [the indigenous people of the Zamboanga Peninsula] slaves each. One family of seven was sold for Seven Hundred Fifty Pesos.'

The document notes the outlawry that followed the Japanese invasion of the Philippines and records massacres of both Christians and Moros. It reports a protection racket run by a man named Laput as a 'screen to cover his looting of Moro and Christian merchants and other busi-nessmen passing through his sector. Laput was later discovered to be a Jap agent placed there for the purpose of stirring up trouble between the Christian and Moro communities to prevent formation of guerrilla opposition to them.'

Crushing emerging guerrilla groups was a more urgent priority for the Japanese than the maintenance of civil order. Strong garrisons protected the ports at Davao, Zamboanga and Cagayan, while smaller outposts were strung across the island's vast interior in the hope of restricting guerrilla movement and the transport of supplies.

A Japanese policy of indiscriminate terror failed to deter civilian cooperation with the guerrillas. As Balis points out, the Japanese humiliated and physically abused the Moros instead of trying to turn their traditional enmity with Christian Filipinos to their own advantage. Believing that the Moros would be 'too intimidated to resist', the Japanese 'underestimated Moro guerrilla war traditions and family pride'.

In their clumsy attempts to terrorise the Muslim Moros, the Japanese utterly failed to understand the militant pride of a people that for centuries had resisted attempts by Catholic Spaniards and Filipinos to convert them to Christianity. As the Allies themselves discovered, the Moros fiercely defended their tribal land, often with weapons and ammunition abandoned by the Americans after the surrender. Japanese patrols that wandered into Moro territory without permission insulted the *datu*, whose followers were prepared to fight to the death to avenge him. Mistreatment by the Japanese turned Moros, many of whom had been prepared to side with the invaders for opportunistic reasons, from potential allies into implacable foes.

In September 1942, a company of Japanese soldiers crossed Lake Lanao by launch and began advancing along the national highway. At the first sound of firing, Moros from the surrounding area began to converge on the intruders. The Japanese, fearing they would be encircled, withdrew to their launches, only to find them on fire. According to a 1944 'G2 Staff Study of Philippine Islands Situation', compiled by US military intelligence ['G2'], the entire company of 126 men 'was wiped out, including a Japanese captain ... [whose] sword was taken and was apparently quite valuable as the Japanese made several efforts to secure the return of it. In retaliation for this massacre, the Japanese bombed and strafed the Tamparan District sporadically for the next three months. However, it appears that the only casualties inflicted were a few carabaos [water buffalo] and chickens.'

Fearful of military reprisals and indiscriminate violence, Filipinos learnt to keep their distance from the Japanese. Self-preservation, rather than active resistance, was the initial motivation for gathering and passing on intelligence about Japanese troop movements. The 'History of the Mindanao Guerrillas' notes that 'civilians, after learning of Japanese brutalities, found it necessary to know enemy intentions and movements to avoid contact and escape bearing the brunt of enemy atrocities. In effect, the very fondness for acts of barbarism on the part of the Japanese forced both the civilian population and the early, loose, scattered guerrilla bands to organize into intelligence groups primarily for security.'

At first localised and ad hoc, intelligence-gathering against the Japanese became steadily more systematic. The 'History of the Mindanao guerrillas' records:

All loyal civilians (the percentage of disloyal ones very negligible), all soldiers and officers were in effect operatives, for in the Philippines, people were naturally curious and to turn that curiosity to advantage became an easy matter ... not only with the Japanese does the spy system work based on 'Everyone can Spy—Everyone must Spy'. Some mercenary elements sided with the Japs, yet the greatest bulk of the population covered the enemy in a network of intelligence.

There could hardly be any movement on his part, unless performed in places absolutely inaccessible to foreign approach, that escaped notice and about which information was relayed through various means . . . to Army Unit Headquarters.

Masquerading as innocent sellers of chicken or wine, civilians and guerrillas would be sent into Japanese-held territory to observe and memorise everything they could about Japanese installations and activities in the area. Such information, acquired at great personal risk, would be indispensable to Americans as they planned the reconquest of the Philippines.

In the aftermath of the American surrender, guerrilla groups all over Mindanao sprang into existence. The 'History of the Mindanao Guerrillas' states that at least seventy were operating by the end of 1942. 'Enemy patrols were ambushed, garrisons attacked, convoys waylaid; puppet officials seized, some jailed . . . there was no stopping the surge of the new resistance government.'

There were several factors that made Mindanao conducive to guerrilla warfare. Except for two highways, the Sayre and the National Highway, there were few roads on the island capable of being used by the armoured vehicles that would have given the Japanese an advantage over the guerrillas. A tangled web of trails criss-crossed the island through forbidding terrain covered with dense forest, mountains, sheer cliffs and other natural obstacles. Unless constantly used and maintained, the trails would disappear completely. Heavily laden Japanese soldiers hacking their way through the jungle were easy targets for guerrilla ambushes.

Having evolved almost spontaneously across the island, the guerrilla bands on Mindanao at first lacked a dominant figure capable of bringing disparate groups together. A number of different leaders emerged, but it was Colonel Fertig who rose to the top. After the American surrender, Fertig had spent four months living within a few kilometres of Japanese forces in Lanao province. In his Master's thesis, 'American involvement in the Filipino resistance movement on Mindanao during the Japanese occupation', Larry Schmidt writes that during this time Fertig 'fostered the image of the strange unsurrendered American colonel'. Schmidt describes how Fertig 'became a *kainginero*, a gardener, and grew mongo beans. He also grew a red goatee on the theory that he would look older, and therefore wiser, among a people who believed age implied wisdom.'

Claiming to have been sent by MacArthur himself to lead the guerrillas on Mindanao, Fertig further boosted his prestige among Filipinos by laying claim to the rank of brigadier general. It was a ruse, but it worked. As John Keats writes in *They Fought Alone*, 'He was Colonel Fertig to Australia, but here, on this island, he wore his stars. On Mindanao, he was, and would remain, The General.' (For all its useful insights into Fertig's thinking, Keats' book is not always factually accurate. In his paper 'Men of destiny: The American and Filipino guerillas during the Japanese occupation of the Philippines', Major Peter Sinclair states that Keats combined Fertig's unpublished manuscript with his own interviews to produce 'a rich narrative rather than a detailed historical record'. Sinclair comments that 'it is hard to determine where the story ends and facts begin', noting that Keats 'changed some of the names in an attempt to protect identities and recreated or created dialogue as a medium to articulate Fertig's efforts in forming the USFIP [US Forces in the Philippines]'. Keats asserts in his preface that *They Fought Alone* 'is not a work of fiction, although it is cast in the form of fiction'.)

Fertig quickly demonstrated his political and administrative skills by unifying all the guerrillas under his command, re-establishing civilian law and order in the areas under his control, and stabilising the local economy through the printing of currency. According to the 'History of the Mindanao Guerrillas', Fertig's Tenth Military District would eventually encompass 85 per cent of the island.

While Fertig's guerrillas performed a useful function in tying down Japanese troops on Mindanao, their most important role was to supply intelligence on the enemy's military strength and especially on Japanese ship movements around the island. The early communication systems were primitive. The 'History of the Mindanao Guerrillas' reports the use of brass drums, cow horns and sea shells to warn soldiers of the approach of the enemy. Another method, the *tagongtong* or 'bush telegraph', consisted of seasoned, metre-long bamboo poles hung at intervals along possible enemy routes. 'Upon enemy approach, the nearest "Tagongtong" is struck with an iron piece. In this way, no movement of the enemy could be made without the knowledge of the people ... Everyone was enjoined to gather all information of the enemy, including the wildest of rumors, for transmission to headquarters for its evaluation and as basis for whatever action need[ed] to be taken.'

It was not until early 1943 that the guerrillas on Mindanao established radio contact with the Americans. In mid-February, a signal reached station KFS in San Francisco. Code words were arranged with the US War Department, and the guerrillas made contact with station KAZ, MacArthur's net control station in Australia. MacArthur responded, confirming Colonel Fertig as commanding officer of Tenth Military District on Mindanao.

Fertig understood that controlling banditry and restoring law and order would be crucial in cultivating popular support for his guerrillas. Between September 1942 and March 1943, Fertig set up effective civil administrations in Eastern Zamboanga and Misamis Occidental provinces, giving pre-war mayors and provincial governors back their jobs, stabilising prices and making sure food supplies were fairly distributed to overcome local shortages. According to Balis, within a month of Fertig being confirmed in his command, 'resistance-controlled areas functioned almost like they did before the war'.

By ambushing Japanese patrols, alerting villagers to their approach, and chasing away bandits, the guerrillas offered protection to local populations, which reciprocated with food and shelter. Such donations of food, Stephen Sams writes, represented an 'enormous sacrifice' by Filipino civilians at a time when the Japanese were exporting food from the Philippines and some Filipinos were starving. Without it, Fertig's guerrillas might have been unable to expand the insurgency beyond the local level. 'The people became the primary means of continuing the war,' Sams writes, and American guerrillas 'exploited the opportunity as best they could. They received their recruits, their sanctuary, and their supplies from the population. In return they provided protection and security. The relationship between the guerrillas and the population was symbiotic.' In Fertig's words, quoted (or created) by his biographer, Keats, the guerrillas had to 'keep the pressure on, everywhere and all the time, killing Japs. Otherwise, no public support. The public wants to see dead Japs. Without public support, no guerrilla.'

Integrating Moro fighters remained a major challenge for the guerrillas. Fertig's solution was to hand responsibility for the Moros to another non-surrendered American officer, Charlie Hedges. Before the war Hedges had worked in Lanao as a logger, employing Moros, learning their dialect and winning their respect. (Other factors might also have played a part. Sinclair suggests that the Moros' willingness to fight with the Americans might have been 'due to a promise made by Hedges to the Moros for the establishment of their own government after the war'.)

Hedges, a reservist rather than a regular soldier, was put in charge of his own guerrilla force and given the rank of lieutenant colonel. A flamboyant figure and expert marksman, Hedges showed the kind of bravado Moros admired in a leader by maintaining his headquarters just across the water from an enemy garrison, in sight of Japanese artillery. According to Keats, Hedges was a 'hard-handed' man who 'took no nonsense from a swarm of Moro tribesmen with filed teeth who would have scared the wits out of [a] banquet hall of bond buyers'. Hedges, he writes, 'managed to gather most of [the Moros of Lanao] under one porous roof by playing off one *datu*'s jealousy against another's'.

A contemporary reviewer of Keats's book described Hedges as 'foul-mouthed as a London dock worker', warning that his language was 'too realistic' for consumption by anything but adult readers. (Rex Blow, on the other hand, remembered Hedges as a 'very nice fellow, very quiet'. Blow himself was not averse to profanity, having once been fined two pounds and ten shillings at Grafton Police Court for 'us[ing] bad language at a telephone box'.)

Receiving General MacArthur's imprimatur was important for Fertig's prestige, but just as important was the ability to deliver much-needed supplies. These arrived, as if by magic, on US submarines. If MacArthur was the Filipinos' ultimate benefactor, Fertig was his proxy, the man with the power to summon and distribute the aid. MacArthur's chief of intelligence, General Charles Willoughby, acknowledged that 'Fertig's influence at present stems from his being the source of supplies from the SWPA and that he is the officially recognized CO of the 10th MD [Military District]'.

Fertig was all too aware of this. According to Keats, Fertig declared:

Any Aid can help me get the guerrilleros in under one roof . . . Anything at all. Magazines with this month's date. Those 'I Shall Return' matches. Paper. Bullet molds, lead, powder, percussion caps. Any little thing that helps give the people reason to hope. That makes them feel they are not alone. That proves I am in touch with MacArthur, and that says, 'Anyone who would get The Aid must go to General Fertig'.

The submarine that arrived off Mindanao on 5 March 1943 brought valuable supplies, including five radio sets, as well as MacArthur's personal emissary, Lieutenant Commander 'Chick' Parsons. Parsons' message to Fertig was for the guerrillas to concentrate on supplying intelligence and not to be drawn into major actions against the Japanese. In Keats's colourful rendition of the conversation, Parsons told Fertig:

'What MacArthur wants is information. Not twenty Japs dead in some gulch. Those radios we brought you are for information. You are to establish a flash line of watcher stations along the coasts, and pass the word to us of Jap ship movements. We will have subs waiting for those ships. One torpedo in half a second can blow up more ammunition than the Japs would shoot at you in a year. Another can kill more Japs on a troop transport than all the guerrilleros in the Islands could even kill.'

'You're talking like an American, Chick,' Fertig cut in. 'Damn it, this isn't America. This is a land where the Japs come to a man's house . . . They slap his face, and tie him up in a chair so he can watch them rape his women. Then they steal his food and leave. By God, that man wants to see those Japs dead.'

But Parsons was adamant. MacArthur was content for the guerrillas to be a nuisance, harassing and killing the Japanese in local operations, but they were not to become so much of a nuisance that the Japanese would decide, as Parsons told Fertig, to 'move in and clean you out'. The guerrillas would be supplied by submarine with radio equipment, weapons, ammunition and medicine to enable them to withstand Japanese attacks and to continue transmitting intelligence, but MacArthur gave orders that the guerrillas must 'only . . . fight to defend themselves'.

For all his tough talking, Fertig understood the limitations of his force. Aware that his guerrillas had neither the training nor the weapons to fight off a major Japanese assault, he focused on ensuring that his headquarters was not encircled and annihilated. Fertig's plan was for his guerrillas to create a matrix of ambush positions to pin down any Japanese unit smaller than a battalion while other guerrillas attacked from the rear and flanks in order, as Michael Balis writes, to 'inflict maximum casualties'.

He ordered that the partisans not engage any enemy units of battalion size or larger. Fertig anticipated that the rapid partisan withdrawals along jungle paths which only Filipinos knew would frustrate Japanese efforts to engage and destroy them. Fertig expected that Japanese terrorism in the lost areas would preserve peasant support for the partisans. He thought that the enemy's frustration over failing to destroy the resistance would force the Japanese to halt their offensive and withdraw their troops. After the Japanese retreated, the partisans would return and re-establish the civil government in former Japanese-held areas.

But there was a flaw in Fertig's plan: Misamis Occidental, the province Fertig had chosen for his headquarters, was separated from the rump of Mindanao only by the 11-kilometre-wide isthmus between Panguil Bay and Pagadian Bay to the south. By taking the isthmus and the nearby coastal waters, the Japanese would be able to isolate Fertig from the bulk of his forces. They would also deny Fertig the land bridge he needed to escape from Misamis Occidental into Lanao Province, where he could hide in the jungle-clad highlands of the interior.

If Fertig was careless in his choice of headquarters, he was also careless in protecting it, failing to take any action even after several Japanese reconnaissance planes were seen flying over his command post in Misamis City.

With the new radio sets, Fertig had been able to build an intelligence system capable of covering the entire coast of Mindanao. The network was also used to coordinate submarine resupply missions. But the new transmitters were more vulnerable than the old ones to enemy direction-finders, and the increased radio traffic enabled the Japanese to pinpoint Fertig's headquarters in Misamis City. 'His headquarters were too close to the coast,' Balis writes, 'and it was vulnerable to a Japanese amphibious commando raid.'

The Japanese struck on 26 June 1943, landing north and south of Misamis City in a pincer movement designed to cut off Fertig's escape into Eastern Mindanao and wipe out the organisation. Three thousand soldiers, supported by aircraft and a destroyer, were met by a few hundred guerrillas who had to fight without support from either artillery or anti-aircraft guns. Panicking guerrillas, facing a far superior enemy force, did what they had a tendency to do: break from the fight and desert Fertig's carefully thought-out defensive positions. It was just as well they did, because it prevented the net from closing around them and enabled the majority to escape.

With communications all but lost and his force dispersed, Fertig took off into the jungle clutching a suitcase containing his radio codes and personnel files. For weeks Fertig dodged Japanese search parties before being rescued by Hedges and a company of Moros, who spirited him across the water to Lanao Province. While hiding out in Lanao, Fertig burnished his status among the Moros by reminding Datu Busran Kalaw that he, Fertig, was the personal choice of General MacArthur to lead the Mindanao guerrillas. It did not hurt his mission that he was also able to show the Moro chieftain, described by Keats as 'lord of the Maranao Moros of Lake Lanao', a copy of *Life* magazine that featured King Ibn Saud of Saudi Arabia proclaiming Islam to be the ally of the United States.

To the Japanese, the Misamis operation appeared at first to have been a great success. With the guerrilla force in disarray, small groups of Japanese troops were sent out to hunt down and kill as many guerrillas as possible. While small patrols allowed the Japanese to search large areas more quickly, the size of each patrol made it vulnerable to attack. When the guerrillas began to pick off groups of enemy soldiers, the Japanese were forced to increase the size of their patrols to battalion strength. Burdened by heavy equipment and reliant on maps, the slow-moving Japanese were less vulnerable to ambush but more easily avoided by the nimbler and more mobile guerrillas.

As Keats explains in *They Fought Alone*, the mass desertions had the paradoxical effect of strengthening Fertig's command, since 'those who fled were now ashamed to return, thus reducing the guerrilla forces to those who might actually fight'.

By October 1943, Japanese commanders were forced to accept that their attempt to liquidate Fertig's guerrilla organisation and destroy the radio network had failed. Weakened by guerrilla attacks and by the steady drain of combat soldiers to other Pacific theatres, the Japanese pulled back to a fortified base at Misamis City, while putting out the story that Fertig had been driven into the hills to starve.

For Fertig, the attack on his headquarters had been a close shave, a near-disaster that confirmed his tactical naivety. A month after his escape from Misamis, South West Pacific Area command created a special Philippines unit inside MacArthur's Australian headquarters, led by Colonel Courtney Whitney. From now on, Whitney would be responsible for directing Fertig's combat and intelligence operations.

Meanwhile, supplies continued to arrive by submarine. According to a report compiled for the Seventh Fleet Intelligence Center, after March 1943 'at about 5-week intervals, small parties of personnel with about 2 tons of stores each were landed at various points in the central and southern Philippines by special submarine missions carried out during their regular war patrols'.

In September 1943 the delivery of a large navy transmitter enabled direct contact between the guerrillas and the US Navy's net control station in Australia. Flashes on Japanese shipping movements could now be sent direct to naval intelligence. In some cases, according to the 'History of the Mindanao Guerrillas', messages reached the navy 'within one hour of ship sighting by the watcher station'.

A month later, Fertig divided his headquarters for security reasons, with a reserve command staying at Liangan in Lanao Province while Fertig and the main command moved 350 kilometres north-east to a more strategic location at Esperanza City, in Agusan Province.

Chapter 9

PLAYING CAT AND MOUSE

———≫●●≪———

McLaren and his companions reached Sindangan, on the far north-west coast of Mindanao, in December 1943. From there a Filipino colonel would take them to the guerrilla base at Liangan. This meant crossing the widest part of the Zamboanga Peninsula and climbing up and over the craggy Mount Malindang range. The only way they could do it was by travelling light and finding food along the way.

The weeks the Australians had spent at sea, often soaking wet, had softened their feet and whittled away their fitness. Wallace and Kennedy were too sick to attempt the long trek. Gillon was recovering slowly from his wounds but one hand was nearly useless and he could only keep up with help from his comrades.

The Spanish had neglected to build an efficient road system across Mindanao, forcing the guerrillas to rely on rough tracks and roads liable to be washed away with every monsoon. The route inland was an arduous slog over sharp ridges and through deep ravines.

Groping for toeholds on mountain slopes and wading waist-deep through rivers, the Australians struggled to keep up with the tireless Filipino colonel. Ray Steele reported that he, Wagner, Kennedy and McLaren travelled part of the journey on horseback. McLaren's experience with the Chinese guerrillas in Malaya had taught him how to move and survive in the jungle, using tricks such as camouflaging his body with vegetation, and seeking out tiny slivers of sunlight to keep his skin from turning grey, but he was as relieved as the rest when the group emerged at last into a highland clearing, at the centre of which was a guerrilla outpost. The hidden sentries let them through, having been alerted through a system of lookouts set up to provide warning of Japanese patrols.

Nestled among the jungle-covered peaks of Mount Malindang, the guerrilla camp was perfectly sited to keep watch on the Japanese base at Misamis City. The Japanese, ever fearful of being ambushed in the jungle, rarely penetrated this far into the guerrillas' highland stronghold. If they did, their approach would be signalled by gunfire from the sentries, a warning to start moving food and equipment to prepared hiding places in the jungle, where the guerrillas could lie concealed within metres of a passing Japanese soldier.

The men in the camp paid the exhausted Australians little attention. Richardson describes 'a barber shop and coffee-stalls, where slightly built Filipinos, wearing soft cloth hats, sat lazily sipping and chatting, while others squatted in the shadows of the houses, gambling'.

It was several days before McLaren and the others were fit enough to begin the last leg of the journey to Liangan. Guerrilla guides led them down the eastern slopes of Mount Malindang, carefully skirting Japanese positions, to the shore of Panguil Bay. After crossing the narrow stretch of water they were picked up and delivered by truck to Liangan, a bustling village at the junction of a creek and a tidal river. For some of the Australians, it was the first time they had ridden in a vehicle since Singapore.

Lanao was unlike other provinces in Mindanao. Not only were there more Japanese soldiers but there were also more Moros, fighting both the Christians, each other and, when it suited them, the Japanese. Keats illustrates the opportunistic nature of Moro allegiances with the following story: '[A] *datu* had enlisted one son in the Japanese forces, and one son with the guerrilla, and quite candidly stated that when he was sure how the war would end, he would recall the son on the losing side and join the probable victors himself.'

Liangan buzzed with guerrilla activity. Armed fighters wandered along streets crowded with stalls selling fruit and vegetables from farms across the bay. Unsurrendered American soldiers were there too, including Fertig's second-in-command, Colonel Robert Bowler. The headquarters of Hedges' 108th Division guerrillas lay a few kilometres inland, up an old railway built by a logging company before the war.

This time there was no fiesta, not even an offer of cigarettes. Bowler and Hedges were not pleased to see them. Steele was told that he and his companions had been ordered back to Australia by the next submarine. Richardson writes that after delivering this information, the two American colonels 'turned on their heels and left'.

The reason for their frosty reception was not clear. Perhaps the Americans resented the imminent departure of six Australian soldiers (Wallace and Kennedy had now joined them, although Blow felt that both were now 'pretty sick') who could have been useful in the fight. Blow himself rationalised that the months they had spent dodging and hiding from the Japanese had made the Americans 'edgy'.

Whatever the cause of the Americans' displeasure, it did not last. In time the Australians would warm to the blunt-speaking Hedges, although Steele remained sceptical of his rank, remarking waspishly to Bowden and Nelson forty years later that 'Charlie Hedges . . . called himself a colonel'.

From his new headquarters in Agusan Province, Fertig continued to organise and consolidate guerrilla units across the island. Mindanao had become a cornerstone of MacArthur's liberation plans for the Philippines, and Fertig's guerrillas were expected to play a significant part in the invasion. A US intelligence report compiled eight months before the October invasion noted that 'the latent power of guerrilla and civilian units . . . if properly directed, will do much to assist our landings, save us thousands of lives, and months of time'.

In Lanao Province, Hedges' guerrillas were stepping up their hit-and-run attacks on the Japanese. Ambushes became so frequent that, in the words of the 'G2 Staff Study of Philippine Islands Situation', '[T]he Japs formed the habit of machine-gunning every curve in the road before they approached it and . . . they always fired mortar shots ahead when they were patrolling in the interior or off the national roads.'

While some Moros remained aloof, others followed their *datu* by joining the guerrillas. By their own accounts, the Australians respected the Moros' fierceness but never fully trusted them. McLaren told Hal Richardson, 'The natives have always got to be able to see you . . . Leadership is everything. So long as they can see one of us up front they'll carry on, but once they see us go down or retreat, then the rot sets in.'

Fertig tried to stiffen his Moro units by putting Americans (or, failing that, Australians) in command. Major Larry Schmidt writes:

The Americans had learned from their early experiments with the Philippine Constabulary that the Moros had a tendency to lionize their leaders, and if a leader possessed the leadership qualities of courage and fairness the Moros would follow him loyally through any hardship. But because the Moros identified closely with their leaders, the leadership had to be stable and leaders not changed often. The

Moros would never serve under a Christian Filipino, and Fertig ...
did not trust the Moro leaders to carry out his orders without some
influence or presence from him there.

Ray Steele felt that at this stage of the war the Mindanao guerrillas
were still 'playing cat and mouse' with the Japanese. 'We weren't powerful
enough to get out and fight 600 to 1000 Japs. All you could do was ...
take a pot shot here and there.' The Filipinos themselves, he told Bowden
and Nelson, 'didn't last very long ... they would stand up alright for the
first five minutes and then they'd start to disappear ... you'd wake up
to the fact that you had no-one left.' The 'G2 Staff Study' acknowledged
that guerrilla units were often 'skilled at ambushing the enemy' but were
'not accustomed to bombing or shelling. Either type of activity will
disperse them.'

In *One-Man War* McLaren recalls an 'old soldier', a veteran of the
Spanish war, telling him during his time on Mindanao, 'Our native
guerrillas will be alive when our civilians are dead ... Our native guerrillas
can run so well!' McLaren told Richardson that if a Filipino guerrilla was
'not in the mood' for fighting, he would think nothing of 'asking to
be excused'.

> When a patrol was being arranged it was not uncommon for a man to
> come sidling along to McLaren and say, 'Sir, my wife is to have a child,
> and I must go to her.'
>
> 'Hell!' McLaren would roar. 'That's the fifth child she's had this
> year!'
>
> Sometimes if he roared loudly enough he could bully the man into
> staying, but an unwilling soldier was never very reliable.

Unreliable soldiers were the last thing Fertig needed in the last weeks
of 1943. Tired of the constant harassment by Hedges' guerrillas, the

Japanese had intensified their patrols along the Lanao coast. Guerrilla outposts on the beaches were regularly coming under fire from enemy gunboats.

In the middle of December, a *banca* arrived with supplies from the US submarine *Narwhal*. Richardson writes that the submarine brought 'radio equipment, rifles, tommy-guns, mortars . . . ammunition . . . some cigarettes and food'. Fertig wanted heavy weapons, and Keats reports him sulking over the delivery of an autographed picture of General MacArthur and a consignment of hammocks.

Chapter 10

THIS IS IT, MAC

———⟫●⟪———

At midnight on 19 December 1943, a Japanese force of an estimated six hundred men attacked Liangan from their stronghold across the bay. According to the 'History of the Mindanao Guerrillas', they came in 'modern landing barges and launches'. Against a superior enemy, the guerrillas could offer only 'slight resistance'. One guerrilla was killed. A second wave followed at 2 a.m., with two groups landing at separate locations in launches. Their destination was Kauswagan, 12 kilometres south-west of Liangan. 'The Combat Co of the HQ battalion, 108th Infantry Regt contacted the enemy at Tugar Creek. After thirty minutes of sporadic firing, the guerrillas withdrew. The enemy occupied Kauswagan at daybreak. At 10.00 o'clock . . . the guerrillas came back on the enemy with mortar fire, BARs and rifles. In the encounter which lasted about an hour, twenty Japs were killed, and one of the guerrilla side.'

Richardson writes that on the night of the attack, McLaren could not sleep. Hearing what he thought was a rifle shot, he dug Charlie Wagner in the ribs.

Wagner tried to drag the blanket back over his shoulder. 'You stupid bastard!' he said, half laughing, half angry. 'You're dreaming.'

Barely were the words out than a burst of machine-gun fire shattered the moonlit calm. Then the crackle of rifle and machine-gun fire blended into a frenzy of sound.

In Sheila Ross's version, Blow, Gillon and Wagner raced down to the beach at the sound of gunfire, leaving McLaren and Steele to follow the logging railway up to Hedges' headquarters in the jungle. After two Japanese flags were sighted half a kilometre along the shore, Blow assembled a party of guerrillas to counter-attack. 'Rex tried to persuade the Moros . . . to join him, but no go: to them he was still an unknown quantity and they made some feeble excuse or other.'

As the guerrillas, minus the Moros, tore into the Japanese, intense gunfire erupted from the rear, accompanied by 'bloodcurdling yells'. Fearing he was about to be encircled, Blow ordered a retreat, only to discover that the 'enemy' attacking them from behind was the Moros 'who had had decided to join the fight after all and in their excitement had mistaken the Aussies for Japanese!'

Richardson reports that the Japanese 'stealthily landed from the sea before the moon rose and crept into the jungle in a flanking movement round the village. There were about one thousand well-armed infantrymen against about three hundred and fifty guerrillas, many of whom were sick and unarmed, and all of whom were taken completely by surprise.' In his tape-recorded interview, Ray Steele confirmed that 'quite a mob' of Japanese got inside the guerrillas' jungle headquarters 'without us knowing' and that he and McLaren were 'cornered'.

The first we knew there was lots of firing going on and we were all asleep. We jumped out of windows, grabbed our arms and ran off. Jock and I were together. We had an 81mm American mortar that the submarine had brought up. I was the only one that knew anything about mortars . . . We went overseas [to Singapore] . . . with three-inch British mortars . . . we had trained with these mortars along artillery lines . . . and adapted them to use them like we would field guns.

The Japanese were experts with the mortar but, according to Richardson, they were not used to having mortars used against them by the Filipino guerrillas. The US 81mm mortar was a valuable piece of equipment, only recently delivered from Australia by submarine. With Steele manning the mortar, Hedges sent McLaren and a handful of runners to scout the Japanese positions. Spotting a lone figure outside a native house, the guerrillas took cover. McLaren recognised that he was wearing the uniform of the 'Filipino constabulary of the American era'.

Within twenty yards of the man [McLaren] paused. His eyes narrowed as he saw on either side of the silent man freshly turned earth that could have come from newly dug defensive positions.

'Look out!' he shouted suddenly, and squeezed the tommy-gun trigger, cutting down the Filipino immediately.

A Juki opened up in its Japanese accent, firing from the native house, proving that the house was a well-prepared trap with the renegade Filipino as bait. If the fresh earth from the fox-holes had not been visible McLaren might have died there.

But McLaren did not die, either in the initial ambush or in the ensuing firefight, when his tommy-gun jammed.

His patrol had gone crashing into the jungle, leaving him with a useless gun. The Japanese opened up with rifles, machine-guns and mortars. But luck was with him, and he ran unharmed through the hail of fire and along the track through the vines and ferns to the village.

Ray Steele was standing by the mortar, concern on his face.

'What's doing?' he asked, as McLaren appeared.

'Put on a range of one thousand and let the bastards have it,' panted McLaren.

Sheila Ross writes that Steele 'set up a mortar with a Filipino crew and went into action while Jock, acting as observer, dashed back-wards and forwards giving ranges and corrections, dodging bullets as he did so'. Steele, by his own account the only one of the Australians who had ever fired a mortar, told Bowden and Nelson that he and McLaren 'let a few mortar bombs go at them'

> but they very soon overran us and to get away we had to slide down a very ... steep hill ... [it was] almost perpendicular. At the bottom was a long wide field of corn before you hit the jungle ... These fellows were hot on our tails and lining along the top ... and we ran the gauntlet to get to the jungle ... It was a little bit hazardous getting across there ... but we made it.

The 'History of the Mindanao Guerrillas' describes the guerrillas' fight to defend their headquarters as 'a heroic but futile stand against an over-whelming number of well-armed Japanese soldiers who emerged from all directions'. At 5 p.m. on 20 December, 'the enemy was in complete control of the Division Headquarters. The guerrilla forces withdrew in disorder to the hills in the vicinity to harass the enemy all night long.'

Meanwhile the Japanese made repeated attempts to take the village of Liangan. Kent Holmes writes that twenty enemy soldiers were killed in a clash with guerrillas at 10 o'clock on the morning of the landings and that the Japanese attacked again at 11 a.m. and at 1 p.m., each time being driven back with heavy casualties.

According to a detailed account of the battle in the 'History of the Mindanao Guerrillas', a Japanese soldier was observed at 1.30 p.m. signalling from the beach 400 metres west of the mouth of the Liangan River. Three 'AIF officers' (they are not identified by name) joined a number of guerrilla officers and a 'small group of Moros' to attack a group of fifty enemy troops gathered at the place where the signaller had been spotted. The encounter was 'bitter', with the enemy pushed back to a creek; eighteen Japanese were reported killed, at a cost of two wounded guerrillas.

Sporadic fighting continued until the early hours of 21 December when 'Japanese troops walked into Liangan . . . unopposed by our troops which had withdrawn across the Tonob Creek earlier in the night'.

The Australians, at risk of being trapped, had been forced to swim across a creek around 200 metres wide that flowed into the Liangan River near the coast. Blow, the strongest swimmer, was loaded up with guns and ammunition.

From a ridge on the far side of the creek, the Australians were able to look back on Liangan. According to Richardson, there was 'no sign of life'. A plywood factory had been razed to the ground, and a pair of two-storey houses built by the logging company appeared to be deserted. Ross writes that the guerrillas were fighting doggedly to hold a bridge. A few of the Australians crept towards the creek and began sniping at the enemy, using the trees of a coconut plantation for cover. Richardson writes that the men were McLaren and Wagner; Ross identifies them as Blow, Gillon and Wagner. A single shot from a Japanese sniper rang out. Charlie Wagner was hit in the head and killed.

Richardson reports Wagner's last words as 'This is it, Mac' while Ross says that he murmured 'They got me', noting that these were 'the same words Rex Butler had used almost exactly four months before'.

Blow told Bowden and Nelson that he, Gillon and Wagner had spent the night sleeping in a coconut grove. When a Filipino woke them with the news that 'lots of Japs' were in the village, 'Charlie Wagner said, "Let's go down and shoot a few."' Blow and Gillon would have been content to leave them alone, but when Wagner insisted on going, they followed. A shot was fired and Wagner fell. In this version there were no last words. Later on that morning 'the Filipinos dug a big hole and we buried him'.

The medical certificate of death signed by Blow states that the bullet 'struck forehead above right eye' and that 'death followed about fifteen minutes later'. Steele's death report notes that while serving with Fertig's guerrillas Charlie Wagner 'did very valuable intelligence work and was able to forward much information' to Fertig and to SWPA headquarters. It also mentions that Wagner was recommended for a decoration for leading the August attack on the Japanese submarine chaser at Bongao.

Wagner was a 'very brave, very aggressive fellow', Blow told Bowden and Nelson. 'If there were a couple of Japs around, he reckoned they should be shot.' Sheila Ross describes Wagner as a 'good IO [intelligence officer], an even better soldier; a superb rifle shot, an expert with the bayonet . . . [a] man in a thousand with the heart of an ox'.

The loss of his jungle headquarters was a heavy blow for Colonel Hedges, who, according to Keats, 'had no time . . . to save his radio or the supplies . . . brought from Agusan'. Retreating in disarray, Hedges 'was pushed yard by yard deeper into the hills, through the bananas toward the mountain jungle where no food grew, farther from the road and the beach, his supplies gone, his supply lines cut and his communications lost'.

Steele's intelligence report states that on 24 December the Japanese left the Liangan area and returned to their stronghold in Misamis City. Eight guerrillas and between fifty and sixty Japanese had been killed.

After the attack at Liangan, the Japanese redoubled their efforts around the Lanao coast. Keats writes that Colonel Fertig received 'reports from Manila that a Major General Harada had been appointed to clean out guerrilla resistance once and for all, and was shortly to embark for Mindanao with an entire division specially trained in anti-guerrilla tactics'.

Hardly a week passed without some part of the north coast being invaded. In the aftermath of each attack, the Japanese spread propaganda that all Americans had been killed and that the guerrilla army had been 'completely wiped out'.

With the Lanao guerrillas under increasing pressure from the Japanese garrison across the water at Misamis City, Hedges was loath to see the Australians leave. The '108th Division Unit History' pays tribute to their contribution:

> In the month of December 1943, five [*sic*] Australian officers that had escaped from the Japanese concentration camp at Singapore arrived from Liangan. Lt. Rex Blow and McLaren were assigned to the 108th Division, Capt Steele and Lt Gillon, all of the AIF, were assigned with the Western Mindanao Corps HQ. Steele was late[r] sent to Australia for intelligence purposes. Unfortunately Lt WAGERN [Wagner] (AIF) was killed during the December 1943 invasion of Liangan. The bravery and combat experience of these officers immensely improved the morale of the men in the Division and the Japanese welcome became more lively with each attack.

In fact seven Australians (not five) had reached Mindanao, and at the time of their arrival Jock McLaren was still a private. Ross writes, however, that during the defence of Liangan the Australians 'proved themselves' and that 'the attitude of the American colonels towards them was now very different'.

Steele told Bowden and Nelson that his group was in 'fairly perpetual contact with Australia, not directly but through Fertig', and that there were 'quite a few discussions' over whether Fertig would 'do a Suarez' by failing to pass on messages in order to keep the Australians on Mindanao.

Sheila Ross writes that over a 'feast of pork and chicken and vegetables', Steele proposed that the Australians stay and fight with the guerrillas on Mindanao and that his suggestion 'met with instant approval'. Steele remembered it slightly differently, telling Bowden and Nelson that most of the Australians were torn over whether to stay or go. Although eager to see Australia again, they were now worried that if they went back, their war would be over. 'We all realised that once we got back we'd be redundant, we didn't have a unit there.' For that reason, 'none of us was that keen to get back'.

When the US submarine *Narwhal* arrived with supplies in February, it brought instructions for the Australians. Anyone sick or unfit was to go back to Australia. That meant Kennedy and Wallace would be returning, Kennedy because he was very sick with malaria and Wallace because, in Steele's words, he was 'pretty damn useless and always saying he was sick anyway'; and, in Rex Blow's, because he was a 'nuisance . . . we wanted to get rid of'.*

---

* Wallace had been sick since leaving Tawi Tawi. Hospitalised for fifteen days with a double hernia, he also suffered from chronic malaria. His book, published thirteen years after the war ended, suggests a reason for Steele's animus towards him. Near the end of their time on Mindanao, Steele gave Wallace a written order to undertake a journey that Wallace considered extremely hazardous. His two companions were willing to obey the command, arguing that 'orders are orders', but Wallace objected. 'That's all very well . . . orders are orders if they are legitimate orders. But this order really isn't legitimate. It's the biggest bag of bullshit I've ever read.' Did word of his insubordination reach Steele? Wallace might have been both a troublemaker and a malingerer, but Colonel Suarez considered his military knowledge and expertise invaluable. His signalling skills were crucial to the success of the coastwatcher system on Tawi Tawi, which was credited by the Americans with the sinking of approximately sixty Japanese ships. Whatever Wallace's failings as a man and a soldier, Steele's description of him as 'pretty damn useless' is not supported by the evidence.

The commander-in-chief of the Australian military forces, General Sir Thomas Blamey, also wanted someone capable of reporting back accurately on the condition of Australian prisoners at Sandakan, about whom almost nothing was known. As the senior officer, Ray Steele was considered the most reliable source of information. According to Steele, 'we decided to toss up or cut cards or pull straws for it. Then at the last minute they said that I had to go—in any case I'd won the bloody straw!' Concerned about what the others would think of his leaving (he worried they might 'think I'm a dingo'), Steele asked Fertig to send a signal requesting permission for him to come back to Mindanao after his mission to Australia. With permission granted, Steele boarded the submarine, fully expecting to return (although he never did).

Miles Gillon, still handicapped by the wounds he had suffered on Tawi Tawi, stayed but would later be taken back to Australia by submarine. That left Rex Blow and Jock McLaren, both of them impatient to fight and eager to make up for lost time. Since joining the guerrillas the pair had been recommended by Hedges for promotion, Blow to captain and McLaren to lieutenant. General Blamey confirmed both promotions.

The February 1944 'G2 Staff Study of Philippine Islands Situation' estimates that at this time Colonel Fertig had 20,000 men under his command, around 12,000 of whom were armed. Fertig himself told MacArthur's emissary, 'Chick' Parsons, that 'as of 5 December 1943 the total guerrilla personnel on Mindanao were 28,400 and the total arms registered 16,000'. (The authors of the 'Staff Study' concede that they cannot account for the difference in the two figures.)

Later estimates put the number of guerrilla fighters higher still. Robert Ross Smith's *Triumph in the Philippines*, published in 1993 by the US Army's Center of Military History, states that in February 1945 'Colonel Fertig had over 33,000 on his rolls . . . 16,500 of them armed'.

Estimates of Japanese strength on Mindanao vary significantly. Robert B. Asprey, author of *War in the Shadows*, writes that the Japanese 'maintained about 150,000 troops on Mindanao'. Asprey's figure is more than ten times higher than the number cited in the 'G2 Staff Study of Philippine Islands Situation', which states that the 'Jap force in Mindanao total[s] about 12,000 men'. A secret 'Philippine Monthly Combined Situation Report' dated 15 April 1944, supplied by the military intelligence section of South West Pacific Area headquarters, put the total at 22,000.

How reliable were these estimates?

From its headquarters in the AMP Building in Brisbane, the intelligence section of the SWPA command depended largely on information provided by the Filipino guerrillas. The 'Monthly Combined Situation Report', produced between December 1942 and September 1944, was a secret résumé of guerrilla and enemy intelligence. According to an official history of the intelligence section published in 1948, much of the information was out of date by the time of publication 'because intelligence nets were initially served largely by runner'. The 'Weekly Summary of Enemy Intelligence', produced between April and December 1944, was designed to supply more detailed and frequent information. As the date for the US invasion approached, raw and 'unfinished' intelligence, mostly obtained from guerrilla sources, was delivered in daily bulletins. According to the official history, 'Guerrilla intelligence reports were of value because of their richness and variety; coverage was widespread throughout the islands; contacts ranged all the way up the economic scale, from dock laborers unloading Japanese ships and mechanics working at Japanese airfields, to General [Manuel] Roxas, who had numerous pipelines to the highest Japanese councils and the Philippine Puppet Regime in Manila.'

The official history states that 'because of the overlapping coverage of the various guerrilla nets and the parallel coverage by separate penetration-party nets, the reliability of information could be cross-checked'.

In 1989 Lieutenant Colonel Dan K. McNeill (later General McNeill) presented a US Army military studies program paper titled 'Eichelberger

in Mindanao', in which he wrote that 'Fertig was a key source of information in Eighth Army's campaign planning for Mindanao'. Naturally,
this information included assessments of Japanese troop numbers. But
McNeill points out that the guerrillas, after years of Japanese subjugation,
'might have tended to provide inaccurate or unsubstantiated reports of
the enemy's strength in order to encourage an expedited Allied landing on
Mindanao'. In other words, they might have understated enemy strength
in order to persuade the Americans to bring forward their invasion plans.
McNeill suggests that General Robert L. Eichelberger, the commander of
the US landings on Mindanao, 'would have been justified in his skepticism
of guerrilla reports': 'After the campaign, it became clear that the initial
estimate of enemy strength of thirty thousand was considerably under
the actual strength. The strength of the Japanese force on Mindanao
[less Zamboanga peninsula] on the day of Eighth Army's initial landing
was probably more than fifty thousand, including twelve thousand plus
civilians who were pressed into military service of one sort or another.'

Even the higher estimate was far below what the Japanese needed to
control the island. According to the 'G2 Staff Study', Fertig's guerrillas had
'complete freedom of action in 95% of the island'. The Japanese 'occupy
in force the cities of Davao, Cotobato, Zamboanga and Cagayan, with
smaller units (100–800) in other communities. Outside of Davao proper,
Jap penetrations are possible only in force.' US intelligence considered
that any attempt by the Japanese to 'seriously curtail' the actions of
Fertig's guerrillas would call for 'ten times as many men' as the Japanese
had on Mindanao. The combination of guerrilla activity, Japan's depleted
resources and its overstretched supply lines made concentrating such
a force on Mindanao impossible. These factors alone meant that the
likelihood of the Japanese sending enough reinforcements to Mindanao
to destroy the guerrillas was regarded by US intelligence as zero.

At the same time, the guerrillas by themselves would never be strong
enough to throw the Japanese out of Mindanao. The result was equilibrium.

Dan McNeill comments that Fertig's guerrillas were 'successful in keeping the Japanese on Mindanao largely at bay' but 'only the combat power of the Allies would eliminate the enemy'.

Constant harassment by the guerrillas wore away at Japanese morale. In a section labelled 'Notes on guerrillas', the 'G2 Staff Study' reports that guerrilla units 'know the trails like a book', and that 'nearby communities are extremely loyal to the units. When units are withdrawn to the hills, the people move with them.'

> They have effectively blocked roads and trails leading into their areas by burning bridges, constructing road blocks and machine-gun nests, and active patrolling. In one Jap penetration from Cagayan to Talakag with 800 men, a guerrilla force of 150 delayed the Jap advance of 30 miles for 8 days, inflicting over a hundred casualties. The Japs stayed in Talakag about three days and then withdrew. Their return to Cagayan was harassed every step of the way, resulting in many more casualties. Such Jap forays do little damage; their casualties raise the morale of the guerrilla units, and the civilians are further convinced of the necessity of supporting the guerrilla forces. Such delaying operations are now being accomplished with a limited ammunition supply, 30 cal[ibre] rifles, a few machine guns, and no trench mortars, bazookas or land mines.

Mindanao's long coastline meant that inter-island travel was quite secure; journeys between adjacent islands could be made in a few hours of darkness and the Japanese simply did not have enough patrol boats to stop and search all the native vessels plying the inland seas. The 'overwhelming loyalty of the Filipino people' ensured that once ashore, Filipinos and Americans were sure to be given help and shelter by locals.

Outside the occupied cities, enemy activities were confined to patrols in force along the main highways, but even such limited forays were becoming more costly to the Japanese as the flow of arms and equipment to the guerrillas by submarine increased.

As Blow and McLaren prepared to rejoin the fight, US strategic thinking was fixed squarely on the invasion and liberation of the Philippines. US military intelligence recognised the guerrillas as a vital asset capable of assisting MacArthur's forces both before and after the landings. But Fertig had to be careful not to overplay his hand, since any major guerrilla offensive on Mindanao risked provoking the Japanese into strengthening their forces ahead of the invasion. The 'G2 Staff Study' states: 'The present policy of GHQ with respect to Mindanao is to supply the troops with arms, medical supplies and radios. Continue the organization and consolidation of positions, avoid any aggressive action which will bring Jap reinforcements into the area, and concentrate on developing coastwatcher stations and intelligence.'

While intelligence remained the overriding priority for the guerrillas, another was sabotage. Among the suggested targets were:

(a) All enemy air fields. It would be possible for a well-planned sabotage organization to practically ground all enemy planes in Mindanao on, or a few days before 'D' day.

(b) Enemy shipping in Davao, Cotobato, Zamboanga and Surigao.

(c) Delay the advance of enemy coming to attack our beachhead by:
   (1) Planting land mines in the roads (the limited road net canalizes motor traffic into bottlenecks).
   (2) Destroying bridges in advance of the enemy. (These bridges are usually small ones over streams, and can be rebuilt in a day.)

In addition to intelligence and sabotage, the 'Staff Study' proposes a number of combat tasks for Fertig's guerrillas in the lead-up to the invasion:

(a) Secure such beachheads as we need prior to our landing.

(b) Seize lightly guarded enemy emergency landing fields.

(c) Delay enemy advance against our beachhead by means of road blocks and delaying actions.

(d) Continue with present construction of airfields.

(e) Diversionary attacks on enemy concentrations coordinated with our 'D' day effort.

These combat assignments marked a significant escalation from the sort of 'hit and run' attacks that had been the guerrillas' stock in trade until now. US intelligence reports expressed confidence that Fertig had the men he needed; that when the time came they would be adequately armed and supplied; and that they would have the support of the civilian population. What Fertig lacked was capable officers. An 'analysis of strength and equipment' in the Tenth Military District (Mindanao) showed just eighty-two American officers commanding a guerrilla force of 19,500 men. The 'Monthly Combined Situation Report' of 15 April 1944 strongly criticised the capability and morale of these officers: 'About 80 Americans hold key positions and run the extensive radio net. The Americans there are mostly enlisted men of the Air Corps, Infantry, and Navy who were able to avoid capture. Their experience and vision is limited. They are tired, have been on the defense too long, and are in need of assistance if the latent power of the guerrilla units is to be fully developed.'

The 'G2 Staff Study' was even more scathing, identifying a 'crying need' for 'American combat officers' to assist the 'tired' officers who were there already. The 'primary purpose' of the latter, it said, was to 'wait the war out as comfortably as possible; their morale precludes any aggressive activity'.

It was this 'crying need' for energetic combat officers—American or, failing that, Australian —that made Hedges and Fertig so keen to hold onto Captain Blow and Lieutenant McLaren.

Chapter 11

GET BACK, YOU BLOODY HERO

———⋙◆⋘———

The Japanese High Command was bracing for the inevitable US invasion of the Philippines. Monograph No. 3, an official account of Japanese military operations in the Philippines between December 1942 and June 1944 (described by the Japanese as the 'quiet period'), anticipated the invasion taking place probably 'in the autumn of 1944' since US forces in the Pacific were 'advancing far faster than we had expected'. In preparation for the American attack, the Japanese army 'began intensive suppressive operations and enforced strict regulations in the important sectors so as to simplify defensive operations'.

Monograph No. 3 notes the particular problems the Japanese army faced in Mindanao: 'Since a large portion of the area was covered with thick forest and undergrowth, which is most suitable for guerrilla activities, we could not attain good results from our raids. Above all, we suffered from the constant rampancy of the MORO tribe in the vicinity of LANAO LAKE. Radio activities and the existence of submarine anchorages were quite evident in this district.'

Meanwhile, guerrilla activity was increasing in expectation of US landings taking place 'in the near future'. The Japanese acknowledged that the guerrillas' 'gathering of information by radio and supply of weapons and ammunition by submarines was carried out skilfully'. Far from the Japanese being able to tighten their hold on Mindanao, 'in fact [order] became worse in some districts'.

On the ground, the arrival of the Australians at the end of 1943 had injected new discipline and spirit into Colonel Hedges' guerrilla force. Jock McLaren began training a group of Filipino guerrillas in the use of the tommy-guns, Browning automatic rifles and machine guns and US 81mm mortars coming in by submarine. The tendency of the Filipinos to go missing in the midst of a battle prompted the Australians to pare back their ambitions for large-scale guerrilla operations in favour of hit-and-run attacks by small groups whose members they could rely on. By the end of January 1944, according to Richardson, McLaren had 'hand-picked a fighting force of about twenty men whom he reckoned he could trust in an emergency'.

As many as two dozen Japanese garrisons or outposts were spread across Lanao Province. After a few months' training, Blow and McLaren decided it was time for the guerrillas to put what they had learnt to the test. To begin with, they targeted the smallest of the enemy outposts. According to Blow, 'we crept up on them one night and wiped them out'. Over the next few weeks the guerrillas attacked and destroyed all the small outposts they could find and then started hitting the Japanese garrison towns.

A Japanese intelligence report, quoted in a footnote to the two-volume *Reports of General MacArthur*, gives a good description of the tactics used by the guerrillas on Mindanao at this time. Issued by Japanese Fourteenth Area Army headquarters, the report covered the period 1–30 April 1944.

The bandits occupy and utilize key points of communications, firing on and making surprise attacks against our military traffic. They flee whenever we attack.

They construct obstacles on the roads and destroy bridges and, when we are engaged in clearing the way or in repair work, they execute surprise attacks.

By cutting wires, kidnapping people, burning homes, and other actions calculated to disturb the peace, they draw out our forces; they execute aggressive attacks on a considerable scale.

The enemy draws us out by using small units and then carries out an enveloping attack with his main force. When our forces outnumber theirs, the enemy, particularly the Moros, lies in wait in jungle areas for our return and attacks fiercely.

The Japanese responded to the harassment by the guerrillas with increasingly aggressive raids along the coast. These attacks, carried out by groups of as many as five hundred heavily armed troops, were designed to kill as many guerrillas as possible, drive the rest inland and eliminate the coastwatch stations from which guerrillas were spying on troop movements and calling in submarine attacks on Japanese ships.

According to the '108th Division Unit History', the guerrillas always knew about these raids well before they happened. Thanks to the guerrillas' network of spies and informers, the enemy 'was never able to carry out operations against the Division without advance notice of their coming being received'. The guerrillas, however, did not always make the best use of their early warning. The Japanese themselves tended to 'propagandise their coming mopping-up operations (as they always called them)' to such an extent that 'no-one paid much attention to their threats until shooting was actually heard'. As a result, it was sometimes too late for guerrilla fighters to get into good positions from which much greater damage could have been inflicted.

One Japanese raid in late January 1944 was aimed at the small but strategically important town of Baroy, tucked in a valley roughly halfway along Panguil Bay. Guerrilla spies suggested that the enemy's objectives lay further up the valley: the town of Malingao, where an old naval wireless set was hidden, and the nearby airfield at Balimbang.

Blow and McLaren set off with McLaren's commandos and about seventy Moros to engage the Japanese, who had come ashore in two parties, east and west of Baroy. Stopping to rest at a jungle clearing, McLaren 'heard two soft reports'. Looking up, he saw two small parachutes open and float slowly down. He recognised it as a signal fired from a Japanese pistol and told his men to take cover. Richardson reports the two Australians venturing out for a look and having to run from enemy soldiers firing machine guns from a native hut. 'The main Japanese force ahead, who had signalled with the parachutes, advanced at the double into the teeth of the [guerrilla] ambush, which, panting but unharmed, the two Australians joined.'

Fleeing from the ambush, leaving their dead and wounded behind, the Japanese succeeded in reaching their objective, finding the hidden radio set (no great loss, according to Ross, as it was old and cumbersome and the guerrillas had others) and overrunning the airfield at Balimbang, which the guerrillas would retake in due course. The Japanese failed, however, in their effort to occupy the important town of Baroy.

More serious damage to the guerrilla radio network was averted when McLaren found a map on the body of a Japanese officer killed in a jungle ambush. The map showed the position of every radio station on Mindanao, all of which now had to be moved.

It was only later that McLaren learnt what had happened at the airfield. Two American engineers, Captain Leo Boelens and Captain Roy Welbon, had been away from the airfield and returned to find it occupied by the Japanese. Both men were ambushed, while a young Norwegian seaman named Knudsen, who had joined the guerrillas after his ship was sunk off

Cebu in the early days of the Pacific war, escaped (with half a finger shot off, according to Richardson).

Ross reports that the two Americans were killed, but Richardson states they were captured. US military records indicate that Boelens was 'killed in action' on 22 January 1944 and that Welbon 'died' on 25 January. Blow, Ross's only source for this phase of the war, remembered the Japanese having 'rather surprisingly' buried the two men, putting 'flowers and crosses on their graves'. According to Richardson, the Japanese occupied the airfield for only a short time before pulling back to Misamis, confident that the scattered guerrilla forces were no longer a threat. Walking through the area after the Japanese had left, Blow and McLaren noticed 'two graves, neatly roped off, with a cross taken from the town church on each one. There were flowers in jars at the heads of the graves. One grave was marked "Captain Boland" [sic], the other "Lieut. Elborne" [sic].'

The Japanese very rarely buried the body of an enemy, and McLaren felt that this was odd. He decided to open the graves so as to identify the bodies positively. The first grave disclosed Elborne's mutilated body. They opened the other grave, to find nothing there. Later Boland's body was found still lying on the airstrip. He had been wounded by bullets and then bayoneted.

'They'll be back,' said McLaren. 'That'll be another score we can even up.'

The opportunity came soon enough. Within a few weeks Japanese troop barges could be seen loading up again for the short trip across Panguil Bay. McLaren took his commandos down to set up machine gun positions on the ground behind the beach. When the barges came to within about 800 yards, Richardson writes, McLaren started firing.

'Oh, don't, sir!' cried one of his native fighters. 'They'll come in and attack us if you fire on them!'

'Get back, you bloody hero, or I'll open up on you too!' shouted McLaren.

While McLaren raked the decks with his machine gun, the guerrillas fired their rifles, but the barges kept coming. Forced to withdraw, McLaren and his men watched the Japanese wade ashore, bayonets fixed, and line up on the beach before marching off on another punitive raid.

This time the Japanese objective was twofold: to destroy an observation post on the hills behind Kolambugan that gave the guerrillas a bird's-eye view of shipping movements in Panguil Bay; and to cut, for good, the supply route from the west coast of Mindanao to Hedges' guerrilla force in Lanao Province.

In order to achieve the latter, the Japanese set up a permanent garrison not far from their landing point. With their fortified base at Misamis City and the new garrison on the Lanao side, the Japanese now controlled both shores of Panguil Bay, making it hazardous for the guerrillas to ship supplies across the water and forcing their ancient trucks to make wide detours to avoid the garrison when transporting supplies by road.

The lookout above Kolambugan was a crucial piece of the surveillance network that, so far, had allowed Hedges to stay one step ahead of the Japanese. From their position directly across the bay, the guerrillas tracked the arrival of Japanese ships supplying the troops at Misamis. This information was passed to US submarines lurking just out to sea. McLaren recalled seeing a 14,000-ton steamship, 'as sedate as a peacetime ocean liner', sliding up the bay. At Misamis two thousand Japanese soldiers came aboard, together with trucks, artillery and Bren-gun carriers, watched through a telescope by the guerrillas above Kolambugan. After three days the ship sailed. Word was radioed to US submarines waiting at the mouth of the bay, and before the ship reached the open sea she was sunk. According to Richardson, the survivors swam ashore on the Misamis side of the bay, only to be killed by locals in a 'bloodthirsty massacre'.

There was little the fighters defending Kolambugan could do against such a determined enemy assault. Most of the guerrillas on the hill were killed, but a few managed to escape. The valuable telescope was saved. The Japanese now moved to consolidate their control by eliminating the guerrilla base at Liangan.

Once again, the strength of the enemy attack forced the guerrillas to abandon the town and withdraw further inland. Hedges's men now faced being driven back towards the enemy garrison occupying the southern part of Lanao. Squeezed between the two, the guerrillas risked being annihilated. McLaren and Blow faced a difficult choice. They could retreat to the safety of the highlands and sit out the following months in their jungle hideaways, but the effect on guerrilla morale would likely be severe. Alternatively, they could ask to be taken out by submarine, as they had originally intended. The third option was to stay and fight. They decided to fight.

The Japanese continued to reinforce Liangan with troops from the garrison at Misamis. Hedges, meanwhile, established a new headquarters just a few kilometres from the original site. A pair of scouts was sent down to reconnoitre the town. In Ross's version, Blow sent them; in Richardson's, it was McLaren. Richardson writes that one was a Filipino guerrilla and the other a 'red-headed, blue-eyed half-caste boy, only sixteen years of age, who worked as personal boy for McLaren'. McLaren saw both scouts 'cut down' by Japanese machine guns. Blow, however, recalled one of the pair getting away while the other was not killed but captured.

'So the only guerrilla casualty was the scout who had been caught,' Ross writes. 'They had long ceased to ponder on the fate of such a casualty; torture was the norm and next time it might be one of them. It could have been worse.'

The guerrillas chose the Emperor's birthday to launch their first attack. They took up positions in the jungle, with McLaren in charge of the 81mm mortar. McLaren seldom took part in any action that did not result in mayhem for the enemy, and the Emperor's birthday attack on Liangan was no exception. Richardson writes that 'the grass was strewn with the dead and dying': '[T]he survivors ran screaming into the sea, mortar bombs falling around them, and rifle and machine-gun fire pouring in from all sides. They never got into action or returned the fire and, taking advantage of their panic, the Filipino prisoners they had taken escaped to rejoin the guerrillas.'

According to Ross, more than a hundred Japanese soldiers were parading when the first mortar shell struck. They pulled themselves together enough to fire off 'over 100' shells, although these did nothing more than 'blacken the odd guerrilla face'. The attack had been a warning to the Japanese that the guerrillas were not the spent force they had imagined, but the damage inflicted was only temporary. Japanese casualties could be quickly replaced with reinforcements from the garrison across the water in Misamis. Nevertheless, Ross writes, the attack on Liangan was 'immensely satisfying—to Rex and Jock as well as their men, the latter afraid no longer'.

Detailed US intelligence reports of guerrilla attacks on Japanese troops refute the insinuation that the guerrillas were 'afraid' to fight. But one fact did emerge clearly from the Emperor's birthday attack: dislodging the Japanese from Liangan would take a force much larger than Colonel Hedges had at his disposal.

Localised attacks continued, however, to inflict casualties on the Japanese. The day after the mortar and machine-gun attack on the parade ground at Liangan, Richardson reports a guerrilla patrol led by McLaren stumbling upon a group of about forty Japanese soldiers 'laughing and whooping' as they bathed in the river. McLaren's men started firing and minutes later 'the river ran red'. Troops came running from the barracks, but by then the guerrillas had vanished into the jungle.

Strategically, Hedges' best hope of being able to throw the Japanese out of Liangan lay with persuading recalcitrant Moros to join his force.

McLaren and Blow both claimed to have been entrusted with recruiting Moros to the guerrilla cause.

Blow, as well as being Hedges' intelligence officer, had now been appointed his chief of staff, replacing a Filipino officer who had been killed. For Blow, 'it made an interesting change, a break from continual skirmishing and a chance to find out more about these difficult people'. Attaching himself to a well-connected local businessman—'a man in his fifties, son of a Basque sea captain and a Filipina mestiza'—who had been governor of Lanao Province before the war, Blow toured the country around Lake Lanao 'making propaganda speeches to the Moros'.

Forty years later, Rex Blow had not softened his opinion of the 'treacherous' Moros. But the Moros admired strong leaders, and Blow himself was a strong leader. His army service record includes a lengthy citation for the Distinguished Service Order. Among other acts of bravery, it records that, in 1944,

Major BLOW was given the task of bringing under control the Moros of the Malabang area in the Lanao Province. For many years the Moros had been a continual source of concern to the Philippine Administration. Major BLOW succeeded in his task, large due to his force of character, his example and his disregard of personal safety. On several occasions, his life was threatened, but by his initiative and coolness, he maintained control and gained the respect of all sections of the Moro population in the Malabang area.

McLaren, an equally forceful character, had no patience for 'propaganda speeches' and went in person to see a local gang leader who, according to Richardson, had been 'murdering, looting, robbing and kidnapping for twelve years'. McLaren was unperturbed by the sight of the chieftain and his 'cut-throat men, armed with the Moro bush blunderbuss' (the same bush blunderbuss that had killed his friend Butler) and asked him directly whether he would fight against the Japanese. The chief, a 'blood-thirsty fighting man' named Pena, refused to give McLaren an answer but agreed to speak to Colonel Hedges.

The later conversation with Hedges, as related by Richardson, went like this:

> 'Now, colonel, before you start I want to make some things clear . . . I may have stolen and I may have looted, but I have never kidnapped.'
>
> 'You lying bastard,' said McLaren softly behind the outlaw's broad back, and Hedges looked down to hide a smile.
>
> After some discussion Pena agreed to join them in force with his men, and he was given the rank of lieutenant.

Pena's first taste of action against the Japanese was when he was asked to attack a machine-gun post that covered the approach to Liangan. Although 'more full of pride than ever', Pena gingerly replied that he would carry out the attack only '[i]f you will come with us, sir.' Hearing this, Blow 'jokingly' said, 'Look out they don't shoot you instead of the Japs, Mac.'

It took two attempts for McLaren and the Moros to overrun the machine-gun post. At the same time, the guerrillas launched a series of hit-and-run attacks on the Japanese garrison at Liangan. Ammunition was now running low. With resupply difficult as a result of the Japanese occupation, Hedges had no choice but to slow down the offensive against Liangan.

Years of disease and malnutrition were now catching up with McLaren. At the fall of Singapore he had weighed around twelve and a half stone (nearly 79 kilograms). Just over two years later, his weight was down to seven and a half stone (47 kilograms). According to Richardson, he was suffering from pellagra and beriberi, which had given him sunken eyes and made his normally thin face resemble a skull. 'Ugliest of all were his

legs, the knees gaunt knobs above stick-like shins where ulcers continu-
ously oozed.' He suffered from chronic dysentery and malaria.*

Aware of McLaren's deteriorating health, Colonel Hedges sent him up
to the radio station in the hills to recuperate. McLaren could not take
the enforced rest for more than two days. Sending a message to Hedges
that he was fully recovered, he asked to be allowed to return. Permission
was refused. Richardson recounts a comical tale of the few days McLaren
spent in the jungle distilling 'guerrilla rum' with bits of equipment he
found lying around in the jungle.

The source of the jungle rum was a drum of tuba spirit 'red with
rust' that, mixed with oil, had been used to power the trucks. McLaren is
said to have claimed that tuba, fermented for around twenty hours, was
'better than Melbourne Bitter' (a comparison more likely to have been
supplied by Richardson himself, since McLaren was a Queenslander!). If
under-fermented, 'it would fill you with gas, so that you sounded like a
Japanese woodpecker machine-gun'. Over-fermenting it turned the tuba
into a 'sour vinegar'.

McLaren ran his tuba twice through a still that had been cobbled
together out of vehicle components and equipment from the old saw
mill, then coloured it with burnt sugar and 'engaged a Filipino to draw
attractive labels'. (According to Ross, one label carried the slogan 'Guerrilla
Rum—ten dead Japs in every bottle'.)

Taking care to send consignments of his product to Colonel Hedges,
McLaren 'lounged back like a Highland chief, sipping the savage spirit
he had discovered'. McLaren claimed to have found tuba 'more effective'

---

* Blow had a supply of anti-malarial drugs but apparently he did not share them.
  Ross, whose account of her brother-in-law often verges on hagiography, notes:
  '[A]t times there was not a tablet of quinine or atabrin [sic] to be had and Rex
  knew that he had to keep his precious stock for himself, since as their CO he
  could not afford to succumb to malaria'. Thanks to his private supply of quinine,
  'Rex managed to keep fairly fit.'

in treating dysentery than the opium used by the Chinese communist guerrillas in Malaya. He also told Richardson that it 'took the heat out of his malaria fever'.

By the time he was allowed back, McLaren had managed to regain some of the weight he had lost after Singapore. But not all his ailments could be cured with jungle rum.

Chapter 12

NEAR DEATH

The Japanese continued to reinforce the garrison at Liangan, while making regular forays along the coastal road and occasional incursions inland. Sometimes these consisted of small fighting patrols ordered to make contact with the guerrillas and then retreat. At other times well-equipped groups of several hundred infantrymen marched into the jungle with a definite objective in mind, such as the mountain radio station from which the guerrillas transmitted information from their network of coastal lookouts.

By April 1944, according to Richardson, the Japanese garrison had thrown up a series of sturdy timber blockhouses connected by underground tunnels from which they would 'aimlessly' clear their machine guns at dusk or 'lob a few mortar bombs into the thick green wall up on the hill-slope'. McLaren, though far from fit, got caught up in a number of skirmishes, on one occasion leaping stark naked from his jungle bed in order to fight off an enemy raid with his Browning automatic rifle.

Getting dressed before joining the attack would have been out of the question, Richardson writes, since it 'might have lost [McLaren] the valuable element of surprise'. The fully dressed Japanese understandably 'milled in panic' as they ran for cover from the 'naked madman and the winking red eye of his gun'.

McLaren had a fighting motto that, a decade later, he was keen to share with his biographer:

'Look here,' he would argue in any discussion of tactics, 'you've got to remember that when you bump into a Jap on the track somewhere, he gets just as big a surprise as you do. You stand there like a couple of gawks for a few seconds, then the man who is first on the draw wins the box of chocolates. Don't you believe this about the Japs being super-soldiers. Their bowels move just as quickly as anyone else's.'

According to the men who fought alongside him, fear never stopped McLaren, but without a personal medical chest to sustain him he succumbed to the usual debilitating diseases—not only malaria but also chronic dysentery and beriberi. By mid-1944 McLaren was a 'very sick man . . . he was lethargic, and lacked the fire that once characterized his actions. He could barely drag one foot after the other.'

Richardson records the arrival in early June 1944 of a US submarine off the coastal village of Pagadian, at the southern end of the isthmus between Misamis Occidental and Lanao Province. Ammunition and other supplies were hauled overland by buffalo to a town called Aurora, behind Misamis. From there the submarine cargoes—including wireless equipment—were brought down to the shore of Panguil Bay for delivery to the guerrillas in Lanao.

But Japanese intelligence was aware of the traffic. As the submarine arrivals became more frequent, the Japanese decided to take action, sending a thousand-strong infantry force to take Aurora. The guerrillas employed their usual tactics, ambushing small groups of enemy soldiers and sniping at stragglers. The Japanese succeeded in reaching Aurora but found the town empty, the guerrillas having melted away into the jungle with their families, food and equipment.

With Aurora now in enemy hands, McLaren was ordered south to join an American lieutenant, Willard Money, who commanded a whaleboat running supplies between guerrilla outposts around the south coast. The two men were to set up a coastwatcher station at the head of Sarangani Bay, on the southernmost tip of Mindanao, facing the Celebes Sea. Richardson suggests that, after finding out about the mission, the Japanese attempted to intercept Money and McLaren before they reached Sarangani Bay.

Feverish and unable to eat, McLaren was in no state to fight. Richardson recounts a dramatic escape, the Japanese arriving with all guns blazing, giving Money and McLaren just enough warning for them to be able to slip the ropes and start the engines. With enemy soldiers running down the jetty, the sea 'spurted under a hail of bullets as the whaleboat moved out of range'.

McLaren's condition worsened overnight, and Money realised he had to find a doctor. As the whaleboat approached land, McLaren 'fell on his side, a great groan of agony bursting from his white lips'. Two locals, identified by Richardson as a Moro chieftain and his wife, agreed to take the ailing McLaren to their house. Although there was a Japanese garrison only a few miles away and the nearby country was swarming with informers, Money believed that McLaren would be safe under the chieftain's protection.

His hosts brought him food, but McLaren was too sick to eat. According to Richardson, a medical student who had studied at Manila University before the war came to the chieftain's house, but the only remedy he could suggest was massage. McLaren lay inert while the student worked on the painful area around his stomach. At one point McLaren winced with pain, his thoughts lucid enough for him to realise that he was suffering from appendicitis.

Before he became sick, McLaren had talked to Rex Blow about the illnesses a guerrilla with no access to proper medical care could not afford to have. One of them, he remembered, was appendicitis. He knew that without an operation he would soon be dead, but who was going to operate?

Richardson writes that the Filipino medical student was summoned back to the chieftain's house, where McLaren asked him whether he would agree to operate. The student, who had left the university without completing his medical training, said he could not, whereupon McLaren reached for his pistol, placing it beside his head and warning the terrified student, 'You'll stand by me and help me, or I'll blow your bloody head off!' Thoughtfully, he then wrote out and signed his own death certificate to absolve the student in case anything should go wrong.

When McLaren moved to Queensland after the First World War, he had worked as a veterinary surgeon in Bundaberg (in 1938, he had married Catherine Ahern in Childers). He therefore had the technical expertise needed for the operation. Although groggy from pain, Richardson reports that he 'supervised preparations for the extraction of his appendix'. While the chieftain and his wife tore up bedsheets to form bandages and made an operating table out of floorboards, McLaren 'ordered two large dessert spoons to be bent to serve as retractors. They were sterilized, together with a pair of scissors, forceps, a needle, and a razor blade.' Banana leaf fibre would be used to stitch the wound. When everything was arranged to his satisfaction, McLaren had himself hoisted on to the makeshift operating table with a mirror positioned over his abdomen 'so that he could see the area to be cut'. There was no anaesthetic.

As Richardson tells the story, McLaren used the razor blade to make the incision, prising the muscles apart 'as he had often done in operating on horses and cows' and inserting the spoons to hold them. An 'old midwife' gripped the spoons while the medical student, 'white and sweat-beaded', passed him the instruments. McLaren found the ruptured appendix, cut it away and drew it out through the incision before stitching himself back together with a 'fair-sized sewing needle'. It was not until he began stitching that McLaren felt any pain, with 'each dragging insertion [an] agony to him'.

The operation took four and a half hours. When it was over, he 'lay back and let his body go limp in an ecstasy of trembling. He was suddenly proud of his feat, especially proud that he had manipulated the muscles apart instead of cutting through them. If he had cut through them they would have taken a long time to regain their normal strength and power. Now, he thought, he would soon be in fighting trim again.'*

McLaren's convalescence was brief. Within a few days of the operation, news reached him that Japanese soldiers were half an hour away and heading for the chieftain's house. Refusing the chieftain's offer to take him to a jungle hideaway, McLaren picked up his tommy-gun, pistol

---

* While Richardson's account sounds incredible, there have been other recorded cases of self-appendectomy. Two such operations are described in the appendix to this book. McLaren's feat was widely reported when he was awarded the Military Cross in January 1948. Newspapers quoted him saying: 'I knew I had appendicitis and that if I did not do something I would die . . . With the aid of a mirror and an ordinary knife I took out the appendix. The operation took four and a half hours. It was hell, but I came through all right. I used jungle fibre to stitch the wound. Natives stood by during the operation.' Some reports were sceptical, quoting McLaren's remarks but suggesting that he might have 'directed' rather than 'performed' the operation, and giving credit to a 'Malayan native guerrilla' for removing the appendix, despite McLaren's unequivocal claim to have done it himself.

and ammunition belt, grabbed the jar containing his appendix and vanished into the jungle, aiming to make contact with the American officer in charge of the local 106th Division guerrillas, Lieutenant Colonel Frank McGee.

Chapter 13

THE *BASTARD*

———⊷⬦⊶———

Hal Richardson describes Frank McGee simply as 'a First World War veteran of Scottish-American blood', but McGee's story is nearly as colourful as that of McLaren himself, which it frequently mirrors.

In 1944 McGee was fifty-five years old. A graduate of West Point, he was thirteen years older than McLaren but still extremely fit. In his Master's thesis, Major Larry Schmidt describes McGee as possessing 'great physical stamina' as well as 'a quick mind, an excellent memory, and great tenacity of purpose'—attributes that, along with a Scottish ancestry, he shared with Jock McLaren.

Awarded the Distinguished Service Cross during the First World War, McGee had retired on permanent disability with the rank of captain. According to Schmidt, he 'had a silver plate in his head from shrapnel wounds', suffered 'excruciating headaches' and slurred his speech. After the war McGee spent twenty years as a planter on Mindanao, returning to the United States every two years 'to have the silver plate in his head adjusted'.

Before the Japanese invasion of the Philippines, McGee had supplied the US War Department with intelligence reports about Japanese activities on Mindanao. Despite his age, he volunteered for active service when war broke out. Frank McGee's name is listed in the 1944 'G2 Staff Study of Philippine Islands Situation', just below those of 'AIF OFFICERS. Capt. K.A. STEELE, Lts R. BLOW and GILLOR [Gillon]'.*

Like Colonel Fertig, Frank McGee did not join the American surrender in May 1942 but went into the hills, determined to fight on. Eventually he joined the guerrillas in Cotabato Province and was given command of the 106th Division. By the time US forces invaded Mindanao, McGee was attached to the 24th Infantry Division as officer in charge of all guerrillas in the sector. He would be killed by a sniper's bullet less than a month before the Japanese surrender.

Cotabato had long been hazardous territory for the guerrillas. As elsewhere on Mindanao, the Moros were capricious, and some were known to be collaborating with the Japanese. According to Richardson, McGee's 106th guerrillas held only a 'precarious footing' in the province. Colonel Fertig was under no illusions about the difficulty of bringing the Cotabato Moros into his guerrilla organisation, telling McGee (in a letter

---

*   The entry for Frank McGee embarrassingly confuses his war record with that of another senior American officer, John McGee, who surrendered to the Japanese in 1942 and was interned at the Davao penal colony in Mindanao. Put on a ship for Japan, John McGee escaped by jumping over the side. He was rescued by a Filipino fisherman and found his way to guerrilla headquarters, but his request to act as liaison officer between the guerrillas and the US invading force was rejected by Colonel Fertig, with a sneering remark about John McGee being 'a former POW with ideas on how to win the war'. John McGee took great offence at the remark and was eventually evacuated from Mindanao by submarine. It is unlikely that either John McGee or Frank McGee would have appreciated being mistaken for each other.

quoted by Major Schmidt), 'I need, desperately, an American officer to take command of the Cotabato area. This thing cannot be handled well by remote control.'

According to Schmidt, Fertig 'never had any doubt concerning the motives of the Moros. They had little sense of patriotism as the Americans would have understood it, and they had no loyalty whatsoever to the Philippine Commonwealth. Their loyalties were unpredictable. Some did actually feel loyalty to the United States. Others were ardent collaborators with the Japanese.' Many Moros were 'tenaciously independent' and opposed to domination by any outside power. But while the ultimate goal for most might have been separatism, this did not preclude (and perhaps even encouraged) interim allegiances that suited both parties. 'Once this was understood, Fertig was able to take a practical approach to his dealings with the Moro chieftains. Who offered what benefits; whose currency was more valuable; who pays spies more and which markets for rice were nearer? These questions could be negotiated objectively.'

When Jock McLaren went looking for Colonel McGee, Cotabato was still a dangerous place. McLaren's exploits had already won him a degree of fame—or notoriety—among his American superiors. As Richardson tells it, McGee greeted him with the words, 'I knew I'd see you soon, McLaren. Come and have some chow.'

By mid-1944 McGee was receiving regular deliveries of food and equipment by submarine. Now recovered from his do-it-yourself appendectomy, McLaren started building a boat to use as a ferry. In September 1944 he was given something better: an 8-metre whaleboat brought by submarine from Australia. He chose some of his Moro fighters to form the crew. McLaren fitted a 20mm cannon in the bow, a .50-calibre gun in the rear and two twin .30-inch guns amidships. He told Richardson that he added an 81mm mortar, prompting Rex Blow to warn him that if he ever fired the mortar, it would 'blow her stern off'.

According to Richardson, Colonel McGee asked McLaren to take his boat—which he had named the *Bastard*—around the coast to Sarangani Bay to keep an eye on some airfields built by the Japanese in anticipation of the coming US invasion. 'Bastard' was one of McLaren's favourite expletives, recurring throughout Richardson's book. Few words were more evocative of the man himself. With her guns hidden under tarpaulins and sacking, the *Bastard* anchored in small coves, her drab hull blending in with the jungle. It was while skippering his whaleboat that McLaren saw US bombers attacking the airfields—the first Allied air raid he had seen since the surrender of Singapore.

In March 1944 the Joint Chiefs of Staff had told General MacArthur to draw up plans for the invasion of Mindanao, to start on 15 November. In response MacArthur came up with a plan to invade southern Mindanao as a prelude to a larger amphibious landing on the island of Leyte to the north. Taking these two islands would provide US forces with secure communications for an assault on the much more strongly defended island of Luzon, the biggest island in the archipelago and site of Japanese headquarters.

The US Sixth Army invaded designated beaches on Leyte on the morning of 20 October 1944, after a four-hour barrage by naval guns. The success of the initial landings enabled MacArthur to wade ashore at 1.30 p.m., proclaiming: 'People of the Philippines, I have returned! By the grace of Almighty God, our forces stand again on Philippine soil.'

As the Sixth Army consolidated its position on Leyte, Fertig was advised by radio not to expect an invasion of Mindanao. MacArthur wanted the guerrillas to begin attacks against Japanese garrisons and to stop the Japanese from moving troops to Suriago Province, the part of Mindanao closest to Leyte.

The US landings on Leyte and the nearby island of Samar had immediate consequences for the guerrillas on Mindanao. All over the island the Japanese pulled back from their far-flung outposts, concentrating their forces in more easily defended garrisons and leaving roughly two-thirds of the island in the hands of the guerrillas.

For the Japanese High Command, the broader impact of the loss of Leyte was profound and irreversible. A study of the Leyte campaign by the US Army Center of Military History concludes that 'once the decisive battle of Leyte was lost, the Japanese themselves gave up all hope of retaining the Philippines'.

MacArthur's own account, published after the war in the *Reports of General MacArthur*, states that the Japanese 'suffered irreparable defeat in the Leyte campaign. Every phase of their ambitious Sho plan for the defense of the Philippines met with complete and irretrievable failure. Driven to near panic by the threat of losing the Philippines, Japan's wartime leaders in Tokyo had risked their remaining offensive power in one last effort to save their empire. Whatever chance the Japanese had to regain the initiative in the Pacific was lost on Leyte.'

But if the eventual outcome of the Pacific war was not in doubt after Leyte, there was still a lot of fighting to be done, and Jock McLaren, in Richardson's words, 'wanted a little excitement before the war ended'.

Some unwanted excitement came when the *Bastard* was spotted at anchor by a formation of US Navy Hellcats (Richardson says there were twenty). Seeing the planes diving towards him, McLaren, in a frenzy, 'whipped off his clothing to show his white skin, and dragged the American Stars and Stripes from a locker. He stood up amidships, naked, waving his flag desperately, his native crew crouching against the bulwarks in terror.' Just in time, the American pilots realised that the naked Scotsman was one of theirs and pulled out of the dive—another near escape to add to a seemingly endless list.

After sailing the *Bastard* back around the coast to Pagadian, at the head of Illana Bay, McLaren made his way overland to the guerrillas' headquarters on the shore of Panguil Bay, facing Misamis. With the Japanese pulling back to more fortified positions, the entire coastal strip along the Lanao side of Panguil Bay now belonged to Fertig's guerrillas.

'By January 1945 Colonel Fertig's command included a force of about 38,000 men,' MacArthur wrote. 'His radio and intelligence network consisted of some seventy transmitter stations and an excellent and extensive coast-watcher system. GHQ was furnished with a constant stream of information which, within its limits of accuracy, helped considerably in the planning of operations against the Japanese in the Philippines.'

McLaren saw US Navy bombers attack Japanese airfields, inflicting heavy damage on the airstrips. Thanks to the detailed intelligence provided by Fertig's guerrillas, there was no need for reconnaissance flights to precede the raids. The bombers achieved total surprise and were able to destroy most of the enemy aircraft on the ground.

Orders now came for McLaren to take the *Bastard* back around the coast in order to cut off supplies to the Japanese garrisons at Malabang and Parang. Richardson does not say who gave the orders, but in his tape-recorded interview with Bowden and Nelson, Rex Blow describes seaborne attacks on both garrisons:

We'd been getting information about the port down at Parang, and apparently there were just a few Jap machine gun posts and a couple of hundred Japs down there. So we decided we'd go down and stir them up. And so we travelled down by day, and that night we camped just outside the harbour. In the morning we steamed in early and . . . we just sort of circled around and shot anything that moved and . . . just in the afternoon as we . . . got back and got our boat under cover . . . two or three Jap planes came along, obviously looking for us. And I think we were pretty lucky that they didn't see us . . .

[Another] day Jock came along and he said . . . you're having a bit of trouble with these people over here at Malabang. And I said, oh, yeah,

Jock, there seem to be a couple of outposts there on the beach that want doing over. Oh, well, all right, says Jock. So we all climbed aboard and away we went and, again we just stood off and . . . peppered them.

Although Blow is missing from Richardson's account of the Parang attack, his service record includes a commendation from the headquarters of Tenth Military District, A Corps, Western Mindanao, dated 1 January 1945 and signed by Fertig's second-in-command, Colonel Bowler. The commendation cites raids carried out at 'Pollac Harbor, Cotabato' (i.e. Parang) and Malabang by Blow, fellow Australian Leslie Gillon and an American naval officer, Lieutenant Thomas Sinclair.

The text states that on 14 December 1944 'two US Navy motor whaleboats under the command of Lieut. T.L. Sinclair, USNR, Major Rex Blow, AIF, and Major Leslie Gillon, AIF, attacked enemy installations at Pollac Harbour, Cotabato, Mindanao, with 20mm cannon fire'. During the attack, 'three small enemy craft were badly damaged, good intelligence information was obtained and casualties were inflicted on the enemy . . . The next day, the waterfront installations of the enemy at Malabang, Lanao Province, Mindanao, were attacked by the same boats and crews with similar good results.'

Their actions were reported to both South West Pacific Area headquarters in Australia and to the US Seventh Fleet, with 'the officers named above, and the enlisted personnel of the two boats . . . commended by this headquarters'.

McLaren was an officer at this time, not an enlisted man. Why was he not named in the US commendation?

In Richardson's account of the attack, McLaren had hatched a crafty plan to surprise the garrison: as well as flying the Japanese flag, he put 'his' crew in 'Nippon Navy uniform'. At the approach of the *Bastard*, the Japanese 'called excitedly to their comrades as they ran down to the jetty to welcome the new-comers'.

The whaleboat drew steadily nearer. At one hundred and fifty yards McLaren pulled on the cord and the Japanese flag came down with a rush, to be replaced by the Stars and Stripes. Immediately, the 20-millimetre gun in the bows opened fire on the milling Japanese and three small craft near the jetty . . . [After the attack] the *Bastard* put out to sea, leaving bodies scattered along the jetty and the three small craft burning and sinking, never again to carry supplies for the Japanese.

In November 1945, three months after the war had ended, McLaren was recommended for the Military Cross for his service with the guerrillas on Mindanao. The citation notes that 'in December 1944 Captain McLaren was in command of an armed whale boat. On two occasions that month, Captain McLaren entered by day the harbour of Parang and, in the face of heavy enemy fire, succeeded in damaging or sinking three enemy small craft.'

For a period of three days in January 1945, McLaren was said to have operated 'with great daring' in enemy waters. Over the following months he kept up a nightly blockade that prevented the Japanese from either evacuating or resupplying the garrison at Malabang. On many occasions he 'proceeded close inshore and engaged at short range enemy-held locations and installations'.

The reference to 'three enemy small craft' suggests that the attack described in Blow's commendation and in McLaren's citation for the Military Cross is the same one McLaren recounted to Hal Richardson. Why McLaren did not mention Blow, and why Blow's commendation did not mention McLaren, is not clear.

McLaren's citation also mentions his service as Blow's second-in-command, commending him for his 'outstanding leadership in battle' and his 'cheerful imperturbability'. McLaren, it says, 'led personally many combat patrols which operated in a most aggressive manner and inflicted considerable casualties on the enemy'. According to his service record, McLaren was awarded his Military Cross on 21 February 1946.

A month later, on 27 March 1946, the US Chargé d'Affaires in Canberra wrote to Australia's Minister for External Affairs, H.V. Evatt, wanting to know whether the Commonwealth Government would be 'agreeable' to the US Army awarding McLaren the Bronze Star Medal for his actions during the siege of Malabang.

On 2 April 1945, according to the proposed US Army citation, McLaren and three unnamed companions came under intense automatic rifle fire while taking a small boat up the Malabang River on a reconnaissance mission. Handing over the tiller to one of his men, McLaren 'crept to the prow despite the heavy hostile fire and manned a mounted 20mm gun. Although constantly exposed to the enemy fusillade he delivered telling fire which silenced the foe and saved his men from further danger as well as enabling the successful completion of his mission.' Through his 'outstanding courage and resourcefulness', McLaren was credited with having made a 'marked contribution to the liberation of Mindanao'.

McLaren never received his Bronze Star Medal.

Chapter 14

THE SHIPS ARE ON THE WAY

Both McLaren and Blow now had a price on their head. According to Richardson, the Japanese published a bulletin with a picture of McLaren (taken from his Singapore paybook) and the promise of a big reward—70,000 pesos for his capture, dead or alive. Blow told Bowden and Nelson that the price on his head was quoted in cloth: 'West Point khaki cloth was very much in demand . . . a couple of thousand yards were on my head and that was quite a lot of money. But I never figured . . . that the Filipinos would give me away.'

Early in 1945, Blow handed McLaren a difficult assignment. The withdrawal of Japanese troops into their garrisons had brought a resurgence of civil unrest and lawlessness. Blow asked McLaren to travel with him through the Moro country around Lake Lanao and, in Richardson's words, 'check all arms' and 'get the guerrilla currency into operation'.

So-called guerrilla pesos, poorly printed and susceptible to mutilation and forgery, had existed in some form or other since 1942, but a Japanese-imposed monopoly over the issue of currency, combined with the outlawing of guerrilla pesos, severely restricted their use. Filipinos knew that anyone caught in possession of the outlawed notes risked arrest and possible execution. At the same time, the guerrillas had issued orders prohibiting the use of currency issued by the Japanese military, but these orders were not always heeded. Blow's instructions to 'get the guerrilla currency into operation' were easier said than done.

In some villages, Blow and McLaren encountered little resistance as they walked through the markets stuffing sacks with fistfuls of Japanese currency. But in other places, Ross writes, they heard the sound of rifles being cocked and glimpsed the flash of knives. At Ganassi, a town on the southern shore of Lake Lanao, McLaren tried in vain to buy food with guerrilla pesos. 'No good,' he was told. 'Nippon money good.' Rebuffed by the Moro stallholders, McLaren retreated to confer with Blow.

According to Richardson, it was Blow who gave the orders for what happened next.

'We'll raid the market and adjust the currency difficulties,' said Blow blandly, a dangerous twinkle in his eye. 'Call in some of the headmen.'

The headmen shook their heads gravely when Blow proposed violence in the money mart. 'It would be too dangerous, sirs. Too risky. Those men are very very fond of their money.'

The war had not eradicated Mindanao's centuries-old ethnic tensions. Blow told Bowden and Nelson that he and McLaren had brought along a 'pretty vicious little band' of Christian Filipinos for protection. With armed Christian fighters surrounding the market, 'between five and six hundred' Moro shoppers and traders looked on as Blow and McLaren filled their sacks with Japanese money. Not a shot was fired, but 'a loud wailing broke out' from the Moros as the two Australians set fire to the sacks. Blow recalled, 'We got away with it.'

Between October 1944 and February 1945, Fertig's guerrillas continued intelligence activities while keeping up their attacks on the Japanese. The heavily garrisoned airfield at Malabang—the best on Mindanao, McLaren told Richardson—had long been an enticing prize, and in November Blow led his guerrillas in an assault that scattered the garrison and briefly captured the airfield. In response the Japanese 'rushed two thousand reinforcements' and dispatched fighter and bomber planes to drive out the guerrillas and retake the airfield.

All over Mindanao, guerrillas were now harassing the retreating Japanese. Convinced that US forces would bypass Mindanao, senior Japanese officers had been slow to organise a concerted defence, with the result that isolated units were cut off and destroyed. With the US invasion imminent, Fertig issued the heavy weapons he had been told to stockpile, although sometimes without instructions. McLaren found himself the lucky owner of a bazooka. 'He fiddled with it for a time, surrounded by curious native guerrillas, then fired it,' Richardson writes. 'He claimed that it took him a week to round up his men.'

According to Balis, heavily armed partisans now 'infested every province. They cut telegraph wires, blew up bridges, and ambushed enemy columns. Partisan raids destroyed almost all the trucks in the Japanese 100th Division at Davao City, denying the Japanese the mobility to quickly restructure their defences if they had to.'

Fertig had been told that US troops would land at Malabang and Parang on 17 April 1945 and ordered an assault on the garrison at Malabang to support the invasion. He gave the task to Hedges, who put together a force estimated at anywhere between 1300 and 3000 guerrillas—Christian Filipinos and Moros—under the command of Major Rex Blow.

Blow—described by Balis as Hedges' 'best combat leader'—spent a month planning the assault. The Japanese garrison at Malabang was divided between the town and the nearby airfield. In his earlier attack Blow had succeeded in briefly occupying the airfield, but without air support his guerrillas had been unable to dislodge the Japanese garrison from the town, where they were holed up inside an old Spanish fort about half a mile from the coast.

After fastidious preparation, Blow launched a fresh attack on 8 March 1945. Around 250 enemy soldiers occupied the fort, which was connected to the airfield by a network of bunkers, trenches and tunnels. According to Richardson, the Japanese were guarding only one side of the airfield. The guerrillas dug in on the unguarded side, with only 'thirty or forty yards' between the two groups. US aircraft from nearby bases bombed and strafed the Japanese. McLaren recalled seeing transport planes dropping supplies on the airstrip and 'racing down in a truck to pick them up from under the noses of the Japanese, while the fighter escort roared over the enemy at treetop height to distract their attention'. A detailed account of the Malabang offensive in the 'History of the Mindanao Guerrillas' reports that by 20 March '400 yards of ground was gained . . . and a connecting trench in the airfield . . . was captured after a heavy resistance by the enemy'.

With the airfield secured, Blow was able to move on to the garrison inside the fort. Lacking heavy artillery, the guerrillas depended on ground attack missions by aircraft from the US Marines base at Zamboanga and bombers from the US 13th Air Force (known as the 'jungle air force' for its skill at operating out of jungle airstrips). Sheila Ross reports Blow being taken up by a 'gum-chewing Yank' who showed off some 'very fancy dive-bombing'. A few days later Blow and McLaren flew on a US Mitchell bomber that 'spent two hours going up and down the coast, bombing and shooting rockets at every likely target from Malabang down to Parang and Cota Bato'.

Blow told the same story to Bowden and Nelson:

Jock and I both went up with [the dive bombers] . . . and dropped the bombs just where we wanted them . . . a couple of mornings later . . . a couple of Mitchells came up, and Jock and I actually got in the Mitchells too . . . and went up with them and, you know, told them what we wanted bombed. It was a bit scary taking off [from] the old Malabang field with a full load of bombs in the Mitchell . . . it wasn't a very good field . . . then after a few days of that the Japs disappeared.

Richardson puts McLaren not on the bomber with Blow but sitting offshore behind the wheel of his armed whaleboat, the *Bastard*, now equipped with a short-range radio telephone. From his box seat in the whaler, McLaren 'saw the bombers come in over the town and, before the smoke curtain descended too heavily, he sent back a description of the bombing and directed bombers to targets he considered could do with treatment'. The Spanish fort was 'soon demolished. Here and there a thick stone corner stood, but for the rest there was only broken stone, shattered timbers, pulverized earth and bodies. Then the Moro guerrillas came charging in from one flank and the Filipinos from the other.'

Balis writes that Blow 'offset' the strength of the enemy's fortifications by 'attack[ing] in different places with small units while the Moros launched intermittent but frightening attacks from many directions at once'.

Although massively outnumbered, the Japanese refused to give up. 'Enemy fire [on 21 March] was very strong during the day,' the 'History of the Mindanao Guerrillas' reports. 'The enemy attempted a counter-attack but were repulsed with heavy losses.'

The next day the guerrillas stepped up combat and reconnaissance patrols while driving home the assault with mortars and heavy machine guns. A day later a Japanese plane dropped a bomb on the guerrillas without causing any casualties. 'Sniping, harassing and reconnaissance patrols towards the enemy line continued.' On the morning of 24 March,

US aircraft attacked again. Moro guerrillas carried out a feint attack from behind while other guerrillas advanced from the front. More aircraft came over in the afternoon. The guerrillas took advantage of the enemy's confusion to move forward. The 'History' reports that at this 'most precise moment', Blow offered the Japanese the chance to surrender.

Tenth Military District
Headquarters 108th Division
In the field
23 March 1945
To: The Japanese Garrison Commander
Malabang
No doubt you are by now informed of the progress of the war. In case you are not—American forces have captured Zamboanga and your garrison is now nearest to American Forces, and no doubt, your turn to be annihilated will come very soon.

However, we have discovered you have women and children inside your garrison and as an American—I cannot but keep sympathizing with them in their predicament—as the nearing action will mean certain death for all—as you must know that cannot be avoided.

However, I am now making the following offer for you to consider:
Surrender of all your soldiers and civilians direct to me.

If you wish to accept this offer—indicate to us in the form [word indecipherable] of the Matling River with a white flag raised on a stick. Bring with you no more than 4 men who will carry their rifle with muzzle towards the ground. Contact one of our officers who is in the line and will immediately send for me and we will discuss terms on the landing field.

I will personally guarantee your safety and if surrender is made, you will of course be concentrated and treated according to International Rules.

However, be warned that any attempt at treachery will have dire results for you in the future—you must know that you have very little chance of receiving any reinforcement or supplies, as you have probably noticed our submarines and launch patrol in waters [off] your shores. We also have unlimited air support now and bombing will be continued.

This note will be shown across your lines by our men and you can send a reply in the same manner.

For the Division Commander:

REX BLOW

Blow's offer was refused.

By the start of April 1945, the Japanese had lost half the ground they had occupied when the offensive began in early March, but they were still holding out. More guerrilla reinforcements were called up. On 9 April, US Corsair fighter bombers from Zamboanga attacked with napalm. (US air support was 'always that little bit late', Blow told Bowden and Nelson.) Most of the guerrilla units gained ground, driving the Japanese in Malabang town into a 'small pocket' near the beach. Orders were given for the final assault to be launched the next day.

The morning began with US aircraft dropping more napalm. The Japanese fought savagely all day. During the night 'between fifty and one hundred' enemy soldiers managed to break through the guerrilla lines, escaping on foot and in dugout canoes to Parang, about 60 kilometres down the coast in Cotabato Province.

News of the capture of Malabang and its valuable airfield reached MacArthur just five days before the initial Eighth Army landings at Illana Bay on Mindanao's west coast.

The cost of the action to the guerrillas was estimated by unit commanders to be seventeen dead and twenty-one wounded, while Japanese losses were 'conservatively' put at two hundred and fifty. The taking of Malabang by

Blow's guerrillas marked what the 'History' called 'the end of Japanese control over Lanao Province and opened up a way to easy landing of American Liberation Forces from Malabang to Parang on 17 April'.

The man chosen by MacArthur to command the invasion of the southern Philippines, General Eichelberger, was determined to ensure that the landings were 'easy'. Richardson writes that McLaren met a 'smart-looking' American colonel after the fighting at Malabang was over. The colonel announced that US aircraft were about to begin 'saturation bombing' of the Malabang area, to be followed by a naval bombardment. McLaren assured the colonel that the guerrillas 'already own all this area' and 'the nearest Japs are ... at least forty-eight miles [77 kilometres] down the coast'. Aware that the guerrillas had already been the inadvertent victims of US bombing elsewhere on Mindanao, McLaren warned the colonel, 'You'll only hit us if you bomb here.'

'Sorry,' the colonel replied. 'Headquarters have made the plans and the ships are on the way.'

Richardson reports that an 'immaculate' Marine colonel flew in the next day and told Blow and McLaren not to worry—the bombing of Malabang was off. Hardly had he spoken the words when 'a sudden roar grew out of the clear morning sky, bursting over the jungle at the end of the strip. With noses glinting in the sun, and diving at an angry angle, came twenty-five bombers. The three men dived for safety as the strip buckled and trembled under the impact of a shower of bombs.'

A number of guerrillas were killed, but Blow and McLaren survived the accidental bombing. According to Richardson, their protests were instrumental in having the invasion fleet diverted from Malabang to Parang—with McLaren leaping from the deck of the *Bastard* in the pre-dawn darkness to confront General Eichelberger in person aboard his flagship!

In the less spectacular version recounted by Ross, Eichelberger summoned the pair to US Army headquarters at Zamboanga where, after a 'well-cooked dinner' and a night in clean sheets, the two 'scruffy' Australians set off on an American PT boat to overtake 'the invasion fleet as it steamed across the Moro Gulf'. Catching up with the fleet, Blow and McLaren scrambled up a 'swinging rope ladder' thrown over the side of Eichelberger's command ship. While on board, Blow 'told [Eichelberger] at once that the guerrillas were in complete control of Malabang and that the general must not do to his men and the townsfolk what had been done to them in Iligan and Dansalan'.

After listening to Blow, Eichelberger made the decision to switch the invasion to Parang, which was softened up first with the bombing and shelling originally intended for Malabang. From Eichelberger's command ship, Blow and McLaren witnessed the bombardment, which made a mockery of their own frugality over the past twenty-two months, during which every round of ammunition had to be brought in by submarine and every shot had to be justified. Ross writes that 'the utter waste sickened [Blow]'. In his conversation with Bowden and Nelson, Blow recalled: '[T]he Americans went ashore, they started off with bombings . . . all the morning, and then the Navy ships poured thousands of shells over the top of us. By then there were about 200 Japs there. But General Eichelberger said, "Well, we're going ashore as if there were 20,000 Japs there." Which is what they did.'

When the battle was over, Blow asked the general how many casualties the Americans had suffered. He remembered Eichelberger telling him, 'Oh, one of my goddamn officers fell in a foxhole and sprained his ankle.'

Dan McNeill tells essentially the same story but without the two Australians; he suggests that the destination of the invasion fleet was changed when 'guerrillas on the island reported that Parang, a better landing area south of Malabang, was free of Japanese'. As a result of this tip-off, 'Eichelberger and his staff quickly revised and reissued their landing plans. Two days later, and almost without incident, the Eighth hit the beaches at Parang.' Omitting any mention of the extravagant naval bombardment witnessed by Blow and McLaren, McNeill comments, 'One would doubt the ability of a joint task force today to execute such a complex task to such perfection.'

The Philippines volume of the official history of US ground forces during the Second World War suggests that it was Colonel Fertig, not the two Australians, who persuaded Eichelberger to change his invasion plans. It states: 'On 13 April Colonel Fertig radioed Eighth Army that X Corps could land unopposed at Malabang and Parang and that the Japanese had probably evacuated the Cotabato area as well.' It goes on to say that while Eichelberger cancelled the naval bombardment of Malabang, he ignored messages from Fertig 'to the effect that no naval shelling would be required anywhere along Illana Bay's shores' and went ahead with the bombardment of Parang.

Stephen Lofgren's short book on the southern Philippines campaign offers yet another version, attributing the change of plans neither to Fertig nor to the Australians.

> With friendly forces in complete control of Malabang [he writes] an opportunity was presented to speed the initial penetration of central Mindanao. Generals Sibert and Woodruff and Admiral Noble quickly changed their plans to take advantage of the new developments. Although one battalion from the 21st Infantry would still land at Malabang, the bulk of the 24th Division was to come ashore at Parang, much closer to Highway No. 1, and thus speed up the entire operation.

The landing at Parang 'went unopposed'.

It is hardly surprising that Blow and McLaren feature less prominently in American accounts of the guerrilla campaign on Mindanao than in their own narratives. And while Balis credits Blow with being Hedges' 'best combat leader', there is no mention of either Blow or

McLaren in John Keats' biography of Colonel Fertig. (Perhaps this, too, is unsurprising given the book's title and a subtitle added to later editions: *They Fought Alone: A True Story of a Modern American Hero*.) Sheila Ross writes that Blow did not meet Fertig face to face until after the guerrillas had taken Malabang.

Whoever it was who persuaded Eichelberger to revise his invasion plans, the US landings on Mindanao allowed Australians for the first time to read the 'almost incredible story' of Blow's and McLaren's adventures since the surrender in Singapore. According to the Sydney *Sun*, the pair had 'established an almost legendary reputation for daring and brilliant jungle fighting' in the Philippines, where they 'trained the guerrillas, killed Japs and disposed of natives who were pro-Nipponese'.

The Perth *Daily News* reported that after escaping from Singapore, McLaren and two fellow Australians 'went storming about Malaya, shooting up enemy patrols'. After escaping from Borneo, the pair 'cross[ed] over to the southern Philippines in a six-foot dugout, killing some Japanese and destroying enemy outposts on the way'. Like many of the stories published about them by Australian newspapers, this was pure fiction. Of the two, only McLaren had reached Tawi Tawi by dugout. The only firearm they had was Blow's .38 revolver. Far from merrily 'shooting up enemy patrols', both men took extreme care to avoid any encounter with the Japanese.

For several months, according to the *Sun*, 'they lived with the blood-thirsty Moros on Tawi Tawi Island'. On Mindanao they were said to have 'lived on the results of guerrilla hunting parties, which would bring in wild pigs, chickens, sweet potatoes and tropical fruits'. At times they were forced to live 'for months at a time on bananas and roots'. In the Philippines McLaren was said to have become 'famous . . . for his skill with the native Bolo—a fearsome knife-like weapon, with which he lopped many Jap heads'. Several reports credited McLaren with having 'killed 30 Japs with his bolo'.

The *Army News* in Darwin recounted an alleged incident with a Japanese sub chaser. 'McLaren was all for attacking it with grenades, but this plan was discarded in favour of an ambush to overwhelm the Japanese on a visit ashore. The move worked perfectly, the Japanese being bowled over like ninepins with automatic rifle fire.'

That the correspondents filing stories from Manila had never actually spoken to Jock McLaren was clear from the *Sun*'s assertion that McLaren (who never lost his thick Scottish brogue) was 'believed to be an Englishman, who was visiting Australia when war was declared'.

With no Australian correspondents on hand to witness the US landings on Mindanao, there was confusion over the status of Blow and McLaren as combatants, some newspapers (such as the Melbourne *Age*) reporting that Blow and McLaren 'headed Colonel Fertig's guerrilla division at Malabang' while others described the pair as having been 'liberated' by US forces.

The capture of Malabang would be their final taste of action in the Philippines. For several months the Japanese had been pouring men and supplies into Davao, on the island's east coast. With American troops pushing vigorously inland, General Eichelberger needed accurate information about the enemy's strength. Blow and McLaren were ordered to guerrilla headquarters at Dansalan, in Lanao Province, to be briefed on an intelligence mission. But a surprise awaited them in Dansalan: instead of being sent to Davao, the two men were told they would be flying back to Australia.

Chapter 15

'YOU TWO WILL BE IN IT'

En route to Australia, Blow and McLaren flew to Leyte in the Philippines and then on to the island of Morotai, headquarters of the Australian forces in the Netherlands East Indies, where they met General Blamey, commander of Allied land forces in the Pacific. Blamey was also commander-in-chief of the Australian military forces, but in practice it was the American General MacArthur who decided how and where Australian troops would be deployed.

Blamey knew a bit about the exploits of the Australian guerrillas in the Philippines and was keen to hear details of what the pair had got up to on Tawi Tawi and Mindanao. Talk about their escape from Berhala Island led to discussion of a subject that had preyed on their minds ever since: the fate of the Australian POWs at Sandakan. Ray Steele had mentioned it on his return to Australia more than a year earlier, and Blow had sent reports about the Sandakan prisoners by radio from the Philippines, but nothing had been done. According to Sheila Ross, it was Blow who broached with Blamey the subject of a rescue mission: 'If he could be dropped in behind Sandakan with a reasonable number of paratroops, Rex told General Blamey, he felt sure he could take both the town and the airfield quite easily, then release the prisoners from the nearby camps . . . an American PT boat could come and take them off.'

Richardson writes that it was McLaren who proposed an operation to rescue the prisoners, and even sketched out for his commander-in-chief how it could be done:

'What about the blokes behind the barbed wire at Sandakan. Can we help them? I think we can.'

Blamey looked down into his whisky. 'We have had a report on the condition of the prisoners and we know where the prison camps are,' he said.

'Look, General,' said McLaren urgently, 'we know that the Jap garrison is at Lahat [Lahad] Datu, and that's nowhere near the prison camp at Sandakan. Why can't we go in with the parachute troops and get the prisoners out to landing barges on the coast? I know a spot where they could beach, not three miles from the camp—and there's a road there, too.'

Blamey looked down at the thin man levelly. 'You think it could be done?'

'Of course it could be done!' said McLaren explosively, and Blamey looked across at Blow, who nodded confidently.

They talked it over, and finally General Blamey said, 'If it can be fitted in with the other operations we'll do it, and you two will be in it.'

That interview took place on 23 April 1945, one week before Allied forces landed on the tiny island of Tarakan. According to Richardson, Blamey ended the conversation by sending both men to Australia on leave—a curious decision, given that Blamey was by then in possession of intelligence reports (which he would not have divulged to Blow and McLaren) indicating the already dire physical condition of the Sandakan prisoners. This alone made a rescue operation urgent. But there were other reasons why the mission could not wait.

To the Japanese, the sole value of the prisoners of war at Sandakan lay in their labour. As long as they were useful for the construction and maintenance of an airfield, it made sense to feed them and keep them alive. But by 1945 the Allies had complete air superiority over Sandakan. The airfield no longer served any practical purpose for the Japanese. As a result, the Allied prisoners, formerly an asset, were now an encumbrance.

By early 1945, the Allies knew that the Japanese had no compunction about killing prisoners en masse to prevent their being rescued and revealing the truth about Japanese atrocities. In December 1944, on the Filipino island of Palawan, one hundred and fifty American POWs were driven into slit trenches and burnt to death at the approach of a US convoy. In February 1945, aware of the risk that POWs and civilian internees would be slaughtered by the Japanese before they could be liberated, MacArthur ordered missions to free prisoners in Filipino camps that lay ahead of the advancing US troops. After several thousand internees had been rescued, it was discovered that Japanese camp commanders had been given orders from Tokyo to exterminate their captives.

Both Blow and McLaren appear to have taken General Blamey at his word. The two men left for Australia convinced that planning was under way for a mission to rescue the Sandakan POWs and that they would take part in the operation.

Their arrival in Brisbane coincided with the Allied landing at Tarakan on 1 May, carried out by the 26th Brigade of the 9th Australian Division. MacArthur expected the island, with its strategically important aerodrome and oilfields, to be taken within three weeks, but fighting would continue until the war ended in August.

Australian newspapers continued to publish stories about Blow and McLaren while they were on leave. Without bylines, and based on material supplied by the Army Public Relations Directorate, these articles corrected some of the error-strewn reporting by syndicated war correspondents in Manila. They also alluded to the Japanese mistreatment of prisoners of war. On 10 May 1945, the *Maryborough Chronicle* reported:

[McLaren's] experience in POW camps was that hospital conditions were the worst he had ever seen . . . in four months 105 of 250 sick men died. Diseases were dysentery, beriberi and pellagra. 'Chinese prisoners were separated from white prisoners. I have seen Chinese beheaded, lashed and branded with the rising sun on forehead and arms. I saw a British brigadier bashed each morning for about three weeks but they couldn't break his spirit.'

Seventeen days after that story was published, the Allies bombarded Sandakan. Of the roughly 1500 prisoners at Sandakan at the beginning of March 1945, fewer than 850 were still alive when US aircraft and PT boats attacked the town on 27 May 1945. The scale of the attack led the Japanese to believe that a landing was imminent and prompted the incineration of the camp, the abandonment of hundreds of sick prisoners and the evacuation of the rest.

In January 1945, 470 prisoners, including some with beriberi or deep tropical ulcers, had set out on the first of the so-called 'death marches' inland to Ranau, more than 250 kilometres away. The prisoners were divided into groups, each with its own contingent of guards. Stragglers were beaten to make them keep up. Those who fell and could walk no further were shot. Around half reached Ranau; most were exhausted and near death.

Two days after the Allied bombardment on 27 May, 536 prisoners—some reduced to as little as six stone in weight—were sent away under guard on the second death march. The remaining 288 stretcher cases were left with a handful of guards among the smouldering ruins of the camp. None of the 288 would survive. By the time the prisoners on the second march reached Ranau, only six from the first march—five Australians and one Briton—were left alive. Of the 2100 Sandakan prisoners alive at the beginning of January 1945, just six survived the war.

Among the dead was Ginger Burnett, who had crawled under the wire at Changi with McLaren and who later turned down the opportunity to join the escape from Berhala Island. Only one Queenslander named Burnett is included among Lynette Silver's definitive list of Sandakan prisoners: QX12664 Private Edgar Robert Burnett. Perhaps McLaren knew him as 'Ginger' to distinguish him from their mate Edgar Wilkie, who escaped with them from Changi. Like McLaren, Ginger Burnett served with the 2/10th Ordnance Workshop.

After the war, Gunner Owen Colin Campbell, one of the six prisoners to survive Sandakan, was asked about the fates of the other Australians in the camp. (Campbell escaped while taking part in the second death march.) He included Ginger Burnett in a list of men he reported as 'having been alive from his own knowledge at the time and place mentioned'. The entry for Burnett read: 'Last seen at SANDAKAN Feb 1945. Left on march with party of 300. In excellent condition.'

The prisoners selected alongside Burnett for the first march were divided into nine groups that left on consecutive days between 29 January and 6 February. Groups 1 to 5 marched directly to Ranau, losing around seventy men along the way. Groups 6 to 9 halted about 40 kilometres further back at the village of Paginatan, ostensibly because there was no accommodation for them at Ranau. Here they stayed for about a month, wasting away from hunger, disease and exhaustion. Of the 138 men held at Paginatan, forty-six would finally reach Ranau.

While they were there, parties of prisoners from the Ranau Camp were forced to carry heavy bags of rice to Paginatan to supply the Japanese garrison and prisoners. It is likely that Ginger Burnett, who had started the march in 'excellent condition', was one of the rice-carriers. The trips took nine days, and those unable to carry their load any further were shot or bayoneted to death. Private Keith Botterill of the 2/19th Battalion, one of the final six survivors, endured six rice-carrying trips. He recalled: 'No effort whatsoever was made to bury the men. They would just pull them five to fifteen yards off the track and bayonet them or shoot them, depending on the condition of the men. If they were conscious, and it was what we thought was a good, kind guard, they'd shoot them. There was nothing we could do.'

Burnett was not one of the five Australians from the first death march who were still alive when the men from the second march arrived in Ranau. He is recorded as having died, aged twenty-nine, on 30 March 1945. The Japanese put his death down to 'Acute Enteritus'.

The second march began on 29 May 1945, almost two months to the day after the lonely death of Ginger Burnett. Sandakan had been regularly bombed ever since October 1944, when the Americans emerged victorious from the Battle of Leyte Gulf, but the attack on 27 May was heavier than previous attacks. According to Major Jackson's report, the Japanese now believed that an Allied division was going to land at Sandakan and that the invasion would happen within three days. Aware that the POW camp was in an exposed position, they feared that the prisoners 'were likely to fall into Allied hands at a very early stage of the operation'. In fact the Japanese had been preparing for some time for a second march to Ranau. Jackson notes that the guards and soldiers 'were already getting extra rations in order to gain condition to sustain them on the march'.

The bombardment on 27 May convinced some of the prisoners that defeat for the Japanese was close. According to Athol Moffitt, some believed that an Allied force had landed at Sandakan and that the POWs were going to be marched to Sandakan township and handed over to the invaders.

Moffitt was a lawyer who served with the Royal Australian Artillery and acted as prosecutor in the Australian war crimes trials that began in

December 1945 on Labuan (he was later a distinguished New South Wales judge). In his book *Project Kingfisher*, Moffitt writes that '[i]ncapacitated men, some hobbling on sticks, joined the march believing their rescue was at hand'. 'When the prisoners reached the road, to their dismay, they did not turn to the left into Sandakan, but to the right. They were on their way to Ranau and, for nearly all, to death.'

Forty years later, Blow remained convinced that a rescue mission had been feasible, telling Bowden and Nelson, 'I think it would have been quite easy to capture the . . . whole of the town, the airport. And OK, the American PT boats come in and take us off. I think it would have been quite easy.' Moffitt's research confirmed that after January 1945 there were no Japanese aircraft operating in Borneo: from February a rescue mission could have been carried out with no risk of enemy air attack.

What neither Blow nor McLaren knew was that by the time Blamey assured them that 'we'll do it, and you two will be in it', MacArthur had already vetoed the operation—codenamed 'Kingfisher'—to rescue the prisoners at Sandakan.

In a speech made two years after the war, Blamey said that a plan to use Australian paratroops to rescue the prisoners at Sandakan had been abandoned because the aircraft needed for the operation were not available. In *Project Kingfisher*, Moffitt suggests that Blamey was being diplomatic in the speech and 'did not wish to open up old wounds relating to his relationship with MacArthur'. These 'wounds' related in part to the deliberate non-use of Australian units in the reconquest of the Philippines—a decision that riled Australian generals and that Moffitt attributes to MacArthur's wanting to be seen as 'the leader, who with US forces alone, was able to avenge the humiliation he suffered in his defeat and retreat from the Philippines'.

MacArthur's refusal to call on highly trained and battle-experienced Australian units for his Philippines campaign prompted a letter from the Australian prime minister, John Curtin, reminding MacArthur that troops from the Australian 7th and 9th Divisions 'have been on the mainland for periods of up to 18 months and have taken no part in the war since 1943' and pointing out that this had been a source of 'considerable public criticism'. Curtin's letter, written in February 1945, went on to warn MacArthur that 'I shall be confronted with a difficult situation if so many Australian troops are to be retained in an ineffective role'.

Had a rescue mission by Australian paratroops using US aircraft been successful, Moffitt concedes that it 'would have raised questions at home for MacArthur ... If US aircraft were used to rescue British and American prisoners, why had they not been used to rescue Americans in a similar situation?'

Analysis by Moffitt of the availability in early 1945 of US C47 transport aircraft—the sort that would have been used in a paratroop drop such as Operation Kingfisher—shows that the relatively small number of planes needed for Kingfisher 'could have been provided at some suitable time between March and April and even early May 1945, if there had been the will and interest to do so'.

The reason no attempt was made to rescue the POWs at Sandakan had nothing to do with the unavailability of transport aircraft, Moffitt concludes, but rather 'there was no will to provide the planes because to do so would not have been consistent with MacArthur's cultivation of his personal image and the prestige of the US forces he commanded. Lack of transport by air and sea had been a convenient excuse for not using units or for not putting into operation plans which he did not favour.' General Blamey, he writes, would have known that unavailability of planes was 'probably MacArthur's excuse for avoiding an operation of which he could not otherwise disapprove'.

But was MacArthur just a convenient scapegoat for an Australian failure? Records of intelligence operations by agents of the Australian Services

Reconnaissance Department (SRD) indicate that the detailed information essential to a rescue mission at Sandakan was never sent. Was this
the result of flawed intelligence-gathering, or was it due to a change in
objectives that meant Operation Kingfisher was no longer a priority for
Blamey and the AIF? When Blamey told Blow and McLaren that there
was going to be a rescue and they would be 'in it', had he already made up
his own mind against the operation? Lynette Silver has pointed out that
if the sticking point was the alleged unavailability of US C47 transport
aircraft, Blamey could have made use of the RAAF's own pool of seventy-
one C47s. On their return to Australia, Blow and McLaren were both
co-opted into the SRD's Z Special Unit, whose priority was the gathering
of intelligence in support of the coming invasion of Borneo. Perhaps,
after all, this is what Blamey meant when he said they would be 'in it'.

Whether or not MacArthur was personally to blame for the cancella-
tion of Operation Kingfisher, his perceived disrespect towards Australian
troops remained a sore point with Australia's military leadership. That
the public at large also felt the slight is indicated by reports such as the
following, headlined 'MacArthur's Report', in the *Dubbo Liberal and
Macquarie Advocate*: 'No reference to the Australian ground troops in
Borneo or New Guinea and Bougainville was made in General MacArthur's
communiqué, which announces that American 37th Division units on
Luzon have captured the town of Banbang, ten miles north of Aritao, in
their push down the Cagayan Valley.'

High Command might have washed its hands of the Sandakan
prisoners, but Rex Blow had not. Three weeks after flying to Australia, he
was back on Morotai, seeking permission from General Blamey to return
to Sandakan. According to Moffitt, who would meet Blow in Borneo in
November 1945, Blow had instructions to enter the Sandakan camp or,
if that was not possible, to use some other means to make contact with
the prisoners. Moffitt writes that Blow was to 'explore possibilities of
escape and to alert the prisoners as to what could happen'.

In his conversation with Bowden and Nelson, Blow recalled that 'the Americans took me in by night and dropped me round the back of Sandakan'. Together with a local guide, Blow paddled inland by canoe, aiming to reach the POW camp on foot. The American PT boat that had dropped him at Sandakan was to return every twenty-four hours to the same spot for a rendezvous. By then rumours had circulated that some prisoners had been moved out of the camp along a jungle trail. As Ross tells it, Blow and his guide walked a couple of hours from the river until they found the trail. Footmarks told the pair that a large number of men had recently passed along it.

While following the trail back to the compound, Blow met several locals, all of whom told the same story: the Japanese had burnt down the camp and the remaining prisoners were being marched inland, perhaps to Ranau. 'Everybody had gone,' Blow told Bowden and Nelson. 'Left Sandakan. All of the prisoners.'

It was clear that many of the prisoners had died along the way: Blow was shown their shallow graves. The locals they spoke to described the shooting and bayonetting of men who could not walk any further.

Blow continued along the trail, refusing to believe that everyone had left the camp, hoping that some might have been left behind and that they could still be saved. But from every villager they met the story was the same: nobody at the camp was left alive. Convinced, in the end, that his mission was futile, Blow turned back. He told Moffitt that he believed he had missed the marchers by only a few days.

From at least the start of February 1945, Allied High Command had known of Japanese plans to kill prisoners of war. By then hundreds of Sandakan prisoners had already been sent on a march that would lead to the deaths of all but a handful. Blow and McLaren were not alone in believing that the fate of the mates they left behind was sealed on the day Allied planes and PT boats bombarded Sandakan.

Chapter 16

PLATYPUS

⸻⸺⸻

Having left Australian troops out of the invasion of the Philippines, MacArthur entrusted the AIF with the job of retaking the former British Borneo territories of Sarawak, Brunei and North Borneo (Sabah).

The landing on Tarakan on 1 May 1945 marked the first step in Operation Oboe, the reconquest of Borneo. The island, shaped like an upside-down pear, was barely 24 kilometres long and 15 kilometres wide, but securing it took the Allies seven hard-fought weeks. The mopping up of unsurrendered Japanese soldiers would continue until the war ended in mid-August. After Tarakan (Oboe 1), landings were planned for Brunei Bay and Labuan (Oboe 6) and the oil port of Balikpapan on the east coast of Borneo (Oboe 2).

General Blamey had advised against the landing at Balikpapan, believing the casualties would outweigh the strategic benefits, but the Australian Government was eventually persuaded by MacArthur to commit troops from the 7th Division to the invasion. The Australians, supported by a small number of soldiers from the Netherlands East Indies Army, would far outnumber the Japanese, whose supply lines had been all but cut by the end of 1944 due to interdiction by Allied submarines. As at Tarakan, however, the Japanese at Balikpapan had built a formidable defensive system, with heavy artillery on the ridges protecting the airfield, town and port.

As Australian and US military teams met on Morotai to plan the assault on Balikpapan, Headquarters I Australian Corps (according to the official history of Australian special operations) 'requested SRD to provide certain information necessary for the planning of operation Oboe II'. The SRD's Z Special Unit was given the task of infiltrating the area, with agents inserted by submarine and parachute. The operation was codenamed 'Platypus'. Like other behind-the-lines operations, the purpose of Platypus was to gather intelligence, survey the terrain, and organise the locals into guerrilla units to harass the Japanese. The operation was to be divided into a number of phases, with phases I to VII carried out before D Day (the landing on Balikpapan) and the remainder on or after D Day.

At the end of June, Captain Jock McLaren was given command of a four-man mission designated Platypus VI. Sent to Leyburn, in Queensland's Southern Downs, for parachute training, McLaren told Richardson that he completed the required three jumps in a single day.

As Richardson tells it, McLaren was summoned for a meeting with Brigadier Wills, controller of the Allied Intelligence Bureau, who said, 'We seem to be up against a difficulty in Balikpapan, Captain McLaren ... We can't get intelligence out of there. Five parties have been sent in, and they have all gone west.' McLaren 'knew that one party had been killed in a plane crash; but the others had not been a match for the shrewd Japanese or treacherous natives'. In fact, the five Platypus operations that preceded Platypus VI had largely succeeded in achieving their objectives, although the first (and least successful) operation, Platypus I, highlighted the dangers that would face McLaren and his three companions.

Platypus I (initially codenamed 'Robin') was carried out several months before the Oboe 2 landings. The aim of the mission was to infiltrate the Balikpapan–Samarinda area and set up an intelligence network capable of supplying reports by walkie-talkie. Led by two New Zealanders, Major Don Stott and Captain Leslie McMillan, the eleven-man party was to gather 'all types of military intelligence, including the layout and routine of the PW camp North of Balikpapan ... escape routes, and any other intelligence task required by HQ SWPA'. Platypus I also had a secondary task, which was to 'contact natives for the purpose of organizing armed and passive resistance movements in preparation for D Day'.

The party left Perth on 12 March 1945 on the US submarine *Perch*. During what the official history describes as a an 'uneventful' journey to the insertion point, the submarine surfaced several times to allow Stott and his men to test the rubber boats, which were found to leak.

At 10 o'clock on the night of 20–21 March, Stott, McMillan and two sergeants, Dooland and Horrocks, were dropped about 35 miles north of Balikpapan. They were to go ashore in two folboats (folding canoes), communicating with the submarine by walkie-talkie, then reconnoitre at the insertion spot and return to the submarine the following night, or the night after, to pick up the remainder of the party.

Things began to go wrong from the start. They were unable to contact the submarine by walkie-talkie. Dooland and Horrocks managed to get their outboard motor running, but the other motor would not start and Stott and McMillan had to paddle their boat. After the two canoes became separated, Dooland and Horrocks tried and failed to make contact with the officers by walkie-talkie. Horrocks's report noted, 'At 0130H we heard a Japanese voice (muffled) on the walkie talkie; at 0145H we heard two English voices loud and clear checking frequency. It was 0200H when we grounded and went ashore.'

On the night of 22–23 March, with the submarine still loitering offshore, a Japanese oil lighter turned up at the prearranged rendezvous spot. Fearing for the safety of his submarine, the commander sank the lighter, which blazed on the surface for several hours before going down. Despite the risk of the burning ship attracting attention from Japanese coastwatchers, the main landing party set off at 10.30 p.m., led by another New Zealander, Lieutenant Bob Morton. The outboard motors 'failed miserably', picking up only as the boats approached the shore. The oil lighter was still burning when the party landed at 1 a.m.

Morton's party spent five and a half hours lugging their equipment inland, only to discover as daylight broke that they had put their stash right next to a well-used native track. Under the gaze of inquisitive locals, they moved their gear to another dump. The walkie-talkies still refused to work, and they could find no trace of Stott or McMillan, or of Dooland and Horrocks. A friendly old 'hermit' agreed to warn them of any Japanese patrols.

In the meantime, the Japanese—tipped off by the blazing oil lighter—scoured the area and found the main equipment dump. After moving the few things they had with them to yet another dump, Morton and his men covered their tracks and continued searching for their missing colleagues.

Bud Feuer is a retired American journalist and a prolific author on military history; according to his book, *Australian Commandos*, the reason the Japanese always seemed to be one step ahead was that the Platypus team 'had been under constant surveillance by Abdul Rahman, a local native in the pay of the Japanese':

On March 23, Rahman had observed the commandos moving their supplies up from the beach. The informer secretly travelled to Balikpapan and reported the incident to the Kempei Tai . . . A company of soldiers was immediately dispatched to the location. The reason that the Japanese so easily found the stores was because pilfering natives had carelessly left discarded food wrappings and other items scattered near the supply cache.

On two occasions Morton's men were caught in firefights with Japanese patrols. One man was wounded and taken prisoner, and three others became separated from the rest.

Grabbing everything they could carry, the three remaining commandos—Morton, Lieutenant Bill Dwyer and Sergeant Bob Dey—retreated deeper into the jungle. According to the official history, they salvaged 'bare personal necessities and 4½ tins of O2 rations. These rations proved most satisfactory, and eventually four men were able to live on them for 2 weeks.' Among the items they left behind were the radio and an impossibly heavy steam generator. While Morton's party conducted some local reconnaissance, lack of food made it impossible to attempt longer sorties. With two hundred and fifty Japanese said to be searching for them, they had little choice but to lie low.

In *Silent Feet*, G.B. Courtney's history of Z Special Unit's operations, Lieutenant Dwyer recalls the struggle to find food as the Japanese cordon closed ever more tightly around them. 'We began to compete with wild pigs for a red berry that grew on certain trees in the forest. They had a terrible taste, but we figured that if the pigs could live on them, so could we. The pigs were able to reach the berries up to a height of about five feet. We cleaned up the rest.'

On 20 April, after four weeks spent dodging enemy patrols, Dooland and Horrocks managed to slip through the Japanese cordon and rejoin the main party. Further efforts to discover what had happened to Stott and McMillan came to nothing. Since the two sergeants had valuable intelligence, Morton decided that the only course of action was for the group to cut their losses and pull out, taking any 'native informants' they could persuade to accompany them.

Some local men were sent to buy a *prahu*, which they obtained for what the official report judged a 'bargain price of 1400 Dutch guilders'.

Pushing off at 8.30 p.m. on the night of 1 May, they began paddling towards Morotai, hoping to be picked up by either an Allied ship or an aircraft. According to the official report, 'The natives were not very willing with the oars, and Lts Morton and Dwyer had to do two-hour shifts at rowing, the other white members of the party not being physically fit.' After two days in the *prahu*, they were picked up by a Catalina flying boat and flown to Morotai for debriefing.

Of the missing four men, Major Stott and Captain McMillan were believed to have drowned when their rubber boat capsized, while the other two, Warrant Officers Leslie Farquharson and Robert Houghton, died as prisoners of the Japanese.

In the end Platypus I was officially judged to have been 'only partly useful'. However, the operation 'was of great importance . . . as it revealed a number of weaknesses in planning that it was possible to correct in subsequent operations'. One of these subsequent operations was Jock McLaren's Platypus VI. McLaren, however, was an experienced enough soldier to know that even with perfect planning, there was plenty that could still go wrong.

According to the official history, Platypus VI had two objectives: (a) to obtain intelligence in the Riko River Bridge area, and (b) to determine the best method of approach to the area by ground. In particular, McLaren was ordered to investigate the 'possible enemy line of withdrawal' from Balikpapan to Bandjermasin on the south coast (a distance of nearly 500 kilometres) and to supply intelligence on Japanese defences in the Riko River area.

The official history begins with the party parachuting out of a Liberator bomber over the Riko River Bridge at 7.30 p.m. on 30 June, but McLaren's involvement in the operation had begun weeks earlier, with a preliminary reconnaissance of the landing area. Delivered by submarine to a point off the coast, McLaren had paddled in by canoe to examine the enemy's shore defences. As well as anti-invasion piles in the shallow water, he noted the coastal gun batteries. Further inland, Richardson writes that McLaren found hills 'honeycombed with bunkers and tunnels . . . concrete pillboxes and a reticulation system of oil to be fired as a flaring defence'.

After his close-up reconnaissance by canoe, McLaren was flown over Balikpapan in a Catalina to search for a suitable dropping zone. Following the path of the Riko River as it snaked between muddy banks into Balikpapan Bay, McLaren eventually spotted a grassy clearing in the jungle that might prove a 'gentle and welcoming spot' for parachutists to land.

While heading back to Morotai, they spotted a native boat just offshore. The flying boat landed alongside, and the local men on the boat were 'persuaded . . . to return with them to Morotai and give information about Japanese installations in the area'. According to Richardson, a second reconnaissance flight nearly ended in disaster when the Catalina was caught in a storm and forced to crash-land at Zamboanga on Mindanao.

Besides McLaren, the Platypus VI team consisted of two AIF signallers, Warrant Officer Sullivan and Sergeant Barnes, and a Malay, Corporal Sarif. McLaren distrusted Sarif, telling Richardson that he considered 'an unspoilt native from the jungle would have been more use to them', but he kept his opinion to himself.

After a successful test run on 29 June, the party set out the following afternoon in a Liberator. According to Richardson, naval authorities controlling the sea approaches to Balikpapan instructed them to abort their first approach to the landing zone. The Liberator went round again, but the crew misjudged the wind speed, causing the four parachutists to miss their target. 'Suddenly,' Richardson writes, 'the air was filled with the "yattayatta" of a machine gun and the spit of rifle fire.'

The official history records simply that all four men overshot the drop zone, with two landing in a village and the others in 'secondary jungle'. One pair 'landed on the NE bank of the Riko river, approximately one mile from the DZ and 50 yards from a Japanese guardhouse'. No one was injured in the landing. Shortly afterwards the Liberator returned and dropped storpedoes (cylinders packed with supplies) on the north-east bank of the river, but the combination of darkness and enemy activity forced the men to abandon their efforts to recover them. McLaren conducted his own reconnaissance of nearby roads before rejoining the party at 4 a.m. Hiding in the jungle close to the drop zone, McLaren smelt smoke from army-issue American cigarettes as Japanese patrols set out at daylight to search for the parachutists—evidence that at least one of the storpedoes had already been found. The next day, with little chance of retrieving any of the remaining storpedoes, the men were fortunate to run into friendly locals who gave them a handful of rice and half a boiled egg each.

Balikpapan was more than 50 kilometres away, on the north-east side of the bay. Aware that the Japanese were searching for them, McLaren decided to move to a safer position on higher ground. Sullivan, who had been complaining about feeling unwell since the landing, was now finding it hard to keep up. The official history notes that he 'became ill with diarrhoea and had a temperature of 103.5'.

The new camp was a 'good defence position' from which the party could 'contact planes by S phone [a ground-to-air radio used by units operating behind enemy lines]'. Using a trick he had picked up from the guerrillas in Mindanao, McLaren ringed the area with trip-wires so that hand grenades would be detonated by any Japanese patrol stumbling across the camp.

Overhead, waves of US aircraft were raining bombs on strategic positions as part of an intensive bombardment like that which had preceded the US landings on Mindanao. The Australian-led invasion of

Balikpapan, Operation Oboe 2, began on 1 July, the day after McLaren's team jumped.

Sullivan's condition continued to worsen. Doubled up from an excruciating pain in his liver, he could not stop vomiting. It was too dangerous for the party's native contacts to venture near the camp in daylight, so food was 'very scarce'. McLaren still hoped that they could be resupplied from the air. Richardson writes that a US aircraft flew almost directly over the camp, searching from high altitude, but that McLaren considered it 'too risky' to attempt to make contact by radio.

The plan for Platypus VI had been for a Catalina to pick the party up from the village of Toenan on the coast south of Balikpapan on 7 July. But on 3 July McLaren decided that Sullivan would have to be moved immediately. The nephew of one of their native contacts agreed to act as guide. McLaren, who three years earlier had been warned by communist guerrillas not to trust Malays, told Richardson that 'past experience of treachery' had made him 'uneasy' about the arrangement but he felt that he 'had no choice'.

That evening, guided by the nephew, the group set off. They had two submachine guns and three pistols, one of each having been lost in the parachute drop. According to the official history, the guide walked 20 metres in front, followed by Burns, McLaren, Sullivan and Sarif. Even after destroying surplus maps and dumping supplies McLaren considered unnecessary, the three fit men all carried heavy loads.

McLaren's intention was to travel through open country under cover of darkness and, during daylight, to follow the guide through the jungle. As they neared open ground, they heard a whistle on their right flank, followed by shouting ahead of them and on both sides. They had walked into an ambush. McLaren, in Richardson's account, 'pulled a grenade from his jacket, whipped out the pin between his teeth and threw the bomb at the line of jungle still ahead of them'. He knew, however, that he could not risk letting the valuable S phone and its secret codes fall into enemy hands. Guessing that the Japanese would hold their fire to avoid hitting each other, he ordered his men to retreat along the track they had been following. But Corporal Sarif 'panicked', according to the official history, and, instead of retreating, turned and ran into the grass on his left flank, straight into the arms of his ambushers.

Sullivan was too sick to run and had to be carried by McLaren. The two men flattened themselves in the undergrowth and held their breath as Japanese soldiers stumbled after them. It seemed impossible for Sarif to have avoided capture. McLaren estimated that more than twenty Japanese had taken part in the ambush, as well as many locals. According to the official history, McLaren was unsure whether his party had been betrayed or whether the Japanese had tailed one of their native contacts.* Clearly, if they had been betrayed, it was no longer safe to head for Toenan. But McLaren felt it was too dangerous to remain where they were and decided the party should push on to its original objective, the Riko River.

By noon the next day they had made it as far as the Sepan River, which flowed east into Balikpapan Bay and on whose muddy banks McLaren had been hopeful of finding a boat. But there was neither a boat nor any sign of habitation, and they were forced to drag themselves through the deep, sucking mangrove swamp that extended from its banks. McLaren cut down bamboo from a nearby hill to build a raft, but the raft was barely capable of supporting Sullivan, let alone all three of them. Realising they were going to have to wade through the mangrove swamps, carrying Sullivan between them, McLaren smashed and buried the heavy S phones and destroyed the codes. Even so, he and Burns were still weighed down with equipment.

---

*   By the time he recounted the story some years later to Richardson, McLaren was convinced that the ambush had been 'carefully planned' and that they had been sold out by their 'treacherous guide'.

Eventually, on the afternoon of 5 July, they arrived at the broader and faster-flowing Riko River. While swimming across, they lost the last of their submachine guns.

With most of their weapons, maps and communication equipment gone, and with Sullivan's condition deteriorating by the day, there was no prospect of Platypus VI fulfilling its mission. Allied forces, led by three brigades of the Australian 7th Division, had now pushed several kilometres inland from the landing beaches and were using artillery and flamethrowers to prise the Japanese out of strongly held defensive positions. There was little that McLaren's party could do except try to make contact with the invading army.

On the afternoon of 5 July, they saw a sampan coming down the Sepan River. Emerging from the mangrove swamp, McLaren beckoned to the occupants, two men, four women and some children, and asked to be taken to Balikpapan Bay. The men told him they were on their way to a nearby kampong and would come back for him after dropping the women and children. Taking no chances, McLaren went with them to make sure they returned. The official history records an uneventful trip downriver, ending with the three Australians reaching Balikpapan at 2 a.m. and McLaren reporting to 7th Division headquarters. Sullivan was diagnosed as suffering from an abscess on the liver and safely evacuated to Australia.

The story McLaren told Richardson is (naturally) more dramatic. According to Richardson, they drifted past hordes of 'begrimed and muddy' Japanese soldiers, many without weapons, trying to escape through the swamps from the advancing Allies. 'Soon they were coming in parties of fifteen or twenty and, as McLaren urged on the native paddlers, the water spurted round the rocking craft and whistled over the crouching men as the Japanese fired volley after volley after them.' McLaren survived the encounter, revelling as always in his own indestructability. Upon reaching Australian headquarters, he presented himself to an officer.

'We got back,' repeated McLaren.

'Who's we?'

'McLaren and party.'

'What!' said the officer. 'But—' he stared at the mud-coloured, unshaven, and stinking middle-aged man standing loosely before him—'but you're dead.'

'That'll be the day,' said McLaren.

According to the official history, Platypus VI was doomed from the moment the storpedoes missed the drop zone. Had they fallen where they were meant to, rather than one and a half miles away, the storpedoes 'would have been recovered immediately'. McLaren's party would then have been able to move quickly to a safer area, with the arms it needed to defend itself and food with which to 'hold the natives'.

Platypus VI was deemed a failure, but there would be worse failures, at much higher cost. Platypus VII, which was to carry out surveillance north of Balikpapan, lost three of its four men soon after they hit the ground, due to what the official history describes as 'poor parachure-dropping technique'. The men were dropped 16 kilometres from their designated landing spot. The team leader landed upside down in a tree and was badly injured while attempting to free himself. Hungry, exhausted and occasionally delirious, he was unable to carry out any reconnaissance and survived only with the help of friendly natives. Platypus VII was judged to be a complete failure.

Despite the damning official verdict, McLaren was awarded the Military Cross (formally entered as a bar to his first Military Cross) for his leadership of Platypus VI. While the citation acknowledges the 'grave handicap' caused by the loss of the storpedoes, it refutes the assessment of the mission as an operational failure. 'When the party was ambushed on July 3, 1945 and one of the members of the party captured, by his coolness and courage Captain McLaren successfully removed the injured man [Sullivan] to safety and continued with the task given . . . Finally on

July 6, 1945 Captain McLaren extracted his party by native craft, passed through Japanese lines and delivered his information direct to the Task Force Commander.'

McLaren enjoyed this style of 'unorthodox', behind-the-lines fighting—he described it to Hal Richardson as his 'vocation'.

> 'The way I look at it is this,' he would say. 'When you are in the lines you are under a direct command, and you do as you're told. When you get into real trouble the command should be able to get you out, but they don't always do it. When you're behind the line and get yourself into trouble, you've got to get your bloody self out irrespective of anybody else. That's why I like it.'

Less than a week after his narrow escape from Platypus VI, McLaren was back in Borneo for another mission. The object of Platypus IX was to 'report on enemy activity in the upper reaches of Balikpapan Bay'. Like Platypus VI, it was a four-man operation.

Richardson reports a preliminary reconnaissance by McLaren, who paddled into Balikpapan Bay in a folboat and observed 'about eighty Japanese craft fleeing towards the far mangroves and mud'. He reported this information to headquarters by radio. The next morning, just before dawn, Japanese troops were paddling across the bay 'in their hundreds' when twenty Spitfires came over the mountains, machine guns blazing, scattering the barges 'like broken twigs'. Later McLaren was sent back to check on some enemy guns on the northern side of the bay that had fired on the Spitfires.

This sounds like the Platypus IX mission that is described in the official history. The official version is that McLaren's party entered Balikpapan Bay on the night of 12–13 July and paddled their folboats to the mouths of the Sepakoe and Semoi Rivers, where they made camp and established radio contact with SRD headquarters.

Although a more limited operation than most of its predecessors, Platypus IX was officially described as 'one of the most successful of the minor phases of Platypus'. The SRD was able to supply 7th Division headquarters with valuable information about the Japanese retreat, as a result of which 'enemy barge traffic in the upper reaches of Balikpapan Bay were disrupted and movement of enemy troops virtually ceased'.

According to Richardson, McLaren also found time to parachute into the jungle behind Samarinda, north of Balikpapan, where he 'crept' around the area 'spying on Japanese movements from behind a jungle screen, and reporting by radio back to Intelligence'. After two days he made his way to the coast, where he was picked up by Catalina and taken to Morotai, only to be up at dawn for another behind-the-lines parachute drop, this time at Bandjermasin, around 500 kilometres south of Balikpapan.

At Bandjermasin McLaren observed the Japanese gathering a fleet of native-style boats and watched them 'blowing up their positions, burning and destroying as they prepared their retreat'. He stayed four days, communicating with the SRD by radio, before returning to Morotai.

These solo adventures are not mentioned in the official history of Platypus, which eventually ran to twelve missions. But Platypus was just one of several operations carried out by Z Special Unit in Borneo during the last months of the war. Less than a fortnight after returning from Platypus IX, McLaren embarked on yet another operation.

Chapter 17

AGAS

⟶•⟶

Agas (the Malay word for 'sandfly') was the codename given to a series of five operations carried out by the Services Reconnaissance Department in British North Borneo between March and October 1945. Like other special operations, Agas had the twin aims of gathering intelligence and organising guerrilla actions by the native population against the Japanese.

The early phases of the operation had mixed results. In its account of Agas I, the official history states: 'The attitude of the natives was most friendly and everywhere a keen desire to help the Allied forces was shown. Forced labour, the taking of crops, rape and general maltreatment by the Japanese had increased the natural disposition of these natives to remain loyal to the previous administration.'

The Australians often had trouble, however, holding on to their local recruits. The history records an attack on the village of Aling, near Linkabau, that resulted in the deaths of thirteen enemy soldiers for the loss of one guerrilla killed and one wounded. 'Shortly afterwards, however, far greater losses were incurred by the desertion of guerrillas. With the exception of ten, all of them expressed a very strong desire to return to their homes. The position rapidly worsened and in spite of every precaution, trained men deserted daily, while others openly stated they would . . . fight only to defend their own villages.'

By the time the last phases of Agas got under way, the end of the war was in sight, and it was clear to the people of Borneo that the Allies were going to win. In its report on Agas III, the official history notes that 'the very greatest asistance was afforded the party by all natives' and that 'no enemy movements or activities took place which were not known to and passed by the party to HQ within a few hours'.

In July 1945 two more Agas missions were launched, a fortnight apart, into the south-east corner of British North Borneo. Rex Blow was chosen to lead Agas IV and Jock McLaren to lead Agas V. The objective of Agas V was to discover enemy strength and positions in the area of Lahad Datu on the east coast of British North Borneo and to initiate armed raids on Japanese posts. According to Richardson, 'This kind of operation was McLaren's meat!'

McLaren recalled his orders being to 'prevent all types of assistance to the enemy by cutting off native labour, food, and information'. In addition he was to 'set up a communications network in the area and organize a thoroughly reliable military Intelligence organization' while acting as a civilian administrator and 'organiz[ing] and train[ing] small bands of saboteurs' to support the invading Allied troops. Owing to the amount of sickness in the area, a doctor would also be sent in, and McLaren would supervise the construction of a hospital and dressing station.

Less than 40 kilometres of ocean separated Lahad Datu from McLaren's old haunt of Tawi Tawi, where storage depots were established to keep McLaren's party supplied by boat with weapons, ammunition, radios and other equipment. The official history of Agas V records that three

Australians, Captain McLaren, Sergeant Douglas Herps and a young signaller, Private Frank Haley, and five 'natives' were 'inserted by workboat ...
about 35 miles east of Lahad Datu on 27 July 1945'. Fate had put McLaren
within a few miles of his old comrade Rex Blow, who had arrived just days
earlier in the neighbouring district of Tawao as the leader of Agas IV.

The penultimate mission, Agas IV had been conceived as an operation
for four men: Blow in charge; two British soldiers, Captain J.A. Halsey
and Warrant Officer A. Campbell; and an Australian signaller, Barney
Schinkel. As the party prepared to set out, something remarkable
happened. As Sheila Ross describes it, Blow was 'issuing some last-
minute instructions before leaving for the first stage of the journey [from
Morotai] to Tawi Tawi when a vaguely familiar figure marched up, came
crashingly to attention and saluted ... It was Koram, Sergeant Koram
now ... the same Koram who had been so instrumental in their escape
from Berhala Island.'

In the interim Koram had delivered a stream of intelligence to the
Allies while pretending to be working for the Japanese. Major Jackson
writes that, after handing himself in to the Japanese, Koram was flown
back to Sandakan, where the Japanese fell for his statement that he 'could
find the cursed PW if the Japanese would give him a chance'.

> For five months he took the Japanese along false trails and always
> endeavoured to visit areas where the Japanese had installations,
> dumps etc. The information that he obtained and the sketch maps
> that he prepared were always thankfully received by the USFIP
> [US Forces in the Philippines] leaders. About December 1944 he told
> the Japs that he had received information that Lt R. Blow ... was
> in the Tawao area and so until February 1945 he roamed this strategic
> area with the blessing of the Japanese. The strength and disposition of
> the Japanese forces in this area was soon in the hands of Koram and
> shortly afterwards with the USFIP.

From Tawao, Koram slipped into Lahad Datu, where he continued to gather intelligence before escaping by boat to Tawi Tawi in May 1945. His information proved so useful that the local guerrilla leader, Colonel Suarez, sent him to report to South West Pacific Area headquarters on Morotai. At the sight of him, Sheila Ross writes, Blow 'turned and gaped, hardly able to believe his eyes'. Blow told Koram that he was heading to Semporna on a mission. He asked Koram 'if he wanted to come too'. Koram did not hesitate. His face 'split into one wide grin and he was off without a word', returning a couple of minutes later with his kit. He brought with him two more recruits, both former constables with the British North Borneo police, named in the official history as Pritam Singh and Ishmael.

After being delivered by PT boat to Semporna in Tawao district on 14 July, Blow set up his headquarters in a house near the jetty and established radio contact with Morotai. Local chieftains were enlisted to 'collect all information concerning the enemy in the Tawao area and to intercept and interrogate all natives entering and leaving the area', while recruiting young men to fight as guerrillas.

Among Blow's tasks was to rescue a Filipina and her children who were being held as hostages by the Japanese, then to do the same for a German doctor and his family. Both missions were successfully carried out under the noses of Japanese guards. But the SRD had not sent Agas IV to Borneo just to free civilians. On 27 July, Koram led a patrol upriver in search of information about an Australian pilot reported to have parachuted from his aircraft near Kalabakan two and a half weeks earlier. At a plantation called Balung Estate, the patrol ran into a group of Japanese soldiers, killing four and wounding eight.

Like plantations all over Borneo, Balung Estate had been turned into what Sheila Ross describes as a 'mini-garrison' housing a permanent detachment of soldiers. Identifying the location and strength of these outposts was part of the brief for Agas IV. Koram found tracks heading both north and south from the estate, information he knew Blow would be interested to hear. In addition, he rounded up a number of former native policemen who, in the words of the official history, 'volunteered to join the guerrilla force'. Until now Blow had relied on boats to move his party around the North Borneo coast. Koram's discovery revealed that the Japanese were using jungle tracks to shift troops from garrison to garrison, avoiding hazardous movements by sea. Such intelligence was sure to be useful to Allied commanders looking to cut off the Japanese retreat.

The morning after the incident at Balung Estate, another skirmish occurred at a place called Batu Tinagat, resulting (according to 'native reports') in the deaths of twenty Japanese soldiers and the wounding of another sixteen. Koram returned the following day to the same spot, and a guerrilla boat 'strafed the shoreline where the Japanese had opened fire the previous day'. Shortly after sunset, they encountered a group of native craft. Unable to see the occupants but hearing 'Japanese speech', Koram gave the order to open fire. Again, 'native reports' suggested a one-sided result: four Japanese dead and eight wounded for no guerrilla casualties.[*]

Information about the missing Australian pilot was vague and contradictory. Koram followed up various rumours and reported sightings, but the most likely outcome appeared to be that the pilot had been captured and taken for questioning by the Kempei-Tai.

Meanwhile, Koram continued to use his influence among the local population to recruit volunteer guerrillas. The official history records

---

[*] SRD missions in Borneo relied on a steady supply of information from local inhabitants, but operatives had learnt to be sceptical of its accuracy. The official history of Agas notes that it was 'not easy to assess intelligence because of native exaggeration of numbers. This exaggeration also applied to bombing and strafing results.' While 'most' intelligence from native sources was considered to be 'bona fide', it came with the significant proviso that 'cross-examination usually proved it to be fourth or fifth hand'.

that at Ulu Seradong 'the Dyak Headman expressed his willingness to organise 100 Dyaks who would later be used to harass the Japanese in the sector west of Tawao'. Successful storpedo drops on 29 July and 11 August enabled Blow to equip the nascent guerrilla force with rifles and ammunition.

It would be some time before the fate of the missing pilot was known. Local informants revealed that after parachuting out of his aircraft near Kalabakan, he had walked to a nearby plantation, where he was arrested by a local man, bound with rope and delivered into the hands of the Japanese military police. According to the official history, he was later shot.

On the same day that Koram had set off upriver to investigate reports of the downed Australian airman, Jock McLaren arrived in the neighbouring district of Lahad Datu as leader of Agas V. As a standard security precaution, SRD operatives on one mission would not have been given details about other missions. But Blow and McLaren were not in intelligence for nothing, and Blow discovered soon enough from his native contacts that another SRD officer was active to the north. On a quiet day when nothing was happening except routine training, Ross writes that Blow 'took the launch . . . determined to pay his opposite number a surprise visit'.

McLaren had been busy setting up his own intelligence system, with locals reporting all enemy activity in Lahad Datu and neighbouring areas. At the same time he was struggling to manage the flood of sick and malnourished people pouring into the district from Japanese-controlled areas, where food was scarce and malaria was rife. Many were in urgent need of medical attention when they arrived at McLaren's hastily erected jungle hospitals. Richardson writes that on his first day handing out the medicines he had brought with him, McLaren had 'more than one hundred patients . . . mostly leg-ulcer cases and evil-smelling sores that had eaten into the flesh . . . bloated beriberi cases and debilitated children carrying the scaly marks of pellagra. McLaren, with his veterinary experience to help him, did his best to cope, aided by a small group of Chinese girls who came to his assistance as nurses.' In return, his patients told him what the Japanese were doing.

The last thing McLaren expected, as he absorbed this stream of intelligence and passed it on by radio to Morotai, was a visit from Rex Blow. In Hal Richardson's account of the meeting, McLaren greeted his old friend and then 'called in one of his team of helpers'. That 'helper' was none other than 'Mata Mata Number 142 of the Japanese Borneo Police Service . . . Corporal Koram'. Blow, Richardson writes, 'looked at him open-mouthed', while Koram 'laughed, his eyes wet with tears, as he shook Blow's hand'.

But that was not how Blow remembered it. As Sheila Ross describes the meeting, McLaren told Blow about his adventures with Z Special Unit, including the parachute drop behind Balikpapan (Platypus VI) for which he had won his second Military Cross. Blow, she writes, 'listened with interest' before recounting his own futile search for the Sandakan POWs. Koram was not even present at the meeting.

In his tape-recorded conversations with Bowden and Nelson, Blow told the story of Agas IV virtually as he had told it to Sheila Ross.

I'd been in to Sandakan and come back, and . . . I'd been organised then to go in with another party into a place called Semporna, where I was going to operate one of these SRD parties . . . It was then that I met Koram, and told him what I was doing, and I said . . . would you come back with me? And, you know, within two seconds he was back with his kit bag, 'When are we going?' . . . they wanted to drop us in by parachute, and I said 'no way', I knew a bit about that country and those things and [said] 'we can take a launch there'. [They said] 'but the Japs are in there operating' and I said, 'Oh, well, we'll take our chances' . . . we had a very heavily armed launch and we patrolled up and down the coast . . . and Koram used to go ashore and . . . contact natives. And we pretty quickly found out . . . what the Jap situation was.

The official history confirms that Koram was a member of Blow's party, not McLaren's: he was a guerrilla leader in Agas IV rather than a 'helper' in Agas V. The romanticised, but probably imaginary, reunion described by McLaren is, if nothing else, a measure of the debt that he and Blow must both have felt towards Koram. The simple truth was that both owed their lives to Koram, who was honoured after the war with an MBE, which he received from King George VI in London. He is named in the 1946 list of MBEs as 'Koram Bin Enduat, British North Borneo Constabulary'. He died shortly afterwards, of tuberculosis.

By the time Agas V came to an end, Japan had surrendered. Ross writes that Blow left Semporna on 31 August—three weeks after the second atomic bomb fell on Nagasaki—for Sebatik Island with money to start 'paying off and disbanding the volunteers'. On his return to Semporna he found the men from Agas V, including McLaren, waiting for a plane to Morotai. The official history records that McLaren's party was ordered out on 10 September 1945, with a clerk left in charge of Talasai and two Chinese nurses looking after the hospital. Similar arrangements were made for another hospital at Dungan. At Semporna, 'all particulars' of these areas were given to an officer from the British Borneo Civil Affairs Unit, along with a list of 'collaborators and undesirables'.

Hal Richardson reports that in the last days of the war McLaren was given the task of taking some surrendered Japanese soldiers into custody. Richardson reports that 'McLaren had no pity for the defeated enemy. He knew how much pity they would have given him.' After handing over his prisoners to the authorities, McLaren was 'severely reprimanded for taking their watches and pens and other personal belongings'. There was talk, Richardson suggests, of 'court martial for this sort of thing'.

The episode confirmed 'beyond doubt' to McLaren that 'his guerrilla days were over'.

With McLaren gone, Blow took over the civil administration of Tawao, making his headquarters in what Ross describes as a 'rickety old two-storey wooden house in a copra plantation just outside Lahud [Lahad] Datu'. Five weeks later he was finally granted leave. On 13 October, a Catalina took Blow and Signalman Schinkel to Labuan, off the north-west coast of Borneo, where Blow met Major Tom Harrisson.

Seconded to Z Special Unit from the British Army's Reconnaissance Corps, Harrisson had parachuted into Sarawak in March 1945 as leader of a large intelligence-gathering operation called *Semut* (Malay for 'ant'). With the war now over, Harrisson had orders for a very different kind of mission, and he wanted Blow to accompany him. Blow turned him down flat, telling Harrisson that he was exhausted and wanted to go home. But, as he told Sheila Ross, 'The bastard had a bottle of whisky and by the time we'd finished it, I'd agreed to go!'

Chapter 18

SEMUT

———>•<———

Changing military priorities at Allied General Headquarters meant that Operation Semut got underway several months later than originally intended. By the time the operation was formally approved, the northeast monsoon made it impossible for the party to be inserted by submarine. This suited Harrisson, who considered the coastal Malays to be 'unreliable' and had always favoured a parachute drop.

After several reconaissance flights in search of a suitable landing zone, the first insertion took place on 23 March 1945 on the Kalabit Plateau, an area described in the official report as the 'mountainous and largely unexplored hinterland of Borneo'.

Due to the late start, it was felt that Semut would be able to do little more than gather and pass on intelligence before the AIF 'landed and took control'. Under Harrisson's leadership, however, the first phase of the operation, Semut I, 'was able to develop so rapidly that it was given the task of organising large-scale guerrilla activities, the medical care and rehabilitation of the natives, and food distribution in the area'.

Written orders given by Harrisson (codenamed A1) to one of his subordinates (H7) in June 1945 confirm the importance of these tasks. H7 is instructed to leave the following day for Long Barang and to '[spend] up to six days there, if job done less (but not less than four). Give all help you can in area and leave a stock of medicines for base use … by other whites … not too much; they should have large supplies dropped at Malinau shortly, and available through area, plus Chinese doctor.'

Harrisson's ten-point orders continue:

Keep your ears open all the way and report back anything of interest straight to me.

At every village and at Barang (where call a full meeting) give a propaganda talk as my direct representative and bearing the word direct from me. Your line of talk:

Now is the time to get really tough with Japs—kill kill kill.

I will help in every way I can.

Those who render good services as soldiers, chiefs etc will be fully rewarded when the war is won.

I shall not myself leave the area until I am satisfied the government has fully recompensed everyone for their services.

Finally, Harrisson tells H7 to 'Stress that we are *orang* [Malay for "people"] INNGRRIS [English] and AUSTRALIE. Bash this in hard. We are NOT Dutch (Blanda). We are not not not not AMERICAN. The Yanks seem, as usual, to have spread the idea that they alone fight the war. Get any such shit out of their heads once and for all.'

H7 is told to 'KEEP this sheet and refer to it each day for lines of propaganda': 'These TEN lines you will plug everywhere you go and however tired, at the end of the day you will summon the village, address them in your unspeakable Malay, and have the Keei or Sungian [Dyak soldiers] to put it across for you in dialect. Speak strongly, and see they do. Natives appreciate strong talk, as you will have noticed. Sungian is a particularly good talker and propagandist.'

The official history of Semut I records that Harrisson's party 'consolidated native morale and built up a definite feeling of hostility towards the Japanese' and that deliveries of weapons gave another boost to morale. 'By the end of July over 1000 men were under arms, some of them equipped with captured Japanese weapons . . . the main problem as their arming proceeded was to restrain these people from taking the offensive in an indiscriminate way. They observed excellent discipline in this respect, once the need for coordination with sea landings was clearly understood.'

As the 9th Division pushed inland, the Japanese retreated along the major river systems. During July a large enemy force was caught when it reached the Trusan River. During constant fighting over the next twenty-one days, at least 320 Japanese soldiers were killed. Efficient wireless communications made it possible for Semut I forces to pick off enemy stragglers from the rear and to ambush them as they made their way inland along the river valleys. (Harrisson reminded two of his officers on 29 July: 'Important get proof all Jap bodies. Our score so high AIF cannot bear it.') The official history reports that, although the the enemy was 'numerically much stronger and better armed . . . Semut I held the initiative at all times, and those Japanese who were not killed arrived at the other end starving . . . Through the whole of this operation, only 2 men, Muruts, were lost.'

A record of decoded signals traffic for the month of July suggests that the situation on the ground was more fraught than the official history admits. On 6 July, Harrisson sent a furious two-part message to his second-in-command, Captain Eric Edmeades, at Trusan:

Part 1

For EDMEADES. Flabbergasted at your attitude in latest sigs. You hold best forces inland. Giving no support to [Lieutenant] Pinkerton on coast. We are attacking main concentration from coast side. You bloody well get stuck into them too. If they are organised well bloody well disorganise them. You apparently have the wrong physology [psychology?]. You have had it too easy. My coast boys plough in at huge formation. Do the same.

Part 2

You appear to have lost control. I found LAWAS in a chaos. Not a man was at his post. Had to reorganise top to bottom. Killing many Japs now. Report immediately all aggressive action you are taking at all points. It will be inexcusable if Japs reach TENOM in strength. Order of the day. Every man into battle. Except poor old sigs. Get going now rpt now.[*]

Frustrated by the poor quality of signals he was receiving, Harrisson issued an ultimatum on 14 July: 'Inform all personnel as follows: In future disciplinary action will be taken against all persons sending in reports or signals without dates times positions directions coordinates and max air identification possible. Invaluable opportunities are being wasted through gross carelessness.'

Signs were painted on the ground to identify friendly villages, with arrows pointing in the direction of the nearest Japanese soldiers as well as their 'distance in yards'. But accidents happened. Harrisson complained bitterly about an RAAF strike on Padas, as a result of which many

---

[*] In his carefully researched history of Semut I, *Voices from Borneo*, Major Jim Truscott describes Edmeades as 'a gallant officer and a great man'. He also points out that Harrisson was 'egotistical and ruthless' and that many of his Australian operatives 'found Harrisson's orders ridiculous'.

guerrillas had 'gone bush'. A signal dated 15 July states, 'RAAF error inexcusable . . . All knew target. Have cancelled all strikes. Report full damage immediately. Too bloody.'

By the start of August, not more than a 'handful' of Japanese soldiers were known to be alive in the Semut I area (comprising northern Sarawak and northern Dutch Borneo). However, large numbers of enemy troops had gathered just outside this area. Harrisson decided to launch a full-scale attack on positions held by the Japanese in strength. According to the official history, a simultaneous attack by two forces totalling eleven 'white operatives' and nearly 400 'native troops' armed with machine guns, submachine guns, rifles and grenades was about to begin when the war ended.

Although hostilities had officially ceased, the cornered Japanese troops refused to surrender. Instead, they advanced on Harrisson's headquarters, looting and pillaging as they went, killing unarmed villagers and ignoring envoys and dropped leaflets informing them of the general surrender. Sheila Ross writes that there was a feeling at 9th Division headquarters that the strength of the Japanese force had been 'greatly exaggerated' and that if 'left alone, cut off from the coast, its members would perish in due course anyway'. Harrisson did not believe this.

By early October, a renegade Japanese force under a Captain Fujino had moved beyond the lower Limbang River, well out of reach of the 9th Division's land forces but close enough to pose a threat to the head-quarters of Semut I. Unlike the Japanese stragglers eking out a wretched existence in the jungle, Fujino's column was an organised unit that now stood threateningly between the rump of Semut I and the coast.

Harrisson was not concerned only for his own men. He knew that Fujino's unit was laying waste to the country, stealing food and killing livestock from the Dyak villages it passed through and leaving famine in its wake. Houses were dismantled for firewood or burnt down. According to his biographer, Judith Heimann, Harrisson 'was not prepared to accept any more nonsense about the war being over and no more Allied casualties to be risked. If Ninth Division would not deal with this renegade column, he would do so himself.'

A few weeks earlier General Wootten (described by Heimann as 'starchy, regular army') had been replaced as commander of 9th Division by General Windeyer. By the time Harrisson met Rex Blow at Labuan, he already had Windeyer's permission to search along the Trusan River for Fujino's column and attempt to bring the Japanese in. This was the mission that Blow had been talked into joining.

Harrisson described how the operation unfolded in a series of detailed reports to 9th Division headquarters. For nearly two weeks, the party tracked the Japanese through extremely rough country up the Trusan valley. They had to carry all their own food, the area having been 'devastated by the Japs, who threw what padi [rice] they could not carry into the river.'

It was not until 2.30 on the afternoon of 29 October, more than two months after the war had officially ended, that a patrol led by Blow caught up with Fujino's column. The Japanese 'as usual, opened fire on every sign of life or movement', but the native troops did not reply, demonstrating great discipline 'under considerable provocation'. At about 4 p.m. two Japanese envoys were sent in, armed for their own protection since 'they considered it possible they would be ill-received' (they were correct). Three-quarters of an hour later, the envoys returned with Fujino and a Lieutenant Kamimura, who 'gave their unconditional surrender to [Harrisson] by word of mouth'.

In fact Fujino had been opposed to the surrender, but his second-in-command, Kamimura (described by Harrisson as 'a stronger man than Fujino'), had 'strongly supported the envoys'. Fujino also confirmed that he had read the dropped leaflets and knew the war had ended. He said the column had been heading for Dutch Borneo because they were in desperate need of salt and they had heard they could find salt there.

(Harrisson pointed out that they had 'passed several salt springs on the track . . . without knowing it'.)

In Harrisson's view, Fujino had imagined that he was clear of all 'white and native troops' and was surprised to find himself caught between well-organised and well-led patrols ahead of and behind him. But for this, and his failure to find salt, it was possible that the Japanese might not have surrendered, despite their debilitated condition. According to Harrisson's report, in the latter stages of Blow's pursuit, 'an average of one [Japanese soldier] fell out and died every ½ mile, from malnutrition and fatigue, despite their adequate supplies of rice, fruit, greens and meat. Suicides were common.'

With the Japanese disarmed and in custody, Blow was handed the role of camp commandant. His final task of the war would be delivering 330 sick and malnourished prisoners to Lawas on the coast. But who was going to feed them? 9th Division headquarters was adamant that it 'will not pay for PW food', while Harrisson insisted that 'the natives cannot be forced to supply food, free, to people who have already wantonly robbed and devastated their country so that some villages are faced with starvation'.

The British Borneo Civil Affairs Unit (BBCAU), the unit charged with administering the reoccupied areas, was equally reluctant to foot the bill for feeding the Japanese prisoners, advising Harrisson that 'No rpt no expenditure can be made from BBCAU funds'. According to his biographer, Harrisson sent a reply 'worthy of the occasion':

Your signal Ack[nowledged] but do not understand. If meant seriously, which of three courses shall I take: (1) Death-march Japs to coast? (2) Pay from my own pocket? (3) Force natives to give remaining food free? In each case can you assure me please: If (1) I shall not be court-martialled. If (2) I shall not be declared bankrupt. If (3), I shall not have my head cut off by infuriated Muruts. If Japs surrender, it will take weeks to get them all down. Must pass through ravaged areas. Reply immediately please.

A blunt signal from Colonel Leach of the BBCAU advised: 'Feed the sods jungle UMBUT [Malay for "plant shoots"].'

In the end, arrangements were made for food to be airdropped at predetermined points along the route. Until then surplus parachutes from the stores were used to barter for food in native villages.

Food was not the only problem confronting Blow. Many of the Japanese prisoners were too sick to walk. Some would need to be carried, but by whom? Even their own officers appeared to consider the sick to be an unnecessary burden. Blow's exasperation is clear from a letter he wrote on 4 November to Harrisson:

> I reckon we give the Doc a bottle of deadly poison—tell him it's liquid monkey glands for the weak & kill the lot of the b—s & no more worries ... it will be a hell of a job having the sick here— may be months ... I think old Kam[imura] and Fuji[no] wouldn't be averse to dropping a few down ravines and into rivers here and there ...

Anticipating trouble, Blow told Harrisson, 'Last night—in bed— tried to imagine myself—strong and healthy—carrying someone over that trail—hell it's almost an impossibility. They say some people do the impossible & seems the bloody Japs are about to do it.'

A typewritten plan for the march shows the prisoners were divided into four groups, each led by an Australian (Blow, Lieutenant Thomas, Sergeant Bennet and Sergeant Nibbs) and a 'native NCO'. Fujino was assigned to the first group, with Bennet as leader, while Kamimura went with Blow in the second group. Nibbs would be in charge of a smaller third group, leaving Lieutenant Thomas to take the remainder, accompanied by a Japanese doctor. The groups were to leave three days apart, and the first three were expected to reach Lawas in fifteen days. No one could predict when Thomas's party would arrive.

Preserved in a folder at the Australian War Memorial is a sequence of identical pencil notes, handwritten in Japanese and English, attesting to humane treatment of the prisoners by their Australian captors in the days before the march. Dated and signed by Fujino and Kamimura, each note states: 'We are quite satisfied with your treatment for us.'

The prisoners' treatment of each other was not so humane. The spirit of mateship that enabled Allied prisoners to survive the Siam–Burma railway was alien to the Japanese, who carried their sick and wounded comrades only under duress. Sheila Ross writes that soon after setting out, Blow 'began finding bodies on the side of the path that had been strangled ... [F]rom then on the Aussie corporal led the march, while Rex with the Japanese officer remained in the rear to see that his orders were obeyed.' Blow told Bowden and Nelson that when the Japanese were informed they would be carrying their sick, 'they said, no, we're not going to carry [the] sick. If they're not well enough to walk ... we might as well kill them. And that's exactly what they did with a few of them ... We made them rig up ... stretchers. You'd go down the trail for a few hours and you'd find these Japs dead. They just knocked their own blokes out if they couldn't walk.'

Captain Athol Moffitt was in Lawas when one of the prisoner groups arrived. In his unpublished memoirs, he recalls them entering Lawas 'in two groups in single file, with an Australian stripped to the waist, one at the head and one at the rear of each group ... march[ing] through the town centre to the waiting 9th Division barges. One Australian was using a Dyak blow pipe (with a spear at one end) as a walking stick.'

Moffitt wrote in his diary:

No man would help another, who fell down or was too sick to walk, and they had to be ordered to help each other. The Aussies made them carry 3 or 4 who could not walk and when the Australians were around a bend, out of sight, they would beat them to make them walk. Once one was missing and the Japs said he died and the sergeant (Z Force) went back and found him hanged on a tree—'You have no friends in the Jap army.' Another, the Japs beat to death . . . I understand now all that is said about the brutality of the Japs to our people, when this is what they do to their own people.

The official history of Semut I contains no mention of this, recording simply that after being disarmed Fujino's unit was 'escorted to Lawas on the west of Brunei Bay, and handed over to the AIF'.

Chapter 19

NO FIXED ADDRESS

The lives of Jock McLaren and Rex Blow continued to follow a curious symmetry. The pair met up after the war—Ross's book includes a photograph of the two men, captioned 'on leave at Surfers Paradise, Christmas 1945'—but neither was able settle in Australia. In 1946 Blow transferred from the army to the colonial service and returned to North Borneo.

Two years later he was back in Australia, his homecoming reported by the Brisbane *Telegraph* under the headline 'Rex Blow returns'. By 1950 he was in North Borneo again, writing to the army medal section in Melbourne for 'any medals and ribbons that I was awarded during the war'. A letter in Blow's file at the National Archives shows that in August 1964 he was living in Bougainville and applying for membership of the Bougainville subbranch of the Papua New Guinea RSL.

Richardson tells us that after hostilities ended Jock McLaren 'hitch-hiked to Tawi Tawi, Zamboanga, Liangan, Iligan, Misamis, Malabang, and as far as Okinawa, Singapore and Kuching . . . He went back to Berhala. The lepers were gone and only twisted iron remained . . . The gate of the prison camp, through which he had walked so long ago, was cobwebbed and broken.'

Like Blow, Jock McLaren was haunted by Blamey's failure to deliver on his promise to rescue the prisoners at Sandakan. After visiting Berhala, McLaren crossed to the mainland and made his own 'bitter pilgrimage' to the ruins of Eight Mile Camp. According to Richardson, he 'began to follow the trail of discarded belongings, and once he had begun . . . he could not stop. For a hundred and sixty-three miles he walked into Borneo, sitting sometimes on the mound that a Chinese had built over murdered bodies. He walked on till he came to Ranau, where the last twenty-eight survivors of that death march had been shot.'

In the following years McLaren's wanderings mirrored Blow's. His entry in the *Australian Dictionary of Biography* states that after the war he 'found no satisfactory occupation in Australia and accepted a post as a government veterinary officer in the Territory of Papua-New Guinea'.

The war had left McLaren a sick man. A journalist on the *Bulletin*, writing under the pseudonym 'Ybsul', recalled sharing a Brisbane hotel room with McLaren for a few months 'just after the Jap war'. At that time McLaren was suffering from a relapse of malaria and 'insisted that sleeping on the floor was the way to a quick recovery. The only ministration he asked of me was to leave two bottles of beer beside him. The day he could drink them, he assured me, he'd be better.'

In 1948 McLaren was admitted to Greenslopes repatriation hospital in Brisbane suffering from what some newspaper reports described as 'general vitamin deficiency, due to harsh treatment by the Japanese'. It was while he was at Greenslopes that he received the Military Cross. 'Ybsul' recalled escorting McLaren to the investiture, where he was presented with 'a brace of MCs'.

Jock was a bit wobbly on his pins after a longish stretch in Greenslopes, but stood like a ramrod while the aide rattled through his citation. General S'John [Governor Sir John Lavarack] said something sotto voce which to this listener sounded suspiciously like 'You should have got a VC, Jock.' After the gubernatorial handshake Jock about-turned so briskly that the decorations fell from his tunic to the grass. The Governor took a smart step forward, waves Jock to remain standing, stooped and picked up the gongs and pinned 'em in place again.

According to the writer, the Queensland premier, Ned Hanlon, was so moved by the citation for McLaren's award that he 'jumped to his feet, grabbed Jock's hand and said, "If ever there's any way I can help you, Jock, come and see me!"'

Within a couple of years McLaren was back in Papua New Guinea. In September 1950, the *Territory of Papua New Guinea Government Gazette* reported that McLaren had been appointed a stock inspector. The appointment was renewed in 1952 and 1954, but throughout this period McLaren kept moving. 'Ybsul' claimed to have 'narrowly missed Jock a dozen times. Neither of us had very fixed addresses.' From time to time McLaren would write a letter recounting some colourful incident that had happened at 'Baiyer River . . . Mount Hagen, Wau, Lae, or some other of Jock's ports-of-call'.

By early 1955, McLaren had left the PNG public service and taken over a coffee plantation near Wau. A handwritten letter in Sydney's Mitchell Library hints at McLaren's struggles to make the plantation viable. In any case, his career as a planter was tragically brief. He died in a car accident on 3 March 1956. According to the *Australian Dictionary of Biography*, he 'accidentally backed his Jeep into a pergola and was killed when struck by falling timber'.

McLaren and Hal Richardson had agreed to split the proceeds of *One-Man War*. McLaren needed the money to keep his coffee plantation going. His death meant that his share, rather than being spent on the plantation, would now go to his heirs. The problem was that McLaren had died without leaving a will. He was separated from his wife, who was living in Queensland, and was believed to have a son in Scotland. In a letter to his publisher, Richardson describes the question of McLaren's legacy as 'complicated'.

In November 1956, the *Territory of Papua New Guinea Government Gazette* announced a tender for the purchase and removal of a 'Single-room Wooden House situated at Wau'. The house was to be taken away within twenty-one days of the tender being accepted. It did not sell. In January 1957, a fresh tender was announced, this time with a more detailed description of the house as '30 feet x 15 feet consisting of exterior walls of weatherboard, wooden floor, divided into four rooms and ceiled with three-ply, roof of iron, 50 per cent galvanized and the remainder black iron painted'.

Was it a single-room house or a house with four rooms? Had McLaren escaped from Changi with two mates or three? Did he serve in one world war or two? Jock was a cloak-and-dagger man to the end.

Appendix 1

OTHERS WHO HAVE REMOVED THEIR OWN APPENDIX

<hr/>

The story of how Jock McLaren removed his own appendix might appear unbelievable (even Richardson's publisher was sceptical), but it is not unique. Seventeen years after McLaren performed his operation with a razor blade and mirror on Mindanao, Leonid Rogozov performed the same operation on himself at the Soviet Antarctic base of Novolazarevskaya.

Rogozov, a surgeon, had sailed from Leningrad on 5 November 1960 with the sixth Soviet Antarctic expedition. Just over a month later, he was part of a group dropped on the ice shelf on Princess Astrid Coast, charged with building a new Soviet Antarctic base. While wintering at the base he became seriously ill. According to an account in the *British Medical Journal* (BMJ), co-authored by Rogozov, he 'noticed symptoms of weakness, malaise, nausea, and, later, pain in the upper part of his abdomen which shifted to the right lower quadrant. His body temperature rose to 37.5°C.'

Rogozov knew he was suffering from acute appendicitis and that his only hope of survival was an operation. The question was: who would do it? Winter was already closing in. The sea had frozen over, and ahead lay months of darkness and extreme cold. The ship that had brought them to the Antarctic would not return for a year. Rogozov was the only physician at the base, and the weather made flying out impossible. He realised that he would have to do it himself.

While McLaren had to cut himself with a razor blade boiled in a rice pot, Rogozov was able to perform the operation using properly sterilised medical instruments. Unlike McLaren, who had no anaesthetics, Rogozov could inject himself with local anaesthetic and had antibiotics to fight infection. He also had a number of confident assistants, none of whom begged him to sign his own death certificate in case the operation went wrong.

Rogozov explained [to his colleagues] how the operation would proceed and assigned them tasks: Artemev would hand him instruments; Teplinsky would hold the mirror and adjust the lighting with the table lamp; Gerbovich was there in reserve, in case nausea overcame either of the assistants. In the event that Rogozov lost consciousness, he instructed his team how to inject him with drugs using the syringes he had prepared and how to provide artificial ventilation.

According to Rogozov, the operation lasted an hour and forty-five minutes, including time for photographs. Gerbovich recorded in his diary that Rogozov 'was calm and focused on his work, but sweat was running down his face and he frequently asked Teplinsky to wipe his forehead . . . The operation ended at 4 am local time. By the end, Rogozov was very pale and obviously tired, but he finished everything off.'

McLaren, more used to operating on dogs and horses than humans, told Hal Richardson that the operation 'took him four and a half hours to complete'.

After five days' rest and recuperation, Rogozov's temperature was normal; two days later he took out his stitches. Within a fortnight the Russian 'was able to return to his normal duties and to his diary'. McLaren did not have the luxury of a leisurely convalescence. Less than a week after the operation, he was back in the jungle with a tommy-gun over his shoulder, hiding from the Japanese.

Rogozov's article in BMJ argues that his self-operation was 'probably the first such successful act undertaken in the wilderness, out of hospital settings, with no possibility of outside help, and without any other medical professional around'—a claim that would probably have irked Jock McLaren. But medical literature records another self-appendectomy that predates both McLaren's and Rogozov's.

On 15 February 1921, an American surgeon, Dr Evan O'Neill Kane, was in the operating theatre of his family-owned hospital awaiting an appendectomy when he decided to do the operation himself. Since he was the chief of surgery, staff had no choice but to comply. There was a serious point to the experiment: Kane wanted to find out whether appendectomies could be done under local anaesthetic, thereby saving patients the risk of a general anaesthetic.

According to an account in the journal *Translational Research in Anatomy*, Kane 'propped himself up with pillows in order to achieve a good view of his abdomen, and had a nurse hold his head. He injected cocaine and adrenalin into his abdominal wall and then he swiftly cut through the superficial tissue, found the swollen appendix, and excised it.' At one point Kane 'leaned too far forward and his intestines protruded out of his abdominal cavity, much to the horror of his staff, but he calmly placed them back inside his body and continued working'.

Kane was said to have taken just thirty minutes to complete the operation—under two hours less than Rogozov and four hours less than McLaren. He could have wrapped it up even sooner, he claimed, but for the 'chaos' in the room. Within a fortnight he was fully recovered and operating again.

Eleven years later, Kane attempted to repair his own hernia under local anaesthetic. Due to the closeness of the femoral artery, it was a far more hazardous procedure than the self-appendectomy. The procedure took more than an hour, and Kane invited the press to watch and take photographs. Although the operation itself was a success, Kane died three months later from pneumonia.

Appendix 2

'ONE-MAN WAR'

———————

If there is one thing Jock McLaren would have hated about Hal Richardson's book, it was the title. Richardson, a former soldier himself, was unhappy with it, informing his publisher in a letter written two months after McLaren's death that he preferred the title 'Private War'.

For all his personal courage, Jock McLaren was no more capable of fighting a one-man war than any other soldier. To an unusual degree, McLaren owed his effectiveness as a soldier—and, indeed, his very survival—to the help he received from civilians willing to hazard their own lives to support the Allies against the Japanese. That he succeeded twice in escaping from Japanese POW camps was largely the result of help given by civilians, few of whom could have been in any doubt about the risks they were taking. Later, civilian collaboration was instrumental to the success of the anti-Japanese guerrilla forces in the Philippines. While on the run from the Japanese on Mindanao, McLaren

could not have undertaken his life-saving self-appendectomy without
the shelter and protection he was given by Filipino civilians. Finally,
as a commando operating behind the lines in Borneo, McLaren knew
that his ability to evade the enemy and to carry out his intelligence
mission relied on winning the support of local tribespeople. In short,
Jock McLaren's 'one-man war' against the Japanese would have ended
before it began without the active collaboration of civilian helpers in
Singapore, Malaya, the Philippines and Borneo.

Why were so many men and women across Asia willing to risk their
lives to help Allied soldiers in their fight against the Japanese? What did
they hope to gain from it? How significant to the Allied war effort was
civilian resistance against the Japanese?

In *Men of Destiny*, Peter Sinclair notes that the Japanese 'inadvertently'
set the conditions for a successful guerrilla movement in the Philippines
by 'ignoring basic governance issues'. Sinclair lists the main issues facing
Filipinos during the Japanese occupation as 'unemployment, lack of
food, and . . . atrocities committed by Japanese forces'. By demobilising
the Philippine Constabulary (it was later reconstituted), the Japanese
also undermined law and order. In many areas the result was to put local
power in the hands of bandits.

Tasked with suppressing Allied intelligence networks and hunting
down fugitive American and Filipino soldiers, the Japanese military
police—the Kempei-Tai—employed brutal interrogation methods that
further alienated Filipinos. In Sinclair's words, the Kempei-Tai's terror
tactics, together with casual violence from Japanese soldiers, 'united the
Filipino population against them'.

Larry Schmidt, in his Master's thesis 'American involvement in the
Filipino resistance movement on Mindanao during the Japanese occupation 1942–1945', argues that the Kempei-Tai 'worked with the
occupation army and civil administrators' to 'turn the people against
the guerrillas through brute force'.

Schmidt describes a method known as the 'magic eye', outlined in a Japanese training manual entitled 'Notes for the Interrogation of Prisoners of War'. A *barrio* or town would be seized and encircled by the Japanese and the men would be herded into the town square.

> After proclamations, denunciations, and general haranguing was finished, a hooded man with eyelets cut in the hood would be brought out: 'the magic eye'. This individual—a traitor, spy or purported captured guerrilla—would scan the crowd and pick out guerrilla spies, guerrillas or sympathizers. These unfortunates would then be publicly tortured, roasted alive, drawn and quartered, buried alive, or, the end result in most cases, beheaded.

The reprisal ratio against civilians varied in different regions and under different commanders, but Schmidt suggests that for every Japanese soldier killed by the guerrillas, the Japanese often killed from 100 to 200 Filipinos. Despite the fearful risks, Schmidt estimates that between 67 per cent and 90 per cent of the Filipino population resisted the Japanese 'in whatever way possible'.

Many demonstrated their support for the guerrillas by providing food and shelter. In their paper 'The Filipino way of war: Irregular warfare through the centuries', Fernando Reyeg and Ned Marsh suggest that most Filipinos understood that 'it was their duty to insure that the guerrillas were fed in order to continue operations', adding that some believed they would be 'reimbursed' for their help by the Americans after they had retaken control of the islands from the Japanese.

Unlike some other Asian populations, Filipinos did not take advantage of Allied defeats to turn against the former colonial power. Nor were they seduced by the mythical benefits they were promised for joining the Japanese-led Greater East Asia Co-Prosperity Sphere. On the contrary, most Filipinos remained stubbornly loyal to the Americans, whose short period of colonial rule bore little resemblance to the Netherlands' centuries-long exploitation of the Javanese. Anxious not to squander this loyalty, American-led guerrilla groups tried not to ambush Japanese patrols in the vicinity of villages. On Mindanao, Colonel Fertig issued strict instructions to avoid encounters that would provoke Japanese reprisals against civilians.

When General Yamashita negotiated the Japanese surrender in August 1945, it was not with MacArthur but with Colonel Russell Volckmann, the American guerrilla commander in Luzon. Volckmann would state that the supply of food, water, technical and intelligence support by Filipino civilians was 'critical' and 'the only lifeline' the guerrillas had.

Major Harry Jackson's report is testament to the lifeline given to Allied prisoners by the civilian population of Sandakan. Jackson's typewritten report contains page after page of names belonging to men and women who helped Allied POWs. Some, such as Siti Binte Jakariah, were the widows of men who had been tortured and executed by the Japanese. Jackson describes her as 'the de facto wife of the late Heng Joo Ming' who was 'executed with Capt Matthews at Kuching. He took a leading part in Dr Taylor's organisation, helped in obtaining radio parts, money etc and harboured Sjt [sergeant] Wallace after his escape. Gave considerable aid to Aust PW.'

Another name on the list is that of Bintang Binte Udung, whose husband, Corporal Abin of the North Borneo Constabulary, was also executed with Captain Matthews at Kuching. According to Jackson's report, Abin was 'the NCO in charge of the Mile 8 police post who gave so much valuable assistance to the Aust PW.'

Jackson had been given three hundred pounds by the Australian Government to disburse among 'natives' who had helped Australian prisoners during the war. He was allowed to pay amounts 'not exceeding five pounds' without reference to higher authority. For any reward greater than five pounds, Jackson had to seek approval in writing from army headquarters.

Before returning to Australia, Major Jackson called on the Resident, Mr Evans, who was reputed to be the 'leading authority on British North Borneo', having 'covered most of it on foot'. Evans 'found it very gratifying to know that the Australian authorities had not forgotten the inhabitants of Borneo who had risked so much to assist the PW' and felt that Jackson's mission 'could achieve much and leave behind an impression that would last for many years'.

Major Jackson especially wanted Evans' advice on 'the scale of payments to be made and his remarks regarding widows whose husbands had been executed or [had] died as a result of aiding the PW'. Evans counselled against lump-sum payments on the grounds that 'it was the practice in the area for relatives etc to move in on any person suddenly receiving an amount of money'. These people, he told Jackson, 'stayed [while] the money lasted and then moved elsewhere, leaving the former recipient penniless'. It would be much better, Evans advised, to pay the widows a pension. As a guide, he told Jackson that the widows of former constabulary members received a pension of between fifteen and twenty Straits dollars a month (roughly equivalent to the wages of an unskilled labourer). When Jackson proposed recommending the same amount for the other widows on his list, Evans 'stated that this was a fair and satisfactory amount'.

Without the courageous help of civilians such as Heng Joo Ming and Corporal Abin, Jock McLaren and Rex Blow would very likely have died at Sandakan. At the unveiling of a temporary memorial to civilian victims of the Japanese on 17 September 1945, the Governor-General of Malaya, Malcolm MacDonald, remembered the '230 civilians [who] were slaughtered because of their loyalty to the Allied cause . . . Many of them suffered death because of individual acts of heroism. They risked arrest, torture and execution in attempts to aid British internees and prisoners of war'.

Walter Wallace, who escaped from Berhala Island and fought alongside Blow and McLaren in the Philippines, left a more personal reminiscence.

Writing after the war to Heng Joo Ming's brother, Wallace recalled, 'Many a time I crept into the jungle while working on the aerodrome and talked with your brother. We did not speak too much on family matters as our time was spent plotting for my escape'. Heng Joo Ming, he said, was 'a gallant man, most understanding and intelligent in every way. I wanted him to come with me as interpreter but he would not leave his family at Sandakan . . . Had your brother travelled with me he would be safe and well today but it was not to be and I am indeed very sorry when I think of his fate. His children should be very proud of him.' Wallace promised to give Major Jackson a full report of Heng Joo Ming's 'gallantry and wonderful assistance to the Allied forces'. Wallace rarely saw eye to eye with Blow and McLaren but, on this subject at least, the three men would surely have agreed.

NOTE ON SOURCES

―――⟶●◄―――

In researching McLaren's wartime exploits, I found the following sources especially useful.

Bowden, T., and H. Nelson, *Prisoners of War: Australians under Nippon* (radio documentary series), Australian Broadcasting Commission, 1984. Among the veterans the pair interviewed were Rex Blow and Ray Steele, both of whom escaped from Berhala Island with McLaren. At the time they were interviewed, the two men were recalling events that had happened around forty years earlier.

Jackson, H., 'Awards to helpers British North Borneo' (report). In October 1946, Major Harry Jackson was sent to Borneo to contact local people who had given help to Australian POWs or their surviving relatives. Jackson's mission had a specific purpose: to distribute cash rewards on behalf of the Australian Government for 'help rendered by residents and natives of that country to Australian prisoners of war whilst in Japanese custody'. While Jackson was fortunate in being able to interview a wide range of eyewitnesses to the events he was describing, it is worth bearing in mind that some of his informants stood to gain financially by convincing him of their version of events.

Ross, S., *And Tomorrow Freedom: Australian Guerrillas in the Philippines*, Allen & Unwin, Sydney, 1990. Ross's book, effectively a short biography of her brother-in-law Rex Blow, relies heavily on the memory of Blow, who was seventy-three at the time of its publication and for whom the author clearly had great affection and admiration.

Silver, L., *Sandakan: A Conspiracy of Silence*, Sally Milner Publishing, Binda, NSW, 2011. Silver's book focuses on the notorious Sandakan POW camp, to which McLaren was about to be transferred when he escaped. A prolific author and historian, Silver has produced twenty books over a span of thirty years.

BIBLIOGRAPHY

Australian War Memorial (physical and digitised items)

Decoded signals out, July 1945, AWM2017.7.134

Civilian administration, including medical papers, AWM2017.7.178

Correspondence with Maj Rex Blow, F/Lt. Paul Bartram, and Capt. Blondeel, AWM2017.7.183

Correspondence with Arthur Tunda, WOII Herbert Hirst (H1), Maj Rex Blow, AWM2017.7.185

Correspondence with Maj Rex Blow and orders Operation Goose, AWM2017.7.186

Papers of Athol Randolph Moffitt, PR01378, including his diaries and unpublished memoir

Sound recording: Rex Blow DSO as a major, Z Special Unit, and a prisoner of the Japanese, interviewed by Tim Bowden and Dr Hank Nelson, S02977

Sound recording: Raymond Eric Steele as a captain 2/15th Australian Field Regiment and a prisoner of the Japanese, 1940–45, interviewed by Tim Bowden and Dr Hank Nelson, S03010

National Archives of Australia

Australian War Crimes Commission—completed questionnaires [Australian and Allied] [see descriptive note for alphabetical list of questionaire participants], NAA: MP742/1, 336/1/2018

'Awards to helpers British North Borneo'—Major Jackson's report, NAA: MP742/1, 328/1/32

Blow, Rex, service record, NAA: B883, QX4648

McLaren, Robert Kerr, service record, NAA: B883, QX 21058

Official History of the Operations and Administration of Special Operations—Australia. Volume 2 (NAA: A3269, O8/B) describes SOA's Operations

War Crimes—Military Tribunal—HOSHIJIMA Susumu (Captain) AWC 733: Place of Tribunal—Labuan, 8–20 January 1946, NAA: A471, 80777 PART 1

War Crimes—Military Tribunal—TAKAKUWA Takuo (Captain) AWC 827: WATANABE Genzo (Captain) AWC 852: Place and date of Tribunal—Labuan, 3–5 January 1946, NAA: A471, 80771

Books, articles etc

Asprey, R., *War in the Shadows: The Guerrilla in History*, vol. 1, Doubleday, Garden City, NJ, 1975

Australian Government, 'Report of Inquiry into Recognition for Far East Prisoners of War who were Killed While Escaping or Following Recapture', Canberra, 2017

Balis, M., 'The American influence on the Mindanao resistance during the Second World War', Master's thesis, Old Dominion University, Norfolk, VA, 1990

Braithwaite, R., *Fighting Monsters: An Intimate History of the Sandakan Tragedy*, Australian Scholarly Publishing, Melbourne, 2016

Courtney, G., *Silent Feet: The History of 'Z' Special Operations, 1942–1945*, R.J. & S.P. Austin, McCrae, Vic, 1993

Davis, M., 'A letter to all guerrilleros: Unifying the Mindanao Resistance Movement and unconventional warfare', monograph, School of Advanced Military Studies, United States Army Command and General Staff College, Fort Leavenworth, Kansas, 2011, https://ia800402. us.archive.org/8/items/ALetterToAllGuerrilleros/ALetterToAll Guerrilleros.pdf (retrieved 15 September 2020)

Feuer, A., *Australian Commandos: Their Secret War Against the Japanese in World War II*, Stackpole Books, Mechanicsburg, PA, 2005

First Demobilisation Bureau, Japanese Monograph No. 3, 'Philippine Operations Record, Phase II (Dec 1942–Jun 1944), https://drive. google.com/file/d/1NSdQBb1TD6y4upcreTinOBBMgqPqRB-1/view (retrieved 15 September 2020)

General Headquarters, US Army Forces, Pacific, Military Intelligence Section, 'G-2 Staff study of Philippine Islands situation' (part of folder 'Intelligence activities in the Philippines during the Japanese occupation'), www.paperlessarchives.com/FreeTitles/ PhilippinesIntelligenceActivitie.pdf (retrieved 15 September 2020)

Gunn, G., 'Remembering the Southeast Asian Chinese massacres of 1941–45', *Journal of Contemporary Asia*, 37:3 (2007), pp. 273–91

Ham, P., *Sandakan: The Untold Story of the Sandakan Death Marches*, William Heinemann, Sydney, 2012

Headquarters, Philippines–Ryukyus Command, G-3 Guerrilla Affairs Division, '108th Division Unit History', June 1944, http://collections. pvao.mil.ph/Collections/BataanDiary/Box_480/108thDivision-10thMD.pdf (retrieved 15 September 2020)

Heimann, J., *The Most Offending Soul Alive: Tom Harrisson and His Remarkable Life*, University of Hawaii Press, Honolulu, 1999

Hill, A., 'Billy Young and the Dead End Kids', Sandakan POW Families Oration, Canberra, 2011

Hogan, D., *US Army Special Operations in World War II*, University Press of the Pacific, 2004, https://history.army.mil/html/books/070/70-42/ CMH_Pub_70-42.pdf (retrieved 15 September 2020)

Holmes, K., *Wendell Fertig and His Guerrilla Forces in the Philippines: Fighting the Japanese Occupation 1942–1945*, McFarland & Company, Jefferson, NC, 2015

Johnston, M., '"Yet they're just as human as we are": Australian attitudes towards the Japanese in the South-west Pacific' (symposium paper), http://ajrp.awm.gov.au/AJRP/remember.nsf/03e59ce3d4a5028dca 256afb002a4ab9/4c1c863cec65148eca256a99001d9f0c?Open Document (retrieved 15 September 2020)

Keats, J., *They Fought Alone*, J.B. Lippincott Company, Philadelphia, 1963

Lofgren, S., *Southern Philippines* (part of a series on US Army campaigns of World War II), US Army Center of Military History, 1992, https://history.army.mil/html/books/072/72-40/index.html (retrieved 15 September 2020)

MacArthur, D., *Reports of General MacArthur: The Campaigns of MacArthur in the Pacific*, 2 vols, Department of War, 1994, https://history.army.mil/books/wwii/MacArthur%20Reports/ MacArthur%20V1/ (retrieved 15 September 2020)

McNeill, D., 'Eichelberger in Mindanao: Leadership in joint operations', US Army military studies program paper, 1989, www.researchgate. net/publication/235205166_Eichelberger_in_Mindanao_Leadership_ in_Joint_Operations (retrieved 15 September 2020)

Michno, G., *Death on the Hellships: Prisoners at Sea in the Pacific War*, Leo Cooper, Barnsley, UK, 2001

Moffitt, A., *Project Kingfisher: The Terrible Story of the Massacres of the Sandakan POWs in Borneo—and the Secret Plan for a Rescue That Never Happened*, ABC Books, Sydney, 1995

Nelson, H., *Prisoner of War: Australians under Nippon*, ABC Enterprises, Sydney, 1995

Nwaogbe, C., Simonds, E., D'Antoni, A., & Tubbs, R. S., 'Surgeons performing self-surgery: A review from around the world', *Translational Research in Anatomy*, vol. 10, March 2018, pp. 1–3, https://doi.org/10.1016/j.tria.2017.11.001 (retrieved 15 September 2020)

Nypaver, T., 'Command and control of guerrilla groups in the Philippines, 1941–1945' (monograph), School of Advanced Military Studies, United States Army Command and General Staff College, Fort Leavenworth, Kansas, 2017, https://apps.dtic.mil/dtic/tr/fulltext/u2/1039888.pdf (retrieved 15 September 2020)

Ooi, K., 'Prelude to invasion: Covert operations before the re-occupation of Northwest Borneo 1944–45', *Journal of the Australian War Memorial*, issue 37, October 2002

——— *Rising Sun over Borneo: The Japanese Occupation of Sarawak, 1941–1945*, Palgrave Macmillan, London, 1999

Powell, A., 'Robert Kerr McLaren', *Australian Dictionary of Biography*, vol. 15, Melbourne University Press, Carlton, Vic., 2000

——— *War by Stealth: Australians and the Allied Intelligence Bureau 1942–45*, Melbourne University Press, Carlton, Vic., 1996

Reyeg, F., & Marsh, N., 'The Filipino way of war: Irregular warfare through the centuries' (thesis), Naval Postgraduate School, Monterey, California, 2011, https://core.ac.uk/download/pdf/36704046.pdf (retrieved 15 September 2020)

Richardson, H., *One-Man War: The Jock McLaren Story*, Angus & Robertson, Sydney, 1957

Rogozov, V., & Bermel, N., 'Auto-appendectomy in the Antarctic: Case report', 15 December 2009, https://doi.org/10.1136/bmj.b4965 (retrieved 15 September 2020)

Ross, S., *And Tomorrow Freedom: Australian Guerrillas in the Philippines*, Allen & Unwin, Sydney, 1989

Sams, S., 'United States-led Philippine guerrilla organizations on
    Luzon and Mindanao', *Global War Studies*, 12(1), 2015, DOI:
    10.5893/19498489.120103

Schmidt, L., 'American involvement in the Filipino resistance movement
    on Mindanao during the Japanese occupation, 1942–1945' (Masters'
    thesis), US Army Command and General Staff College, Fort
    Leavenworth, Kansas, 1982, https://apps.dtic.mil/dtic/tr/fulltext/u2/
    b068659.pdf (retrieved 15 September 2020)

Seventh Fleet Intelligence Center, 'Submarine activities connected with
    guerrilla organizations', www.history.navy.mil/research/library/online-
    reading-room/title-list-alphabetically/s/submarine-activities-connected-
    with-guerrilla-organizations.html (retrieved 15 September 2020)

Silver, L., *Sandakan: A Conspiracy of Silence* [1998], Sally Milner
    Publishing, Binda, NSW, 2011

Sinclair, P., 'Men of destiny: The American and Filipino guerrillas during
    the Japanese occupation of the Philippines' (monograph), School
    of Advanced Military Studies, United States Army Command and
    General Staff College, Fort Leavenworth, Kansas, 2011, https://pdfs.
    semanticscholar.org/7785/d1ff5fafe44869b8c2b4d51b043aded37c18.
    pdf (retrieved 15 September 2020)

Tenth Military District Headquarters, 'History of the Mindanao guerrillas',
    Wendell Fertig Papers, Box 1, Army Heritage and Education, www.
    west-point.org/family/japanese-pow/Guerrillas/History%20of%20
    the%20Mindanao%20Guerrillas.pdf (retrieved 15 September 2020)

Truscott, J., 'Voices from Borneo: The Japanese War' (monograph),
    www.clarsys.com.au/jt/VfromBor1.pdf (retrieved 15 September 2020)

Villanueva, J., 'Awaiting the Allies' return: The guerrilla resistance against the
    Japanese in the Philippines during World War II' (doctoral dissertation),
    University of Ohio, 2019, https://etd.ohiolink.edu/pg_10?::NO:10:P10_
    ETD_SUBID:175834 (retrieved 15 September 2020)

INDEX